Literary Theory Today

Literary Theory Today

Pramod K. Nayar

Foreword
Profulla C. Kar

Asia Book Club
NEW DELHI

Published by
Asia Book Club
New Delhi 110 058
Distributors: prestigebooks@gmail.com
Phone: 9818755529

ISBN: 81-7851-005-7

Printed in India

CONTENTS

For My Parents

Preface

This book is intended as an introduction to Literary and Cultural Theory after Structuralism for students of Literary/Cultural Studies in India. It aims to elaborate concepts, and summarise the arguments of the principle thinkers of particular schools. There is a need, I believe, for a book that does so with an accessible approach free of jargon. This is a modest attempt in such a direction.

The book is established around the main theories. Each chapter is divided into the following sections: Background and Origins, Assumptions and General Methods, Key Concepts and Thinkers, and Relationship with Other Disciplines. After tracing the essential origins and initiators of various strands of Theory (such as Saussure and Freud for structuralism and Psychoanalysis respectively), the individual chapters outline the main methodological principles and informing assumptions of each strand. The arguments of individual thinkers are summarised in some detail. I believe this organisation based on thinkers rather than concepts will benefit the students better, while providing a quick survey of the thinker her/himself in *one* section. The use of the "point form" of writing is meant to help readers obtain the gist of the arguments faster, in addition to being easy on the eye! A short note on other disciplines is available to indicate areas for further exploration. A list of introductory books for additional reading is provided at the end of every chapter. More specialised books, and the works of the key thinkers are listed in the Select Bibliography. Where necessary, short notes on related developments are also provided at the end of the chapter (such as notes on Subaltern Studies and Cultural Studies). Two appendices on newer developments, Ecocriticism and Technocriticism, are also included.

No attempt has been made to provide a critique of the various theories themselves, nor on the "politics of literary theory." I believe that such a critique should *follow* a survey of this kind, rather than intrude into or "dilute" an understanding of these theories.

I cannot close these prefatory remarks without thanking those who have helped me write this book.

My parents, for giving me the very possibility of writing.

Dr. Nilima and Sri Anil Khadakkar, for their affection, interest and encouragement.

Professor Mohan Ramanan and Professor Sudhakar Marathe for their inspirational teaching over the years.

Professor Prafulla Kar, for his encouragement at seminars and other occasions, and for agreeing to write the Foreword.

Dr. Tejaswini Niranjana, who first introduced me to, and instructed me in, Literary Theory.

Professor Rajendra Chenni who read early drafts of this book, offered invaluable advice and suggestions, and who compounded the occasional felony by allowing me to "get away" to work!

Mr. Nagya Naik, Kuvempu University, for a friendship.

My students Nivedita, Utpal Londey, Pavitra and Kiran Kumar at Kuvempu University who read early versions of the manuscript and offered constructive comments.

At Shimoga, Professor Nagaraj Rao and family, Professor C.S. Nanjundiah and family, and Drs. Vaidehi and Anil Kumar for their numerous instances of warm hospitality.

Dr. Ram Kumar Menon, for his gift of Derridas, and his entertaining friendship.

Neeraj Khadakkar, for procuring many important books, his affection and (bewildered) interest.

Sara Valentine, for her insights into punk rock, feminism and Riot Grrrls.

Ajit and Panikkar, for an enduring friendship.

Siraj Ahmad, for the good times.

Professor R.K. Dhawan for broaching the idea for this book.

Ms. Renu of Prestige Books for bringing out this book expeditiously and so elegantly

The staff of the New School University Library (New York) and Elmer Bobst Library (New York University) for their help.

And Nandini, who makes everything possible, everytime.

Pramod K. Nayar

Foreword

The present volume is a broad critical survey of the field of literary and cultural theory since the decline of New Criticism and emergence of structuralism around the 1960s to the end of the twentieth century and beyond. The volume is primarily designed as a helpful reference-text for undergraduate/post-graduate students and research scholars in Indian universities, who are now being introduced to theories of all kinds as part of their academic curriculum. But the scope and range of topics covered here are too vast and complex for only students and research scholars; teachers engaged in inter-disciplinary studies will find the volume extremely useful. Although meant to be a survey, the volume is not a conventional summary of major trends and movements presented in a schematic and simplified manner to the uninitiated. It is rather a serious reflection on the changing configuration of the critical scene in a climate charged with unusual dynamism and vitality. Nayar has tried to map the complex topography of Theory in a careful and intelligent manner without being carried away by passion. He has explained in some detail the various aspects of Theory in both their collaborative and contestatory modes of operation, thus defining the nature of the difficult terrain in the best possible way. Beginning with the emergence of structuralism in the 1960s, the volume traces the trajectory of Theory as it winds its way through the radical period of the sixties and seventies to occupy a prominent place in the academy in the eighties and nineties from where it seems to initiate a new kind of dialogue on issues which were once upon a time important in literary and cultural studies but were gradually submerged under the sway of radically disruptive tendencies. The current interest in nature and ethics in literary studies has accorded Theory a new direction, which, I hope, will continue to influence the study of literature in at least the first few years of the twentieth century. Nayar's narrative of Theory's development takes into account this hopeful trend demonstrated in the emergence of "ecocriticism" and various kinds of studies of environment and nature.

Between structuralism at one end and ecocriticism and techno-criticism on the other end of the spectrum, Theory has a series of over-lapped manifestations. It is difficult to describe the teleology of its progress as its various manifestations happened rather simultaneously. Until the rise and fall of the New Criticism, it was not difficult to map its development chronologically, but during the last fifty years the simultaneous occurrence of several perceptions and insights obfuscated the chronology of events and the sense of demarcation of individual space. From the three main theoretical orientations, namely, New Critical, deconstructive, and New Historicist, other corollaries developed and jumbled the critical space in an intricate way. Thus psychoanalytic criticism, reader-response theory, feminist and gender studies, social and Marxist criticism, post-colonial theory, theory of ethnicity and marginality, and finally, ecocriticism and technocriticism, branched out from these three main channels and spread their tentacles far and wide. Nayar's work throws some light on this intriguing scene and attempts to acquaint the reader with the rudiments of literary and cultural theory as they continue to affect our understanding of literature and culture surrounding us.

It is now difficult to think of literary studies without some appreciation of the philosophical and methodological insights stemming from Theory as a "force field of knowledge," to use a phrase of Walter Benjamin's. The last fifty years have been dominated by Theory which, interestingly, has come down from its high academic pedestal to traffic with the sub-culture of the marketplace. In such a scenario, it is appropriate to present it in an intelligible way, as Nayar has done, so that its import gets across even to those who may have nothing to do with university learning. But Nayar's text is meant to be used at the universities and institutions of higher learning, which Theory has invaded in a big way. In the present educational market, Theory has a higher value than anything else. Whether one likes it or not, one has to know it and to engage with it, even if that engagement is sustained by a spirit of resistance. One needs to know Theory in order to appreciate the complex relationship between literature and culture. Theory is therefore not a rarefied field of knowledge in its abstraction but a means to understand the way various modes of knowledge are constructed and disseminated.

With these preliminary remarks about the place of Theory in our intellectual life now, I would like to comment on some of the specific topics that Nayar has addressed. Nayar begins with an examination of structuralism and semiotics and discusses the way these two aspects of critical methodology of reading have provided a new dimension to reading experience through their meticulous emphasis on linguistic signs and their arrangement in the text. Structuralism goes beyond the principles of linguistic structure to an understanding of the intricate mechanism of a cultural system organized around a constellation of intelligible signs. Thus what initially appears to be a simple structure turns out in close reading a complex network of interrelationships. Nayar has rightly expanded the scope of structuralism and semiotics to include a whole range of narratology examined by such diverse theorists as Jakobson, Lotman, Gennette, Eco, Bakhtin, Propp and Kristeva. But however effective the structural method may be in the exercise of critical exegesis, its philosophical orientation stemming from its emphasis on a totalised structure erected on a solid foundation was highly problematic for those who have invested their time and energy in the business of reading with an eye on the fragility of language. In his chapter on poststructuralism and deconstruction, Nayar has addressed this problem in detail with references to the insights of such philosophers and theorists as Barthes, Derrida, De Man and the Yale Critics. Deconstruction opened up the text which structuralism had closed off and challenged the earlier humanistic assumptions about universalism and coherence by their radical suggestion that all reading is in fact deconstructive, which means that the more one reads the greater is the text's unreadability and that the reader finally confronts a moment of aporia when all traces of the text's materiality dissolved before him. By taking issue with both new criticism and structuralism in their emphasis on the teleology of the textual closure and lucidity of language, deconstruction questions the conventional assumption that reading is possible because language can be made transparent and suggests instead that writing is always under erasure and reading always leaves behind a residue, a trace, or a series of traces. As Nayar has rightly suggested, deconstruction is not just a method of reading a linguistic text but has implications for examining structures of power and cultural sedimentations. It has therefore influenced varieties of minority discourses including feminist readings and theorization and has now become a powerful tool for political analysis of entrenched ideologies and attitudes.

Closely allied to deconstruction, psychoanalytical criticism practised by such critics as Lacan, Norman Holland, Shoshana Felman, Deleuze and Guattari, Nancy Chodorow and others has expanded the scope of textual interpretation by emphasising the subliminal, the repressive and the unconscious. Psychoanalytical criticism is not just a tool for analyzing the mind of the character or the author, but becomes a very sophisticated strategy of studying such problems as cultural neurosis, national longing, sexual deviancy, social tensions and collective frenzy. There is a close relationship between psychoanalytical criticism and feminism as both deal with the origin of desire and its social and cultural manifestations. Nayar has pointed out that the areas that psychoanalysis explores constitute the sub-text of any work of art and therefore as an interpretative strategy psychoanalysis has a pervasive appeal.

It was Freud and later Lacan who opened up the Pandora's box of the feminist problematic and provoked the feminist critics to challenge the entrenched ideologies of masculinity and to develop a criticism of their own as an analytical tool to interpret the works by women. Freud's notions of "penis envy" and "castration complex" which were biological determinisms, according to the feminist critics, were intended to keep women down and make them feel perpetually subordinate to men. Thus a psychology of superiority was deliberately or unconsciously developed among men which resulted in the misinterpretations of female figures in works of art. One of the important tasks of the feminist critics was to correct these misrepresentations by bringing to light the politics of representation in canonical writings. Alongside this stupendous task involving painstaking examinations of male writings masquerading as universal was an equally rigorous task of putting together the varieties of scattered pieces of women's writing since the time of Sapho to the present-day within the living tradition of *ecriture feminine*. Although feminism was initially a politically charged movement to contest forms of patriarchy, both real and metaphorical, it has finally become a mature and responsible cultural mode of perception highlighting the virtues of difference and altered vision which are helpful ways of understanding the essentially heterogeneous nature of human culture. Nayar has traced the history of this movement and has suggested that feminism be understood as a response to the prevailing structure of power and thereby has filiations with deconstruction, Marxism, postcolonialism and environmentalism. As a subversive strategy for undermining the structures of authority spread throughout the entire body-politic, feminism has close affinity with Marxism which is determined to do away with the coercive productive mechanisms of capitalism and replace them with the collective governance of the proletariat. But Marxism of today is not just a movement against economic disparity, but a sophisticated intellectual movement to understand the forces of hegemony, ideology and process of reification in culture. Marxist intellectuals like Althusser, Gramsci, Jameson, Eagleton, Lukacs, Raymond Williams and others have contributed immensely to the contemporary debates about culture and paved the way for the emergence of Cultural Studies as an inter-disciplinary approach to reality. In their definition, culture has not to be understood as a stable entity, but as a liminal phenomenon perpetually in the process of transformation. Thus Williams' tripartite division of culture as "dominant," "emergent" and "residual" has to be looked upon not in terms of a rigid hierarchic formulation but as a way of articulating the close proximity of each component to the other in a system of contiguous relationship implying the scope for permanent slippage of one into the other and mutual imbrication. Thus the Marxist way of interpretation of literary text has added a new dimension to hermeneutics.

One of the effects of Marxism as a radical strategy of subversion is its easy acceptance by New Historicism in the United States and Cultural Materialism in England, which have revived the interest in historical approaches to literary texts and have refined these approaches in the light of new developments in historiography emanating from the works of Foucault, Braudel, Geertz. In his chapter on New Historicism and Cultural Materialism, Nayar has demonstrated by examining the work of Stephen Greenblatt, Louis Montrose, Hayden White, Alan Sinfield, Jonathan Dollimore and Pierre Bourdieu that the revival of the contextual study of the text was necessitated by the disenchantment with the rhetorical analysis of the text by deconstructionists who, it was alleged, had reduced texts into mere language games. By placing the texts, authors and even readers in their respective contexts, these critics have paved the way for fresh ways of writing history with an emphasis on "thick description" of space rather than on the temporal evolution of events over a long period of time. These approaches have spawned such diverse perspectives as subaltern studies, minority discourse, gay and lesbian studies, ecocriticism, and studies of sense as in Alain Corbin's fascinating *The Foul and the Fragrant: Odour and the French Social Imagination*. But it is not right to suggest that deconstruction and New Historicism were always at loggerheads with each other; Derrida in the 1990s turned to global politics and changing history of the time and began to address questions of contemporary events as effectively as he did in his earlier phase while dealing with textuality. His later works such as *The Other Heading: Reflections on Today's Europe* and *Specters of Marx* testify to this changed perspective

What New Historicism and Cultural Materialism have done for the United States and England respectively, postcolonialism has done for the newly independent nations trying to march ahead on the road to development. Nayar has devoted the longest chapter to this topic and for the right reasons. For a country like India which has a long history of colonial rule and a complex relationship with the West in terms of the conflictual encounter between indigenous forms of knowledge and the one that came as a result of the English rule, the subject of postcolonialism generates a natural and appropriate response. Although the term "postcolonialism" has several connotations, the simplest way of understanding it is to take it at its face value, as a way of making sense of what exactly happened during the colonial regime and how that event was taken by the people under subjugation. To try to understand this phenomenon with the advantage of hindsight of history is to penetrate into the thick layers of contradictory forces and to bring them into limelight for a critical scrutiny. As an epistemic concept developed the western-educated Third World intellectuals like Said, Gayatri Spivak, Homi Bhabha and others who negotiate between the two worlds—the first world and the third world—and speak in terms of hybridity, in-betweenness, migrancy, the self-consolidating Other and such tropes, postcolonialism defines itself as both an assertion of national self-identity and a critique of that identity which is paradoxically engendered by the forces from which it tries to make itself free. Nayar is right in suggesting that one of the major tasks of postcolonialism is to deconstruct nationalism which seems to replicate the same ideology of holistic essentialism as colonialism had represented. Fanon's examination of national culture can be cited as an appropriate example of this kind of deconstruction. But whatever may be the nature of postcolonialism as a theoretical construct, the postcolonial enterprise has rendered a valuable service to some of the third world countries by enabling them to be critically introspective about their conditions and to confront the challenge of coming face to face with the myriad contradictions of their own indigenous past. In other words, postcolonial thinking has brought about a new historiography for a new country like India to make her try to understand the complex nature of her genealogy and to rewrite her fractured narrative.

In a book about literary and cultural theories a chapter on postmodernism may seem at first somewhat out of placc, as postmodernism is a large concept incorporating within it several components which are already taken care of in this text. But on reflection one could see the rationale behind such an inclusion. As this volume is mostly meant for students of Indian universities, it is expected that some discussion on the twin concepts of modernism and postmodernism is made so that the students get clear perspectives on these two seemingly recognisable but difficult-to-distinguish concepts. Modernism is so inextricably bound up with the history of the West and its aspirations that it is difficult to say whether it has ended or still continues. Habermas thinks that modernity is an incomplete project and will go on forever; Lyotard subscribes to the idea of rupture and believes that modernism died at the beginning of the 1960s and postmodernism replaced it. But the debate has not yet been closed. Those who believe in the thesis that postmodernism has affected all branches of knowledge and has altered the human culture in a significant way look upon it as a liberating force which has encouraged innumerable disruptive movements throughput the world against collective authoritarianism and thoughtless globalisation. But to say that postmodernism is against globalising tendency is also wrong, as we know that those who support the idea of a global culture through the free flow of goods also emphasise the value of the local, the ethnic and the exotic in the global commercial and cultural transaction. One can see in Baudrillard's writing an attempt to come to terms with this problematic. Nayar has taken into account the way postmodernism as a cultural ideology has affected several disciplines including literature and the other arts, politics, sociology, economics, ethnography and even cybernetics. It is indeed refreshing to see postmodernism as no longer a mere aesthetic concept but as a social and cultural force having a ubiquitous impact almost everywhere.

The various categories of deconstruction that have emerged from the ethos of poststructuralism relate to the progressive weakening of the hold of the traditional institutions on the mind of the people who no longer feel contained by structures of control erected by society. One such institution was the family, organised by the power of the legitimacy of heterosexual love, sanctified by religion. But the sexual revolution of the present time supported by other minority movements has challenged the sanctity of this institution and has made a strong case for gay and lesbian rights for same-sex relationship which was hitherto considered unnatural and perverse. Radical feminists like Luce Irigaray and Helene Cixous have celebrated not only same-sex relationship, but also, more radically, auto-eroticism based upon their close examination of the female body as a self-sufficient and self-fulfilling organ of pleasure. Thus lesbianism within the broad movement of feminism could be considered as a radical symbolic protest against forms of sexual tyranny perpetuated by heterosexual love. Similarly, the battle of the homosexuals with the morality-enforcing agencies operating in favour of "normal" sexual relationship sanctified by "legitimate" heterosexual love could be taken as a form of protest against the imposition on them of certain sexual codes which they think are subtle strategies for maintaining the conventional moral order as a hallmark of patriarchal authority. Therefore the current burgeoning of interest in lesbian and gay theories has to be explained in the context of the proliferation of similar minority theories coming out of the subculture of the marketplace. Nayar marks similarities between these theories and African-American theories providing the conceptual grid to the American Blacks. By citing the works of D.A. Miller, Judith Butler, Gloria Anzaldua and others who have written extensively on this aspect, Nayar has demonstrated that what started as a silent revolution in the late Sixties has now become a powerful force in literary and cultural theory which cannot be ignored. The alliance of gay and lesbian theories has produced what is called "Queer Theory" which has broken down the sexual barrier between men and women and has focussed on unequal practices of gender roles. It is interesting that Nayar has suggested towards the end of his chapter on a need for a rethinking of pedagogy in the light of the composition of the class in terms of the sexual preferences of the students. This is certainly a radical idea and therefore needs careful examination.

A conspicuous example of the tremendous success of a minority literary theory is the one coming out of the African-Americans. In his chapter on African-American aesthetics and literary theory, Nayar has examined the genesis of such a theoretical discourse which evidently had its origin in Africa and developed as a self-conscious movement called Negritude outside the domain of the United States and got assimilated into the Black Arts movement in the United States which was a combination of aesthetics and social protest and was a typical product of the experience of slavery which had transformed the suffering of the Blacks into the texture of their art form, be it music or literature. The Harlem Renaissance of the 1920s which had coincided with the rise of high modernism in the West was the first major event in the history of the African-American consciousness which highlighted the need for an independent literary and cultural theory germane to the peculiar nature of the Black experience. The second Harlem Renaissance occurred in the 1960s with the emergence of the radical Black Arts Movement which was militant in tone but a significant attempt to channelise the robust Black social energy into creative expression. Since then both literature and theory produced by African-Americans have made a major contribution to the multicultural America where various kinds of minority discourses have made their mark through critical engagement with the majoritarian ideologies. Literary and cultural theorists like Henry Louis Gates, Jr. and Houston Baker have enriched the scope of American Studies in their theorisation of the African-American experience in terms of cultural production and dissemination. Within the broad discourse of Black aesthetics and theory is incorporated another minority articulation called Black feminism which Alice Walker defines as "womanism" as a way of removing from it political overtones. Black literary theory, as Nayar has outlined, employs strategies of orality, parody, ludic imitation, burlesque, magic and primordial African myths like the "signifying monkey," as well as the music of jazz and blues to convey to the world that there is a rich tradition which supports and keeps alive the vibrancy and dynamism of Black culture.

With the chapter on African-American aesthetics and literary theory, the volume seems to be technically closed, but Nayar decided to continue to say a little more, on what he perhaps cautiously considered to be topics for the new millennium. In Appendix 1 and Appendix 2, he speculates on what the shape of things would be like as we look back with the hindsight of vision and look forward with some uncertainty at the vast uncharted plain opening up before our eyes without any clear signals. There seems to be an element of exhaustion in the climate resulted from an over-use of Theory and its abstractions. But there seems to be a rethinking now on what could be done to recover what were lost and how to set our future goals if we are expected to read and write and think in an environment dominated by what Baudrillard called "hypertexts," which are a euphemism for "cybertexts." As I mentioned in the beginning of this Foreword, there seems to be emerging in literary and cultural studies a consciousness for a return to nature and to an ethical turn in reading and writing. That is why, Nayar's brief comments on "ecocriticism" and "technocriticism" as appropriate topics for speculations for the future are significant pointers to our responsibility as readers engaged in the activity of production and dissemination of knowledge. It is indeed heartening to know that sensitive scholars like Lawrence Buell, Joseph Meeker, Mary Mellor, Cheryl Glotfelty and many others have started redirecting their energy to making people conscious of their environment from the perspective of nature for the sake of nature, as distinct from the anthropocentric and androcentric perspectives of the earlier period. Similarly, the effect of the Internet revolution and the proliferation of cyber-texts in the chat-rooms of booming cyber-cafes throughout the world may pose a threat to reading, writing and serious intellectual dialogue. But there may be a silver lining here; an exhaustion may set in sooner than expected and a nostalgic return to books and to the human world of the classroom and to the ethical perspectives in reading, writing and speaking will reorient us to an old-fashioned world of human filiations taught by great writers. Perhaps the beginning of the next century will give a new direction to literary and cultural studies through an emphasis on the twin elements of nature and ethics. The indications available from the samples of critical theory available for us represent such a trend appropriately closing off the long and tortuous trajectory of the twentieth century and looking forward to a positive new beginning of the next.

Nayar's volume sketching the development of literary and cultural theory in the West and their implications to teaching and reading in the other parts of the world will no doubt be a useful text for students of literary studies who are in the midst of a serious paradigm shift of their discipline as a consequence of the systematic influx of ideas from other disciplines and the willing acceptance by literature of these ideas as part of its effort to enrich its texture through a process of continuous dialogue with every branch of knowledge.

PRAFULLA C. KAR
Professor and Chair
Department of English
M.S. University of Baroda
Vadodara, India

Chapter One

Structuralism and Semiotics

Structuralism, a form of criticism that flourished in the 1950s and 1960s, sought to understand a work of art in the context of the larger contexts or structures that contain them: genre, culture and language. It sought to answer questions like: how does a poem generate meaning? Or, how does a narrative work?

I Background and Origins

Structuralism finds its origins in the work of the early twentieth century linguist Ferdinand de Saussure. In his 1916 work *A Course in General Linguistic*s Saussure called for a scientific study of language rather than a historical one. Saussure's attempt was to "reduce" language to a set of propositions based upon formal relationships that define and exist between various elements of language. In the nineteenth century, historical linguists focussed primarily upon the origin and development of languages and the relations between them. They employed a *diachroni*c mode, that is a study "across time," rather than focusing upon the patterns and functions of language *as in use today* (which would be a *synchronic* study). Saussure turned away from this pattern of study of languages. Structuralism is an attempt to see everything in terms of Saussurean linguistics. Things as diverse as the fashion system, a poem, toys, a myth, a wrestling match can be seen as a system of signs.

The sign is constituted by the *signifier* and the *signified*. The signifier is the *word*, the alphabets arranged in a particular order. The signified is the *concept* that the signifier stands for. That is, ROSE is the sign made up of (i) the *letters* that make up the word "rose," (ii) the *concept* or image or meaning that the word *evokes* when one sees or hears the word.

Saussurean linguistics has three fundamental assumptions:

(1) **Arbitrariness**: The meanings we attribute to words are entirely *arbitrary*, and prescribed through usage and convention only. There is no inherent or "natural" connection between the word and the meaning. The word has no quality that suggests the meaning (except perhaps in onomatopoeic words like "hiss," "grr" or "cuckoo"), nor does meaning "reside" in the word. Therefore language cannot be said to stand for, or reflect, reality or the world: language is *a system in itself*. Language refers only to itself, since all words lead to other *words*. To phrase it in its proper terminology, the relation between the signifier/word and signified/meaning is purely arbitrary.

(2) **Relational**: Linguistic elements are defined in relationships of combination and contrast with one another. No word has its meaning in isolation. It possesses meaning through its *difference* from other words in the organisational chain (the syntagmatic arrangement of words). Thus "cat" means cat only by virtue of its difference from "cap" or "hat." Saussure announces: "In the linguistic system there are only differences."

(3) **Systematic**: Language constitutes our world, and our very existence. The whole is greater than the parts. We therefore should look not at what people say, but what makes speech *possible* at all. We need to analyse how meaning is produced through the acts of language. We need to understand the set of structures *in* language that enable us to speak and make sense. In short, we need to study signs and sign systems. Language is thus *form* not substance. Saussure called the life of signs in society "semiology."

Saussure argued for a distinction within language. The system or structure of language and the conventions that rule and govern speech is *langue*. The *actual utterance* in the social context is *parole*. To make sense of an utterance (parole) one should be aware of the underlying system at work (langue). This relationship between a communal and shared root (language and the conventions of language) and an individual practice (the act of speaking or expression) was at the root of all cultural practice for Saussure.

The relation between the signifier and the signified, as we have seen from assumption (1) above is purely arbitrary and, (2) completely functional. Signs are therefore structured in relation to each other in accordance with the principle of differential relations, and of opposites (binary oppositions). The relations between opposites are charged with deep meanings in human culture. Only historical convention ties the signifier to the signified. Therefore the sign itself has no immanent/inherent relation to the external referent (the world, or reality). Language is both the *process* of articulating meaning (called signification) and its *product* (communication).

II Assumptions and General Methods

Structuralism is informed and characterised by the following assumptions and methods:

(1) Literature is an artefact of culture and is modelled on the structure of language. Language constructs the very nature of our perception of reality.

(2) This premise allows the structuralists to investigate the manner in which literary texts are structured like a language, or what they call its *grammar*.

(3) Literature is a system within and in relation to other systems in a particular culture, all of which are based upon the linguistic model.

(4) Structuralism seeks the processes of meaning-production, that is, *how* the text constructs meaning.

(5) The text is seen at three levels:
   (a) as a system *in itself* with its own constitutive elements and laws (grammar)
   (b) as one element within the literary system as a whole. That is, the generic contexts of a text—the novel, a poem etc.
   (c) as it relates to the culture as a whole.

These correspond to the levels of structuralist reading: at the level of the individual poem, at the level of the genre, and at the level of the cultural matrix.

We can now move on to a survey of structuralism at work. The following sections provide an approach to the key issues addressed by structuralism by exploring the various "branches" and thinkers who have adopted structuralist principles. These include *Russian Formalism*, the *Prague School*, *Semiotics*, and *Structural Narratol-*

ogy. Thinkers covered here include Roman Jakobson, Mikhail Bakhtin, C.S. Peirce, Barthes, Umberto Eco, A.J. Greimas, Julia Kristeva, Yury Lotman, Gerard Genette, and Tzvetan Todorov.

III Key Concepts and Thinkers

Russian Formalism: The Russian Formalists, working around the 1920s (eventually disbanded by the Party), revolved around the work of the *Moscow Linguistic Circle*. They relied upon the nineteenth century linguists and theoreticians Aleksander Veselovski and Aleksander Potebnia.

1. They were more interested in methods, and mechanisms of "literariness."
2. They sought to establish a "scientific" basis for the theory of literature. They proceeded from the assumption that the "human content" (emotions, ideas) had no literary significance in itself but merely provided a context for the functioning of language and literary devices.
3. The Russian Formalists undermined the assumption of the mimetic nature of literature. They argued that the prime task of literary criticism is to analyse the constructional devices whereby daily objects are transformed into "new" (see *defamiliarisation* below).
4. However, they did not accept the structuralist notion that literature was a system like language, suggesting, on the contrary, that literature was a work *in language*. They believed that literature was an *autonomous practice* whose uniqueness lay in its ability to transform everyday experience/objects into something perceptibly different. Poetry is therefore a controlled violence upon language. It must be stated right away that much of the work of Viktor Shklovsky, Boris Eichenbaum and Boris Tomashevsky is apolitical and shows little Marxist orientation.

Viktor Shklovsky: Shklovsky defined literature entirely in linguistic terms, calling it "the sum total of all stylistic devices employed in it." Advocating the idea of "*defamiliarisation*" Shklovsky in his epochal essay "Art as Technique," argued that the chief effect of literary language (a subspecies or a special use of language for the Formalists), was to "make strange" everyday objects and experience. This causes us to see "differently," thus inducing a change in our consciousness itself. This defamiliarisation enables us to experience the "*artfulness*" of an object (the object itself being unimportant) and draws our attention to the material process of language itself.

Boris Tomashevsky: Working primarily on a theory of narrative, Tomashevsky distinguished between *story* (fabula) and *plot* (sjuzet).

(i) The story is the *actual sequence* of events as they have occurred, and is merely raw material for artistic work. Plot is the artistic representation of these events.

(ii) Plot may use repetition, reordering, and juxtapositions to heighten literary effect (suspense, for instance). Plot therefore prevents us from regarding the events as familiar.

Boris Eichenbaum: Eichenbaum is better known as a literary historian and narratologist. In his famous essay on Gogol's "Overcoat," he emphasised the autonomous nature of the work of art, and analysed the tale without any reference to extra-literary referents. Eichenbaum elaborated the concept of skaz ("to tell"). Third person narration and the syntax of direct speech marked Skaz by the character. He rejected traditional concepts of form and content, suggesting that the notion of "technique" was more relevant than the one of "form."

Mikhail Bakhtin: This Russian thinker was "discovered" by the West decades after his work in the 1940s. He is known principally for his books on Dostoevsky and Rabelais. Publishing under the name of his friend, V.N. Voloshinov, Bakhtin was the first thinker to provide a full critique of Russian Formalism (in his book *The Formal Method in Literary Scholarship*).

(i) Bakhtin's main target here was Saussure's emphasis on the formal aspects of language rather than the social parole. Language for Bakhtin was inherently *dialogic*. Language and words made sense only in its communication/orientation directed towards an Other. The sign was not, as Saussure argued, a stable unit but an active component of speech in certain social contexts. The sign therefore was the scene of struggles and contradiction since social conditions were always amorphous and heterogeneous with conflicting interests.

(ii) In his attempt to reread Saussure, Bakhtin focussed on parole rather than langue, arguing that one cannot analyse texts as though they were independent of the context. Language is essentially a matter of utterances rather than of sentences. Any attempt to understand parole must take into account the circumstances, assumptions and the time of the *enunciation* of the speech act. This leads Bakhtin to formulate the idea of the chronotope (see below). Thus for Bakhtin all language was imbedded in social, economic, political and ideological systems. With this Bakhtin highlighted the *material* nature of language.

(iii) In his work on Rabelais, Bakhtin focussed on the concept of the *carnival*.

(a) The carnival, the site of laughter, is ambivalent. It is the people's laughter not sanctioned by the power structures, the government or institutions. There is no "object" of this laughter.

(b) For Bakhtin there is no life outside the carnival, people are both spectators and participants: they are both the subjects and the objects of laughter.

(c) The carnival embraces death (as in macabre laughter, black comedy and the grotesque). It embraces "lowness," incorporating bodily functions (including the "dirty" ones: copulation, urination and defecation). The body is an essential part of the carnival's ambivalence. Carnival figures like the clown existing on the border between art and life illuminate the ambivalent.

(d) The mask used by the clown, unlike the mask of the Renaissance period which symbolised hypocrisy and deception, is here the "distorting" element. It plays with contradiction (I am me and the mask, am I the mask? Or is the mask someone else? Does it make me someone else?) The mask is thus transition, metamorphosis, the transgression of natural boundaries, and mockery. The carnival is thus the subversive: it, or rather its laughter cannot be objectified or theorised. Carnival logic undermines academic/institutional *discourse* because the carnival resists the academic repression of ambivalence.

(iv) In his *Problems of Dostoevsky's Poetics* Bakhtin introduced the idea of the polyphonic novel.

(a) As opposed to a monological text which has a homogeneous and relatively uniform logic, Bakhtin speaks of the multi-voiced discourse of Dostoevsky which renders much of his work open-ended.

(b) The "*dialogical*" word includes the other's voice in itself, is "translinguistic" because of the interplay of numerous voices and sounds (like a carnival), none of which is repressed. The novelist surrenders his "knowledge," placing himself on the same level as his heroes. Arguing that the poetic used "tropes" whereas a novel used *dialogised heteroglossia*, Bakhtin suggested that reading a novel in terms of "poetics" might do an injustice to the richness of the novel. This dialogised heteroglossia where many languages rooted in particular and different kinds of experience (e.g.: a profession, an ethnic group, social class, generation) prevents languages becoming "naïve." There are, therefore, many languages of truth.

(c) Bakhtin also emphasised the "*unfinalisability*" of works, as embodied in his famous statement: "Nothing conclusive has yet taken place in the world, the ultimate word of the world and about the world has not yet been spoken, the world is still open and free, everything is still in the future and will always be in the future."

(v) Bakhtin defines the chronotope, inspired by Einsteinean relativity, as "the intrinsic connectedness of temporal and spatial relationships in literature." In Rousseau, for instance, the world is self-sufficient, homogeneous and identical with itself—outside time and change. In a dialogic work, as in Greek romances, the plot unfolds over various geographical locations, and the lives of people on these different spaces are described. In the novel both the individual and society undergo real and unfinalisable becoming. Time is a heterogeneous and even unrepresentable element. Time renders space more fluid.

The Prague School: The Prague School of linguistics, inaugurated in 1926 as the *Prague Linguistic Circle* (PLC), was constituted by

Roman Jakobson (who moved from Russia to Prague and eventually the USA), Jan Mukarovsky, Felix Vodicka and others. In the 1930s critics like Rene Wellek and Josef Vachek joined them. Among the contributors to the seminars and presentations at the P.L.C. were Edmund Husserl and Emile Benveniste. They represent a "transition stage" (as Terry Eagleton terms it) between Russian Formalism and the later structuralism. Essentially functionalistic in their view of language, the Prague School, saw poems as "*functional structures*" in which the signifiers and signifieds are governed by a set of relations. The Prague critics argued that these signs must be analysed *in and as themselves*, without relating them to any external reality. They insisted on the structural nature of a work, where the poem or novel must be seen as a dynamic whole. Each text has one "dominant" level that influences and affects other levels. They also distinguished between the ordinary reader and the seasoned reader of literary texts. They sought to combine Saussure's synchrony and diachrony in their commitment to literary history. In this latter focus, the Prague School adopted the model of literary communication with the three factors of writer, literary work and reader.

Jan Mukarovsky: He emphasised the tension between literature and society present in the artistic product (the artefact). The artefact can be seen only against a general background of significations and as a deviation from an established linguistic norm. Thus, the *aesthetic function* is an ever-shifting boundary, where the "circumference" of the sphere of art is in a dynamic relationship to the socio-historical conditions. There is no aesthetic function that is independent of the socio-historical context of the human reading/interpreting/evaluating it. Mukarovsky also distinguished between the *material artefact*-the physical object of a painting or a book, and the *aesthetic artefact*—the human interpretation of the physical object. Arguing that interpretation and evaluation of the artefact changes with changes in the social conditions, Mukarovsky suggested that eventually it might cease to be regarded as a work of art at all. For him structuralism was essentially "an epistemological stance," the manner in which concepts are formed and *put into operation*.

Roman Jakobson: One of the most distinguished thinkers in linguistics, philology and aesthetics, Jakobson was responsible for the development of semiotics as a critical practice. Since his work is extremely wide-ranging in scope, Jakobson's contribution to semiotics and structuralism alone are discussed here.

In the Jakobson model of communication (either oral or written) the following SIX constituent elements play pivotal roles:

CONTEXT
REFERENTIAL

MESSAGE
POETIC

ADDRESSER . . . . ADDRESSEE
EMOTIVE *CONATIVE*

CONTACT
PHATIC
CODE
METALINGUAL

(i) A message is sent by an addresser to an addressee. To facilitate this, they need to use a common code, a conduit/channel of communication, and the same frame of reference. Each of these elements has a corresponding function in the communicative act.

(ii) Language seen from the *addresser's* point of view is emotive (expressing a state of the mind). Seen from the *addressee's* perspective language is conative (seeking an "effect").

(iii) If communication concerns itself with the *context* it is referential (which privileges the information content of any utterance) if the communication is oriented towards the *code of communication* it is metalinguistic (the query "do you understand me?" typifies this nature).

(iv) When the message focuses on the *words of the message* itself, that is when the communication draws attention to itself, it is poetic.

(v) And finally, when the communication focuses on the *act of contact* it is phatic.

(vi) Jakobson's work with aphasics (people with a particular kind of speech disorder) resulted in his analysis of figurative language. Adopting the two distinct uses of language namely selection and combination, Jakobson elaborated the terms *metaphor* and *metonymy*.

(a) In *metaphor* one sign is *substituted* for another, entailing a transfer of meaning between two unrelated domains. An example would be the use of the words "jealous" and "green." Here to "go green" commonly implies the state of being jealous. However, there is no logical or semantic link between the two. That is, the two words/ideas of the emotive state and the colour are actually unrelated

(b) In *metonymy* one sign is *associated* with another, where it utilises a term that is a property of the key word, or is related to it contiguously (example: "sail" for "ship," since sail is a part of the ship). In poetry the metaphor is used more often than metonymy because the stress in poetry is on similarity and/or startling opposition. Metaphor therefore involves a transfer of *sense*, whereas metonymy involves only a transfer of *reference* (part for a whole, but not a totally unrelated term/domain). *Selection and substitution constitutes the metaphoric pole, and combination and contextualisation the metonymic pole.*

(i) "Poeticity" or the poetic function is a necessary part of the study of language because language and reality (or, in Saussurean terms, sign and referent) do not coincide. In order to study the poetic rhythm Jakobson developed phonology, and was one of the first to analyse the sound, phonemic oppositions, opposition in sound and vision, between pitch and rhyme in poetic discourse.

Semiotics: Semiotics is the study of signs and significations. Originating from the theories of Saussure, semiotics analyses social and cultural life in terms of signification. Semiotics studies the way in which signs signify in literary texts, documents or in advertisements.

C.S. Peirce: (pronounced "purse") Peirce worked on logic and semiotics (this latter term he translated from the Greek), frequently linking the two. He argued that signs are the vehicles for thought *as well as* the articulation of logical forms. Peirce differs from Saussure in an important way. Peirce's semiotics is based not on the *word-as-sign* but on the *proposition* as that which allows comprehension and intelligibility. It is therefore a theory of the *production of meaning* and not a theory of language.

(i) A sign, for Peirce, is what represents something for someone. This is a *sign-function*:

Sign **A** denotes a *fact or object* **B** to a *reader* **C**

A sign always has these three aspects, it is never an isolated entity. A sign is an example of *Firstness*, its object—of *Secondness*, and the interpretant (the mediating element)—of *Thirdness*. The First is therefore a quality, a feeling or possibility. The Second is an individual who interacts with the environment and who may actualise the possibility. The Third is a general term, a rule or law that represents the determinate quality of a regularity or principle. The interpretant is the indispensable element needed to link the sign with its particular object. That is, the presence of C is necessary for A to stand for, or represent B. Without C the connection between the sign A and the object-referent B is incomplete. Here Peirce is suggesting the role of the *reader* as the medium that produces meaning in her/his act of interpretation. But a sign may also indicate something else. Thus the sign "STOP" may indicate an intersection, a main road, or a dead end. The interpretant may thus extend (or abuse) the sign to make it mean something else. This is the "unlimited semiosis" of Peirce.

(ii) Peirce's semiotics adopted many such triadic structures. Peirce classifies sign types under three types. The *icon* is a sign, which is in one, or more respects the same as its object (e.g.: a portrait, where the qualities of the sign are assumed to be the same as the qualities of the object represented). An *index* is a sign physically linked to or affected by its object. For example, take a weather-cock or a sun-dial. A cry of "Help!," or a knock at the door, smoke indicative of a fire, are also examples of signs that function as indices. The index evidently has a "dynamical" relationship with the object. The *Symbol* is a conventional sign used in speech and writing. Its relation to its object is of "imputed" character. Also, no symbol can be a sign without being interpreted. Peirce later modified and reified this triadic structure of the sign (see below):

1. QUALISIGN (A quality which is a sign)	SINSIGN (an event which is a sign)	LEGISIGN (a conventional sign)
2. ICON (a sign which denotes the quality of its object)	INDEX (a sign which is affected by its object)	SYMBOL (a conventional sign)
3. RHEME (represents a possible object, a qualitative possibility)	DICENT (a sign which denotes the actual existence of the object)	ARGUMENT (a sign of a law)

A.J. Greimas: Greimas' work has been an effort to analyse all forms of discourse. Greimas emphasises the idea that language is an "assemblage of structures of signification" which implies that the language system cannot be "given" in advance but must be *articulated as discourse* (discourse, for Greimas, is "language as taken on by the person who is speaking"). In order to analyse this discourse Greimas develops a range of concepts.

(i) At the auxiliary level we have three things.
   (a) The minimal meaning unit the "*seme*,"
   (b) The contextual semes or "*classeme*,"
   (c) The link between utterances and paragraphs, the "*anaphora*."

(ii) Developing a "*structural semiotics*," Greimas undertakes an analysis of the production of meaning in a particular context.

(iii) Meaning is neither intentional nor hermeneutic: meaning is a process of signification. Discourse and discursive action produces "*actants*." There is no other subject behind discourse: a subject is constituted by the very *act of discoursing* itself (what Greimas terms the discursive instance). The syntactic actant is not "the *person* who is speaking" but "the *person who is speaking*" (note the shift in emphasis onto the *act of speaking as producing the subject*).

(iv) In order to describe the manner of actant action in discourse Greimas introduced other concepts.

(a) *Modalities* and modalisation is that which characterises any situation of the actant. It is the given in any situation. For example, "The king wanted to go home" or "he was angry yesterday" refer to the modality of *obligation* and the temporal modality of a *condition* (being angry) respectively. "Wanting to," "having to," and being able to refer to specific levels of existence: "knowing" or "being able to" is the level of *actuality,* "doing" or "being" to the level of *realisation.* Evidently modalities are related to actions (which are necessarily discontinuous and momentary).

(b) In order to describe a continuous state of emotion, moods or temperament, Greimas introduced the concept of "*aspectuality.*" Aspectualities denote disorder, instabilities and imprecise states in the human.

(c) *Isotopy* refers to the parallel levels of meaning within a single, apparently homogeneous discourse. Thus it indicates different elements (actions and utterances) to be related to the same discourse. Isotopy may be *actarial* when passages describing different actions are finally seen to be related to the protagonist. They may be *discursive* when different sentences are found to refer to the same subject. They are *figurative* when the same text is discovered to conceal different allegories. Or isotopy may be *thematic* when the text refers to a knowledge/story/truth extending beyond the present narrative knowledge. Greimas' contribution to narratology will be discussed in the section on structural narratology.

Umberto Eco: Eco proceeds from the Peircean assumption of "*unlimited semiosis.*" Though unlimited semiosis indicates that signs always refer to other signs (and that a text is open to infinite interpretations), Eco seeks a middle ground between univocal meaning and infinite meanings. For Eco unlimited semiosis is meaning established with reference to conditions of possibility. A univocal type of code is one where one system of elements is translated into another system. For instance the Morse, where a system of dots and dashes corresponds to the letters of the alphabet.

(i) Eco is interested in the langue-parole constitution of language. The "*code*" corresponds, in Eco to the structure of the language. It (the code) correlates the "expression plane" of the language with the "content plane." This is Eco's "*S-code*"—the equivalent of the organisation of the elements of parole. S-codes may be *denotative* (the literal "reading" of a statement or sentence) or *connotative* (when another code is detected underneath).

(ii) The meaning of a sign-vehicle (the word) must be treated as independent of a supposedly real object (the "referential fallacy"). Thus "table" refers not to any particular/single table but to *all tables*. Codes have a social and cultural context. The response of an individual to a particular sign-vehicle imparts information about the particular "cultural unit" (the context). Evidently, then, signs can take on a multiplicity of meanings; each derived from the competence of the user. A sign not only stands for something, but must also be interpreted. What this idea suggests is that langue as a code becomes equivalent to the competence of the language user. Thus Eco is here providing a dynamic understanding of codes.

(iii) Eco develops the *Q-model* of the code, which he suggests is a model of "linguistic creativity." The Q-Model supposes that the system can be added to, and that further data may be inferred from incomplete data. The code is therefore modified in accordance with the *competence of the language user rather than being defined or determined by the code itself.* Eco's theory of sign production focuses on the "*ratio facilis*" and the "*ratio difficilis*."

   (a) *Ratio facilis* refers to the elements that can be easily assimilated by the code, and corresponds to the Peircean symbol (see above).

   (b) *Ratio difficilis* refers to elements that cannot be easily assimilated by the code (the Peircean icon). In the second type the sign of the object is motivated by the nature of the object itself.

However, Eco argues that even the most motivated of signs have conventional elements. Any "outside" sign (that is an unconventional, unfamiliar sign, beyond the code) soon *becomes conventionalised.*

(iv) Eco's typology of sign production is as follows:

(1) Physical labour: effort required to produce the sign

(2) Recognition: object or event is identified as expressing a sign-content

(3) Ostension: an object or event is shown to be a symptom/exemplar of a whole class of objects or acts.

(4) Replica: describes the more difficult or "motivated" signs which eventually become conventionalised (mathematical signs and symbols, musical notations)

(5) Invention: a new sign, unavailable in the code or convention. This is also the basis of creativity.

Thus Eco's model emphasises the creative and ever-adaptable nature of code and language itself.

Roland Barthes: Barthes' structuralist or semiotic work eventually shifted positions to take on a distinctly poststructuralist tone (his famous essay, "The Death of the Author" is generally the marker of this "turn"). Barthes' work on myths in *Mythologies* is his best-known semiotic phase. Arguing that myth is a product of speech (parole) rather than of langue, he defines myth as "neither a lie nor a confession, it is an inflexion." How a myth articulates is important for Barthes, for it does not need to be demystified. In fact, if the ideology of the myth is obvious then it is not effective as a myth at all.

(i) Barthes argues that language is a relatively autonomous system. The literary text is opaque and unnatural. The denial of the opacity of language and the notion that true art is verisimilitude is a bourgeois fallacy. A "zero degree writing" (the title of Barthes' book), in contrast, *calls attention to itself.* It reveals itself as language and as a sign system.

(ii) In his study of fashion, Barthes analyses the rhetoric of fashion writing. We have the "*fashion signifier*" where meaning derives from the object (e.g.: cap), its support (the head) and the variant (caps/hats). The *fashion signified* is the external context of the fashion object ("woollen equals winter"). Fashion is never a simple relationship between the signifier and the signified, since fashion is always connoted and not denoted. The *rhetoric of the signifier* of the clothing code opens up a poetic dimension (the garment by itself has no demonstrably productive value). The *rhetoric of the signified,* on the other hand, concerns an imaginary world—of fashion. The rhetoric of the sign is the rationalisation of fashion: the transformation of the description of the fashion garment into something necessary because it (apparently) fulfils its natural purpose, and naturally fulfils its purpose because it is necessary. Barthes' structural analysis of narrative is discussed below in the section on structural narratology.

Yury Lotman: Lotman belonged to the Tartu school of semioticians. For Lotman, the literary text is a stratified system where meaning is a function of contexts governed by sets of similarities and oppositions, which are themselves relative to one another. The nature of the signifier, the sound patterns and rhythms determine meaning. Though poems do carry enough information, poetry is the most condensed form of communication ("semantically saturated") because it has the least number of signs meant to facilitate communication, but manages to produce more intense meanings/messages than any other discourse. A literary text has lexical, phonological, graphic, metrical and other "systems" each of which sets up certain expectations through their accepted "norms." Other systems deviate from, modify or transgress these expectations set up by one of the systems, producing, as a result, the literary effect. Meaning is hence the result of different "determinants" acting together. Each sign in a literary text participates in several different such systems simultaneously, where the associations are *syntagmatic* (or horizontal) to produce a "system of systems." This dizzying effect of defamiliarisation produced through contrast and difference may even be the product of the "*minus device*," where the startling *absence* of a particular device or system may suggest a meaning (because the *other systems* led to and created a context in which this device was *expected*).

Julia Kristeva: Kristeva first came into prominence for her work on Bakhtin. Seeking to counter the "necrophilia" (as Kristeva called it) of phenomenology and structural linguistics, she suggested "semanalysis," a portmanteau term derived from semiology (Saussure) and psychoanalysis (Freud) to address an element beyond language but in an extremely self-critical fashion, questioning its own suppositions and ideological gestures. With semanalysis, Kristeva reintroduced the body into language by arguing that (1) the logic of signification is already present in the material body and (2) bodily drives make their way into language.

(i) For Kristeva the entrance into language is not just the result of lack or castration but also motivated by *pleasure* and *excess*. Anality is a process of rejection (due to excess) and separation (as Freud argued) that prefigures a separation that leads to signification. Birth, for instance, is separation inherent in the body: one body is violently separated from the other, the maternal body's excess leads to separation. The maternal body also regulates the first laws (the availability of the breast, for instance). This maternal regulation operates *before* the advent of paternal law (which, for Freud and psychoanalysis, sets up the child's identity).

(ii) For Kristeva there are two elements in signification.

   (a) The *semiotic* (which, it is important to note, is distinct from semiotics in Kristeva) elements in the signifying process are the *drives* they discharge into language, and are associated with rhythm and tone. It is a subterranean element that *does not signify*. It corresponds to the "*genotext*" which is the very foundation of language. The semiotic is equated with the *chora*, the unrepresentable place of the Mother. It is a kind of origin but an unnameable one (for, if named it would be placed in the symbolic realm). The chora stands for the material, poetic dimension of language.

   (b) The *symbolic*, on the other hand, is the element of meaning that *actually signifies*—the syntax and grammar. This symbolic corresponds to the level of the "*phenotext*," which is the language of communication, the level at which we normally read when seeking meaning. The threshold of the symbolic is the "*thetic phase*," the point at which the subject takes up a position and identification/identity. The genotext and phenotext together constitute the *signifying process*.

The semiotic challenges the symbolic and the two are involved in what Kristeva characterises as a *dialectic oscillation*, between symbolic identity and semiotic rejection. This occurs in the following manner: without the symbolic we have only incoherent, random and (perhaps) indecipherable "delirium," without the semiotic we would have empty language (we speak because of a driving semiotic force). It is this relation between rejection and stasis that produces the speaking subject. It is thus a *subject-in-process*. Kristeva's work consistently seeks to bring the speaking body back into language, and language into the body by arguing that the pattern-logic of language is already found in the body, and the pattern-logic of otherness (alterity) is already found in the subject.

(iii) Kristeva's three models of discourses that challenge identity are *Poetry, Maternity* and *Psychoanalysis*. Poetry points to the language/process of signification: it draws attention to its own construction. Its attention to the sounds, rhythm, rhymes in language indicate the semiotic element in signification. It thus reactivates the semiotic within the language, to place the subject/identity under question. Poetic language thus disrupts meaning, and opens the way to a new range of meanings. Maternity and the maternal body are the embodiment of the subject in process. It cannot be divided into subject/object. It suggests the alterity (otherness) within, the simultaneity of the inside and outside (I and the Other—the *child* inside *me*). The subject (maternal body) is bound to the object/Other through Love and not Law. Psychoanalysis gestures towards the difference inside the subject. Psychoanalysis elaborates the semiotic, indicates the semiotic alterity inside the subject. Kristeva's later work on love, abjection, melancholy and eros is perhaps more Lacanian and poststructuralist.

Structuralist Narratology: Structuralist criticism enabled the development of a rigorous model of reading, breaking up the text into its constituent elements to uncover the method by which the text constructs meaning. Narratology, the science of narrative, has benefited a great deal from structuralist insights as the work of Tzvetan Todorov, Barthes, Greimas, Vladimir Propp and Gerard Genette illustrates.

Roland Barthes: In his *The Structural Analysis of Narrative, s/z* and several other works, Roland Barthes developed a structuralist mode of reading literary and cultural texts. Barthes divides the story (Balzac's "Sarrasine") into 561 "lexies" or units of meaning. These lexies are classified using five codes. For Barthes, these five codes are the equivalent of the langue, informing the structure of all narratives. The five codes of Barthes are:

(1) Proairetic: which informs the sequence of events in the story and provide indications of actions. Thus the sequential logic of kidnapping, falling in love or the temporal sequence of "they proceeded at 5 AM" are *sought* by the reader.

(2) Hermeneutic: governs mystery and suspense and initiates queries like: "Who committed the murder?" and "What is happening?" To put it loosely, this code informs the reader's what/why/where/how questions.

(3) Cultural: appeals to the fund of common assumptions, knowledge and which do not require explanations or glossing. Literary, medical and psychological knowledge is implied here.

(4) Semic: is the code of connotations, and may include stereotypes like the mad scientist, the wicked priest and so on.

(5) Symbolic: closely linked to (and therefore difficult to distinguish from) the semic, this moves from textual details to symbolic ambivalence, the contrasted elements (binary opposites) such as male/female, night/day, good/bad (Peter Barry argues that the symbolic is merely the semic on a larger scale).

Vladimir Propp: This structuralist worked on Russian folktale to develop a narratology that was eventually modified by Greimas. He divided the fairy tale into 31 basic "*functions*." Arguing that no function excludes any other, Propp suggested that the functions always appear in the same order in the tales. All tales contain the basic function of "lack" or "villainy" and proceed from it to another function (rescue, battles) that constitutes the denouement (e.g.: the "filling up" of the lack or the destruction of villainy). Propp identified SEVEN basic *roles* adopted by the characters in the fairy tales, each of which corresponds to a particular function or set of functions: the *hero* (seeker or victim); the *villain*, the *princess* (the sought after person) and her father/mother, the *despatcher*, the *donor*, the *helper* and the *false hero*. The same character can play more than one role and each role may be played by more than one character.

A.J. Greimas: Greimas in *Structural Semantics* developed a model of narrative by positing "*actants*" as fundamental structural units. The actant is neither a specific narrative event nor a character. There are for Greimas SIX actants paired as binary opposites: *Subject/object, Sender/receiver, Helper/opponent*. The subject is paired with the object s/he seeks, the object is sought by the subject, the sender sends the subject on the quest for the object, the receiver of the object to be secured by the subject, helper of the subject, and opponent of the subject. These actants describe and "carry out" three basic patterns in any narrative:

(1) desire, search, aim (subject/object)
(2) communication (sender/receiver)
(3) auxiliary support *or* hindrance (helper/opponent)

Greimas thus thinks in terms of the relations between the elements. The narrative follows this framework: a contract is established between sender and subject to bring about a new order, or reinstall peace or discover/seek something; the subject who becomes competent along the axes of desire, duty, obligation and knowledge goes on the quest; and as a result of her/his actions restores order or brings in a new one, for which s/he is duly (justly) rewarded or punished. Greimas' scheme may be summarised thus:

Contract (or prohibition) → violation → punishment
or
Lack of contract (disorder) → establishment → reward

Tzvetan Todorov: Todorov argued that the smallest unit of a narrative was the "proposition." There are FIVE such propositions informing narratives: Equilibrium (e.g.: peace), force (e.g.: enemy attack, illness), disequilibrium (war, death and destruction), force (enemy defeated, cures found), equilibrium (peace returns). These propositions form a sequence, a succession of sequences form a text. The sequences themselves are embedded in the form of a story-within-a-story or a digression, linked to each other or even alternating to produce effects of suspense and tension.

Gerard Genette: The most important of the structural narratologists, Gerard Genette, has argued for the autonomous nature of the literary text. Genette's work has been of particular use to literary critics for his attempts to develop models of reading texts in a rigorously analytical manner. The analysis of narrative has been Genette's abiding concern, as his voluminous work on the subject adequately demonstrates. Here we shall look at the more important notions of the narrative suggested by Genette.

Genette, for instance, argues that the *narrative voice* has many levels. The voice is constituted by the following elements:

(1) Narrative Instance: This refers to the *actual moment and context* of the narration, the "temporal setting" of the enunciation of the narration. This context of the narrative moment is crucial to understand the meaning of that utterance.

(2) Narrative Time: This is the time indicated by the tense (of the verb) in the narrative. The narrative instance also indicates the time of narration *with respect to the events narrated*. For example, the narrative may be about a *future event*, where the narrative time is prophetic. Or, in certain novels the time of the event is the time of the narrative itself, where the event is narrated *as it happens*. In third person narratives there is no such time of narration, because the events are recounted from a perspective *outside* the narrative itself. Thus narrative time refers to the time of the narrative.

(3) Narrative Levels: This refers to the relation of the acts narrated to the act of narration itself. For example, is the narrative a story within a story?, for instance. The narrator may tell us about the events which lead to his narrating to us the story of a character: "Dear reader, when I was in Paris I met this young man . . . we became friends . . . and then he suffered a terrible tragedy . . . it happened this way: . . . " Here the early remarks are a prelude to the narrative of the events that befell the narrator and his friend, which are to be narrated soon, as the final ellipsis indicates.

Genette discerns four important levels of narrative. They are:

(1) Order: The sequence of events in relation to the order of narration. An event may have taken place before the actual narration (*analepsis*, or flashback); it may not yet have taken place, and is merely anticipated/indicated/predicted by the narrative (*prolepsis*); discordance between "story" narrated and "plot" (actual order of events as they occurred and *not* the order in which they are narrated: *anachrony*); or there may be a movement between one narrative level and another (metalepsis).

(2) Duration: The rhythm at which the events take place (does the narrative expand episodes, summarise them?). There are four speeds of narration:
   (a) ellipsis: infinitely rapid,
   (b) summary: relatively rapid,
   (c) scene: relatively slow,
   (d) descriptive: no progress in the story.

(3) Frequency: The extent of repetition in a narrative (how many times has an event happened in the story?).

(4) Mood: This is distinguished by Genette into two further categories:
   (a) distance, or the relationship of the narration to what it narrates. This distance may be *diegetic,* or a plain *recounting* of the story (the presentational level which is immediate as language or gesture), or *mimetic,* or *representing* the story (or character, situation, event);
   (b) perspective or what is commonly called "point of view" or focus. Focus determines the *extent* to which the narrator allows us to penetrate into the character or the event. Narrative focus alternates and shifts throughout the narrative and may be of two kinds (1) *paralipse*: where the narrator withholds information from the reader which the reader *ought to receive* according to the prevailing focus; (2) paralepse: where the narrator presents information to the reader which the reader according to the prevailing focus *ought not to receive.*

(5) Genette favours "*focalisation*" over the traditional "point of view." Focalisation while not completely free of the visual con-

notation, is broadened here to include: *cognitive, emotive* and *ideological* orientations of the narrator. Types of focalisation may be based on TWO criteria: (a) position of narrator relative to the story, (b) degree of persistence. Focalisation also includes TWO aspects—the *subject* or *focaliser* (one whose perception orients the presentation and the *object* or the *focalised* (what the focaliser perceives/presents for the reader). Focalisation based on the *position of the focaliser* is of two types:

(i) *external*: with its vehicle the "narrator-focaliser." This is both *panchronic* and *panoramic* (across time and space)

(ii) *internal*: with its vehicle the "character-focaliser." This is naturally more restricted because a character's range of vision is always circumscribed by her/his location vis-a-vis places, people and events.

Focalisation whether external or internal can be *within*—presenting the thoughts and emotions of the character, or *without*—presenting only the outward manifestation of the object. Frequently, novels have both modes of focalisation (it must be admitted that the "within/without" distinction in Genette is quite blurred in practice). There may also be "*retrospective focalisation*" where the character focalises her/his past.

(6) Every narrative, for Genette, has the following elements: the *story*, which is the actual order of events in the text, *narrative discourse* and the *narration* (which is the telling of the story). The statements made constitute narrative discourse. The narration is the *act* of making the statements. Narrative discourse is thus imbedded in the narration of the story, but is *not identical* to either of them. This element of narrative discourse is Genette's work in his later books.

(7) A narrator may be of any type: homodiegetic, heterodiegetic, intradiegetic, extradiegetic, autodiegetic. The extradiegetic narrator is "above" the story. The heterodiegetic narrator is one who does not *participate* in the story. When characters become narrators they are intradiegetic. If such an intradiegetic narrator is also one of the characters in the story narrated by him or her (i.e. when the narrator tells her/his story to someone else in the context of the novel (e.g.: Charles told Sam: "let me tell you

what happened when I went to Delhi to meet my friends at the university . . . " what follows is Charles' role as an intradiegetic narrator of his own story to Sam, all *within the context of a novel that you as a reader are reading*) then s/he becomes a homodiegetic intradiegetic narrator. When a character narrates her/his own tale (e.g., in an autobiography) they may be described as autodiegetic narrators.

(8) Genette also develops a whole typology of intertextuality (the notion that a text refers to, echoes, is influenced by a range of texts, thus making each text a site of numerous convergent texts) in his later work, especially in his seminal *Palimpsests* and *Paratexts*. "Transtextuality" is textual transcendence and cuts across genres. *Hypertexts* are late texts that follow (directly referring or writing back to an earlier text, such as Coetzee's *Foe* that refers back to Defoe's *Robinson Crusoe*. This early text is a *hypotext*. *Paratextuality* refers to the relations between the body of text with its titles, epigraphs, illustrations, notes, and first drafts. *Architextuality* refers to the genre demarcations. *Metatextuality* refers to the relationship between a commentary and its object.

IV Relationship with Other Disciplines

Structuralism influenced a host of disciplines. Claude Levi-Strauss adopted the structuralist methodology to analyse myths. He argued that the individual myth/tale (Saussure's parole) did not have a distinct or inherent meaning, but may be interpreted only in terms of its relation with its relation to other elements—myths in the entire cycle of myths (the langue). Levi-Strauss' "Structural Anthropology" was the earliest adaptation of structuralism and Saussure to another discipline. Psychoanalysis, especially in the early work of Jacques Lacan, Marxism in the work of Louis Althusser and the culture-critic Colin MacCabe also adopted structuralist principles. Roland Barthes writing on the fashion system also analysed the dress codes through linguistic principles.

Further Reading

Hawkes, Terence. *Structuralism and Semiotics*. London: Methuen, 1977.

Holquist, Michael. *Dialogism: Bakhtin and His World*. London and New York: Routledge, 1990.

Rimmon-Kennan, Shlomith. *Narrative Fiction: Contemporary Poetics*. London: Methuen, 1983.

Scholes, Robert. *Structuralism in Literature: An Introduction*. New Haven: Yale University Press, 1974.

Scholes, Robert. *Semiotics and Interpretation*. New Haven and London: Yale, 1982.

Todorov, Tzvetan. *Mikhail Bakhtin: The Dialogical Principle*. Trans. Wlad Godzich. Manchester: Manchester University Press, 1984.

Chapter Two

Poststructuralism and Deconstruction

In many ways poststructuralism is an extension to radical extremes of the premises suggested by the structuralists. The structuralist assumptions that (1) reality is available only through language and that (2) language and meaning are, in turn, the product of difference (see Saussure, above) influence poststructuralism. Poststructuralism argues that we live in a world where there is no possibility of certainty in belief or identity: there is no fixed or stable point of reference. We live in a decentred world, in which we cannot know where we are, since all positions seen relative to the centre have been called into question with the decentering of the centre itself.

I Background and Origins

It is ironic that we begin our discussion with a section titled "origins," for it is the notion of origins that is the subject of the most rigorous deconstruction! Poststructuralism while not restricted to deconstruction is identified primarily with it. Other thinkers such as Michel Foucault, Jacques Lacan and even Edward Said have been treated as part of the poststructuralist turn. Let us first try and locate a point of departure.

In terms of texts and authors, Roland Barthes' later writings such as the famous essay "The Death of the Author" are remarkably poststructuralist in their methodology and assumptions. Barthes here announced that all texts are connected to all others in an unending chain of intertextual relations. He announced that the text is *produced* (and not consumed) by the reader, the death of the author causes the birth of the reader. A text is thus plural in origin, and polysemic in nature. There is no definite "margin" or "centre" to a text: every text is a weave of many other texts.

The work of Jacques Derrida in the 1960s is generally considered of crucial moment in the rise of poststructuralism. In three seminal works—*Of Grammatology, Speech and Phenomena* and *Writing and Difference*—Derrida called into question the notion of centres, unity, identity, signification. Working at a point where he is intensely self-conscious and self-critical of his own writings, Derrida demolishes the boundaries between literature and non-literature.

The adoption of Derrida by the American academy, most notably in the work of Paul de Man, Geoffrey Hartman, J. Hillis Miller and Harold Bloom, announced the arrival of deconstruction as an institutional phenomenon and a critical approach to literature (though Derrida himself has been careful to claim that deconstruction is not a methodology). The "Yale School," as the American deconstructors were called, developed a series of readings, which analysed texts, especially literary ones. This was the excessive textual orientation of deconstruction. The second generation of deconstructive critics such as Barbara Johnson also produced thinkers who sought to link deconstruction's "radicalism" with other theories like Marxism. Gayatri Spivak, Derrida's translator, has consistently worked at the interface of Marxism-deconstruction-feminism. Michael Ryan, Andrew Parker and Marjorie Levinson have successfully yoked the two. Deconstructive tendencies are also evident in the "schizoanalysis" of Gilles Deleuze and Felix Guattari.

After a survey of the basic assumptions and "methodology" of deconstruction, let us move to a discussion of the prominent thinkers. These include Roland Barthes in the poststructuralist phase, Derrida, Paul de Man and the Yale critics, and Michel Foucault.

II Assumptions and General Methods

(1) Poststructuralism, or more specifically deconstruction, involves close textual analysis and argument to reveal the rhetorical or logical contradictions in texts, to demonstrate how the apparent and explicit logic of a text is undermined or contradicted by the hidden text (or subtext).

(2) Method: three stages may be located in a deconstructive practice.

(a) Deconstruction analyses the binary oppositions (man/woman, inside/outside, and black/white) to reveal their hierarchical nature.
(b) It then overturns this hierarchy to reveal how what appears privileged is actually undercut by the suppressed term of the hierarchy.
(c) As a third stage deconstruction displaces *both* terms thus preventing a new hierarchy. To this end deconstructive reading may seize upon a minor detail (a footnote or epigraph, a marginal reference in the "main text"), works this detail *through* the main text to demonstrate how even this minor/marginal note may subvert the main text: thus reversing the main/peripheral hierarchy of the text's organisation.

(3) Reality itself is textual for deconstruction. Derrida's famous (and much misunderstood) formulation "there is nothing outside the text" suggests that all history, identity and reality is available only through their *textualisation*, i.e. through their insertion into language.

(4) Language itself is never stable. Meaning is the result of difference, and this process of differentiation is endless. Meaning is never *present* in the sign, simply because the sign refers to (yet) another sign which is *not here*. Thus reading or interpretation is the slow movement through the chain of signs, seeking a temporary meaning from/at each halt. The process never ends. This suggests that every signifier (word/sign) leads not to a stable end-signified, but to more signifiers. The signifier has merely excluded some other signifiers temporarily so that it can be itself. No signifier is thus without the *trace of other signifiers*. (The "trace" in Derrida is discussed in the section on his work. See below). This implies that meaning is never fully graspable, and the final meaning is always postponed (deferred).

(5) A sign may be reproduced any time any place (the iterability or repeatability of the sign). Thus it can be made to mean differently each time it repeats in a different context. It is never *absolutely* the same sign that we encounter at each moment of its repetition.

(6) If meaning is never self-identical or *present* it follows that human identity—which is the result and product of language—is also never stable, unified or self-identical. The notion of the human subject itself is called into question with this move.

(7) Origins, margins and ends are concepts that search for roots, single/unified subject-positions that are now discovered to be multiple, fragmented and always referring to something else. The "presence" of identities or meaning is a metaphysical illusion, for all presence is tainted with the impurity of the absent and the excluded. The desire for dichotomous structures that imply origins and derivatives/linearities are now replaced by multilayered, rhizomic states that proliferate endlessly without boundaries or origins (this latter work on the rhizome is the contribution of Deleuze and Guattari). The term "structure" which presupposes a unity, a centre and margins is a much critiqued term in poststructuralism

III Key Thinkers and Concepts

(1) **Roland Barthes**: in his works like "The Death of the Author," Barthes demonstrates a departure from his structuralist legacy. In *S/Z* he argues that a literary work could no longer be regarded as a stable structure. Distinguishing between *writerly* and *readerly* texts, Barthes argues that a "readerly" text, exemplified by a realist novel is consumed by the reader, s/he has nothing to do with the production of meaning. A writerly text, such as a modernist novel, is one that has to be produced by the reader to generate meaning.

(2) The difference is also the difference between the kinds of pleasure evoked in the process of reading. A writerly text induces a "*jouissance*", a violent ecstasy closer to death and fragmentation. Reader and the text disintegrate, and this loss of self in disintegration is an orgasmic experience. This is what Barthes terms the "pleasures of the text" (these ideas are generally known as Barthes' "erotics of the text" for his explicit link between reading and the sexual act). A readerly text induces mere "*Polaris*," an easy enjoyment which is stable. Barthes speaks of the "closed" and the "open" texts. Open texts are plural, dif-

fused, there are no beginnings or ends, they refer to numerous other texts. Hence there is no such thing as "originality" of a text: every text, as noted before, is a weave. It is the reader who unites the various elements of the text.

(3) Barthes also distinguished between the *work* and the *text* (in his essay "From Work to Text"). The arguments may be summarised as follows.

   (i) The work is the physical object "held in the hand." It becomes a text with the reading by the reader. A text is thus an exercise in language.

   (ii) The text is unlimited, unrestricted to genres, open to many interpretations, and is repeatable elsewhere. It upsets the rules of hierarchy and rationality.

   (iii) A text is an *endless* play of signifiers, which prevents a definite or final meaning or "core." The reader thus plays a text. If a work is "affiliated" to an author, the text has no author, and can be "redone." The reader is born at the death of the author-centre. The death of the author-centre also, in a sense, frees the literary text from authority: one need not limit or unify the text to what the author intended or meant in the work. The author is no more the originator of the text or the repository of all its meaning. The author is a mere tool for language to operate, and the meaning of a text rests in the *process of reading* (which is itself never "finalised").

   (iv) References, citations, echoes in a text suggest the plurality of meaning. These references are untraceable, and thus leave the text without any "final" shape.

Jacques Derrida: He is undoubtedly one of the most influential thinkers in the history of Western thought. Moving from a text-oriented deconstructive practice through analyses of politics and institutions (in works like *The Other Heading, The Laws of Reflection*) to social philosophy (with his great work on Marx, *The Spectres of Marx* and the recent *Politics of Friendship*) Derrida has been hated and admired (David Lodge asks: "Is there life after deconstruction?") for his ability to yoke philosophy, science and literature in virtuoso displays of critical readings. His 1966 paper "Structure, Sign and Play in the Discourse of the Human Sciences" is widely taken as the moment when deconstruction arrives in the Western academia. The radicalism of Derrida's work may be unforgivably summed up as asking philosophical questions of literary texts (as in his essays on Joyce or Mallarme) and literary questions of philosophical texts (as in his writings on Plato and Rousseau).

(1) Derrida's work begins with the notion of difference expounded by Saussure (that signs derive their meaning only in their difference from other signs). Thus, meaning is not always *present* in a sign; it is relational and dependent upon its (the sign's) presence among a chain of other signs. For Derrida interpretation is the movement along this chain, where every signifier leads not to a definite "end signified" but to another signifier. Meaning is never present in one sign alone—it is dispersed (or "disseminated," as Derrida terms it). Meaning in deconstruction is, as Eagleton glosses it, "a kind of constant flickering of presence and absence together."

(2) Each sign thus contains a *trace* of other signs that are themselves absent. Trace is Derrida's substitute for "sign." The trace is a theoretical unit of writing; it operates in the innermost places of writing. It is omnipresent, but cannot be captured. The trace is the sum of all possible relations which constitute the sign. The trace takes many forms, at different levels. It may work at the level of the phoneme, the morpheme, or the word. The trace thus makes writing possible. Leitch in his gloss on the trace terms it the "microlevel of the sign."

(3) Derrida argues that not only is meaning available *only* through difference, a finality of meaning can never be attained, because each signified simply refers you to other signifiers. Hence meaning is both differing and deferred endlessly. To suggest the togetherness of these two features of the sign and meaning Derrida coins the term *differance* (to say both differ *and* defer). This is a typical Derridean move: the use of terms that always mean two things, and leaving a clear meaning undecidable (hymen—both inside and outside, pharmakon—both poison and cure, supplement—both necessary addition for completion and excess).

(4) In terms of philosophy, Derrida's attempt has been to undermine a "*metaphysics of presence*" in Western thought. Notions of truth, being, reality are dependent and predicated upon the idea of an essence, origin (*arche*), centre, or end (*telos*) all of which seek to deny difference, absence and Otherness. This leads Western philosophy to privilege speech over writing, because speech implies the presence of a speaker (unlike writing, which can be referred to and reproduced in the absence of the author). This is what Derrida terms the "phonocentrism" or "logocentrism" of Western philosophy.

(5) Such a metaphysics, argues Derrida, represents the West's sentimental desire for a guaranteed authority, a finality of essence and meaning—the "*transcendental signified*." This transcendental signified is the logos where all truth originates, rests and which is irreducible and unquestionable (this transcendental signified is usually God). Logos is the Word of God, the origin of truth, a truth which is pure, coherent and "completely whole." By this move Western thought is able to reject arbitrariness and the impurity of all meaning. Derrida's deconstruction has taken its first step with its interrogation of such a metaphysics that privileges presence, absolutes, centres and origins over absence, "relativeness," margins and limitless plurality. One cannot escape this language either. However, one cannot "inhabit" it without interrogating it. Thus Derrida suggests that we use all terms and concepts "*under erasure*," since we have to use it and interrogate it *at the same time*.

(6) Speech is a form of writing for Derrida. He points out the differential relations that produce meaning in speech (as in writing). He suggests that we unravel meaning by ignoring impurities of tone/accent/pronunciation in speech just as we ignore style, letter size, fonts and shape to grasp the "essence" of an alphabet by its difference from other alphabets. Derrida demonstrates how the so-called inferior qualities of the written word, such as temporal delay, spatial distance from its author (as we have seen above), are features associated with speech too. Thus Derrida reverses the hierarchy of speech/writing.

(7) Derrida's much critiqued formulation, "there is nothing outside the text" needs some elaboration. Before Derrida, the notion of a text was that of something with margins, an author, a beginning and end, overall unity and identifiable content. This text was different from reality, history, consciousness and life. Derrida argues for a text that "overuns" borders, by referring to other texts. A text is a differential network that refers to other differential networks. It is not a finished corpus of writing, not held by margins or covers, because its "traces" extend beyond these confines. Every border marks a difference, and no border is guaranteed or guarantees the inside/outside distinction: everything is inside (as traces) *and* outside (as absence). The text thus has no borders, and there can be no limits to intertextuality. The world, constructed and available in language (which is, one recalls, a system of differences endlessly multiplying), is an infinite Text. All things (contexts) get textualised—political, economic, and social—and become intertexts.

(8) For Derrida the entire field of signs is "writing," or *ecriture*. Here writing is *not restricted* to the graphic sense of the word, but refers to the *figural* sense: *writing is the term used to denote any system that is based on difference and deference (differance)*. The study of such writing, Derrida terms *grammatology*, the very science of *differance*. It implies an analysis of the *play* of terms, of the linguistic interdependence of each sign on other signs (Derrida's *traces*), and of the infinite possibilities of every sign (the limitless play of signifiers which do not come to rest at any transcendental signified). The net result is to suggest that meaning is the arbitrary effect of difference and writing. Writing always refers back to another being or trace, which is absent.

(9) For literary criticism, Derrida's work has been adopted to unravel the contradictions of a text. A text always exceeds the author's intentions due to the inherent instability of language. That is, language distorts and contradicts the explicit logic-systems of a text in a closer deconstructive reading. The underlying, implicit text may present an alternative logic that contra-

dicts the perceived and suggested one. There are a few assumptions that help us understand Derrida's literary exercises:

(i) No hermeneutics of literature is really possible, explication and interpretation is temporary, indefinite and slippery.

(ii) No truly critical "metalanguage" is free from the metaphoricity of the text, i.e. no criticism is free from the *literariness* of the text it hopes to explicate. Each is "*contaminated*" with the other.

(iii) In any text there is a clash of metaphors. Literature always relies upon the concealment of the dead signs, which always escape any such attempt.

(iv) Since signs are repeatable out of context, any time, any place, they cannot possess any singular authority. Any sign can be "grafted" into another discourse in another context. For instance, an "economic" sign such as "circulation" or "interest" is also used for literary purposes. The repeatability of a sign (what Derrida terms "iterability") is more fundamental than its attachment to a particular context.

(v) All this constitutes what Eagleton succinctly described as "reading against the grain." Deconstruction seeks to uncover the dead or buried *unconscious* text underneath the apparent or surface one, and then show how this unconscious text subverts and contradicts the conscious one. Derrida has therefore always been concerned with marginal comments, puns, footnotes or an inadvertent word-slip which he then analyses to an extreme point (a method commonly termed "foregrounding") where it contradicts the "main text." By this Derrida demonstrates how the *marginal* or the peripheral is *in effect* the main text, it constitutes the main text. Thus the hierarchy of main-text/footnote, text/commentary are subverted in Derrida. A simple example would be deconstruction's work on the word "*guest*." Guest is cognate with "*host*" (they have the same Latin roots), which in turn comes from the Latin *hostis* meaning "enemy." This implies a subtext where the arrival of a guest at the house of a host may possibly read as an unwelcome event—the arrival of the enemy. With this knowledge, try reading Wordsworth's "Daffodils" with its "host" of flowers now!

To sum up, Derrida's deconstruction looks for a text's paradoxes, contradictions, shifts in tone/sense/connotation, conflicts, absences and silences (what a text does not say). A deconstructive critic uses all these puns, double meanings, sexual connotations that slip in unguardedly into an author's language. Their penchant for etymology is very evident. Etymology helps reveal alternative meaning of a word, and thus prevents any unique, solitary or definite meaning being attributed to it. We now move onto the deconstructive literary critics who have adopted Derridean modes of reading for critical analyses.

American Deconstruction: Derrida's greatest support has been the Yale Department of English. Paul de Man, Hillis Miller, Geoffrey Hartman and Harold Bloom took to deconstruction in a major development for literary studies. The "Yale School" became synonymous with a deconstructive practice in the 1970s.

Paul de Man: One of the most important members of the Yale School of deconstruction, de Man developed a rigorous critical practise of reading texts, which may be termed "rhetorical reading."

(1) For de Man language is always *figurative* and not referential and there is no unrhetorical language. Figures of speech (tropes) allow the writer to *say* something and *mean* something else. Tropes destabilise logic, deny the possibility of a straightforwardly literal or referential use of language. De Man's famous example illustrates this. To the question "tea or coffee," one replies, "What is the difference?" Here the *actual and understood* meaning is that it makes no difference if either tea or coffee is served. But this contradicts the logic of the *literal* meaning, which is: what is the difference between tea and coffee? Thus the linguistic sign is merely the site of an ambivalent and tension-filled relationship between the referential and figurative meaning.

(2) Reading for de Man is always a *misreading* because tropes constantly interfere between critical and literary texts. Literary texts are self-deconstructing because every text calls attention to the

literal meaning, which is contradicted by the implied or surface meaning.

(3) Even criticism is returned to the common textuality of literature. All language—economics, political theory, law and philosophy—work through metaphors just as any *literary* text. In order to convince us of its logic and rational arguments, all language/ discourse relies upon metaphor. That is, just when a text seeks to be at the most persuasive and logical, it reveals its own fictive character through its language. However, literature is the area where this irony and ambiguity between the literal and figurative, logical and irresponsible (because fictive, self-reflexive) is most visible. Critical writing can never be simple paraphrase or description. Between the literary and the critical text a trope mediates. Thus critical writing is always suspended within the linguistic games of truth and falsehood. *Any language in any text is rhetorical and figural, i.e., literary*. All reading is thus misreading. A text is literary to the extent that it allows misreading.

(4) De Man's method has been to analyse rhetorical figures in a text and to demonstrate how the text is aware of itself as a rhetorical construct. De Man teases out the hierarchical oppositions within a text to reveal their linguistic and philosophical bases. He reveals how a text's literal/narrative level actually repeats the figurative/rhetorical substructure. Thus de Man's deconstruction is closest to Derrida's when he tries to show that a text's *own rhetoric undermines what the rhetoric tries to say*. These are the moments of *unreadability* for de Man because the ways of knowing and interpretation are dependent upon *ways of saying*; i.e. all questions of epistemology and certainty are exercises *in language*. This is the *aporia* or the pathless path of deconstruction. An aporia is an impasse, where there is *the assertion and simultaneous negation of opposing systems of logic or rhetoric*. Here nothing can be harmonised or rejected. What is unsaid or repressed in a text (the unconscious) returns in the act of reading, thereby calling the apparent/visible meaning into question by contradicting it. We cannot resolve the issue by privileging either the said/conscious or the unsaid/repressed unconscious; it

is impossible to do so. It is never the binary opposition of "*either/or*," but rather the impasse of undecidability, the simultaneity of the incompatible "eitheror." Indeed deconstruction is the recognition of this impasse, for as Derrida puts it "deconstruction is a testing of the impossible."

Geoffrey Hartman: Hartman advocates the use of incomplete references, and seeks a critical language that is highly figurative and critical at the same time. His is a rich if eccentric style of writing that is self-conscious and constantly calls attention to the manner of his own writing. Thus erudition, vast scholarly references and cliches are present together in Hartman's work, thus suggesting that his own writing is an intertextual construct. Hartman is completely textual in his orientation (as indicated in the title of one of his several books "Saving the Text"), preferring to laboriously explicate the literary work rather than connect the work to politics or institutions. Hartman and others represent the American turn to deconstruction as a purely textual exercise.

(1) Hartman argues that there are two extreme tendencies in modern criticism. The scholar-critic relies excessively on elucidation of texts. The philosopher-critic uses the text as a step in attaining absolute thinking. One has to bring these two strands together. According to Hartman, this is what deconstruction achieves.

(2) Hartman regards criticism as inside literature, best argued in his essay "Crossing Over: Literary Commentary as Literature." He argues that critical reading should not seek meaning but should reveal the contradictions and equivocations in a text. Since criticism is *inside* literature, it must also be as *unreadable* as literature, i.e. the language of criticism must be as figurative, allusive and elusive as the poem it seeks to interpret.

(3) Hartman rejects the "death of the subject" and the idea of unlimited freeplay. For Hartman the Derridean notion of the completely undecidable is unacceptable.

(4) Proceeding from (3) above, interpretation is a "consciousness of the self" for Hartman. This consciousness must be raised to critical heights and interrogate the turning of the mind *upon itself*. This self-reflective and self-conscious style has been Hartman's hallmark, most visible in his great book on Wordsworth.

J. Hillis Miller: One of the most distinguished critics writing now, Hillis Miller's work has moved from phenomenology in his early work *Poets of Reality* to deconstruction in *Fiction and Repetition, Ariadne's Thread* and *Topographies*.

(1) For Miller all signs are rhetorical figures. Language is, right from the beginning, fictive. By going back to etymology, Miller disturbs the apparent stability of the sign and opens out many more possibilities of interpretation. The reader is forced to move from one rhetorical figure to another, in an endless *mise en abyme*, or a "lateral dance" (Miller's term for reading). This movement from one figure to another is the allegory, which suggests both a difference and a spacing in time and space.

(2) Repetition and difference are a favourite figure in *Fiction and Repetition*. The repetition that Miller favours is the Nietzschean kind, where everything repeats, but repeats differently. Analysing English novelists like Hardy and Dickens, Miller demonstrates how a single figure or trope recurs in a text (the image of graphology or writing in Hardy's *Tess of the D'Urbervilles*, for instance) and with each recurrence appears different. Miller's aim is to show how all presence is based on difference and repetition and not on any metaphysical base. This is the abyss (*mis-en-abyme*) of a text: where etymology, tropology (the study of tropes) or ambiguity is essentially a problem or effect of language. The abyss is an inherent result of the differential nature of language itself.

(3) In *Ariadne's Thread* Miller uses the trope of lines—the linear progression of narratives, the line by line reading and physical arrangement of a text itself, the lines of physiognomy of characters, their family lines and genealogies etc.—to develop a whole series of deconstructive readings. The lines themselves are both inside and outside and *anastomosing* (criss-crossing, mixing up of lines, thus confusing points of origin, entry and exit points). Miller here revives Greek and Latin etymological connotations of lines, characters, texts and signs to show how they all imply the same, and hence can never be resolved as one or the other.

(4) Arguing that the self is only a locus of floating signs, Miller demonstrates that the self/sign repeats *differently* in different contexts, and that the self/sign never comes to a rest: the destination of the sign is never reached, but is always postponed—a "*destinerance*" (another Derrida term combining destination, deterence and deference). Likewise in his essay "Tennyson's Tears" (in *Topographies*), Miller argues for the essentially playful, differential and abyssal nature of language.

(5) For Miller deconstruction is a retracing from figure to figure. It seeks through this, "the element in the system/text which is alogical," and which will unravel the text. Deconstruction, in Miller's well-known definition, annihilates the ground on which the building stands by showing that the text has "*already* annihilated that ground, knowingly or unknowingly." Literature, which calls our attention to the figural nature of its own language, is the highest form of deconstruction for Miller.

Harold Bloom: Bloom has combined Freudian psychoanalysis, Cabalistic and rabbinical (Jewish) thought and deconstruction in a series of brilliant works, culminating in his most recent book, *Shakespeare: The Invention of the Human*. Bloom is less textual than Miller or de Man.

(1) Bloom argues that since Milton English poets are aware of their belatedness, of having arrived late on the scene, after many poetical "fathers." This is the "*anxiety of influence*" the poets suffer from. These writers experience a certain Oedipal hatred of their father, and want to deny their paternity. All poems must therefore be seen as written against the poetic father. This Bloom terms a "*misprision*," a misreading of the past masters to produce a new interpretation. A wrenching of the predecessor poets must be undertaken for the younger, late-come poet to assert his position (it must be pointed out that Bloom's model speaks only of male poets).

(2) A revisionary reading is then developed by Bloom using the Cabala as a source of poetic theory. There are three stages of revision in Bloom's psychopoetics:

(i) *Limitation*, or taking a new look,

(ii) *Substitution*, or replacing one form with another,

(iii) *Representation*, or restoring a meaning.

When a "*strong poet*" writes he goes through these three stages. These strong poets battle and come to terms with the anxiety of influence using six psychic defences. These are the primordial forces behind the revisionary origins of poetry which correspond to and appear as the six tropes in their poetry. These may be mapped as follows:

Primordial forces	Rhetorical Figures	Psychological
(1) Clinamen	Irony	Reaction-formation
(2) Tessera	Synechdoche	Reversal
(3) Kenosis	Metonymy	Regression
(4) Daemonisation	Hyperbole	Repression
(5) Askesis	Metaphor	Introjection
(6) Apophrades	Transumption	Projection

Bloom's work has thus sought to recast deconstructive readings within a "historical rhetorics" (a term coined by Peter de Bolla) of poetic imagination and Freudian theory.

Other Poststructuralists: Poststructuralist concerns are also found in the writings of Michel Foucault, the psychoanalysis of Jacques Lacan and the work of Gilles Deleuze and Felix Guattari. Lacan and Deleuze-Guattari will be discussed in the chapter on Psychoanalytic criticism.

Michel Foucault: The analysis of discourse and discursive practices that constitute, inform and reinforce power structures have been Foucault's concerns in his works on the clinic, the prison system and the "history of sexuality." Foucault's methodology uncovers the discourse of "right," of sanity that helps incarcerate the Other as wrong, diseased or mad. Foucault's concern was poststructuralist because he sought to understand how a system is put together through the process of *exclusion*, of *marginalisation*. It was also poststructuralist because, like Derrida and others, Foucault posited a subject as *constituted by discourse*. He is not interested in who speaks, but rather in the rules that make speech possible. In any episteme, certain things may be spoken/written and accepted as truth. Thus for Foucault, the task, as he phrases it in *The History of*

Sexuality, is "to discover who does the speaking, the positions from which they speak, the institutions which prompt people to speak."

Power and knowledge—which helps identify and classify individual subjects as mad or ill—always go together for Foucault. Foucault's methodology to analyse the working of power/knowledge has been summed up by Barry Smart thus:

(1) An analysis of techniques of power embodied in local, regional and material institutions such as the family, the market, the clinic and the prison.

(2) An analysis concerned with the exercise and practice of power, the field of its application and its effects. Foucault concentrates on the various complex processes through which individuals/ subjects are constituted as effects and objects of power.

(3) Foucault argues that power is not the possession of a group or an individual. It is a network, spread through society. The individual is both the *effect* of power and the *element of its articulation*. Or, the individual is the site and the instrument of power.

(4) Analysis should proceed from a microlevel to reveal whole histories, techniques and tactics of power. There can thus never be a general, all-explanatory theory of power. Connections must be made between the mechanisms of power and economic and political institutions at individual levels.

Thus the analysis of power seeks to understand, in Foucault's own formulation, the "production of effective instruments for the formation and accumulation of knowledge—methods of observation, techniques of registration, proceedings for investigation and research and apparatuses."

For Foucault, three historical processes constituted the construction of a disciplinary system and a disciplined society.

(1) **Demographic-Economic**: The changes in size, density of population and production systems (i.e. the economic basis) in society. Disciplinary methods to make more men productive produce more wealth were then evolved.

(2) **Juridico-Political**: The legal and political systems of governance and control were structured and predicated upon relations of power, which ensured and guaranteed submission of individuals and bodies. These also undermined subtly the mecha-

nisms set up to *limit* the exercise of power. Foucault is here suggesting that the exercise of power managed to evade the safety devices installed to prevent excessive use of power and domination.

(3) **Scientific**: Methods of formation and accumulation of knowledge began to be employed for domination. The need to quantify and classify spurred this mode of inquiry. The census, the clinic, the school, the prison, were scientific in approach, *and* helped implement power relations effectively.

As an example of Foucault's analysis let us look at his reading of the discourse of sexuality in his epochal *The History of Sexuality*. The 17th century was the period of sexual frankness, when codes governing obscenity, indecency were lax. The later 17th century—which Foucault characterises as the age of sexual repression—cloaked sex with silence. Yet there was a proliferation of discourses about sex (scientific and medical, for example). A whole set of practices emerged as a result: the compulsory confession and the importance of penance as a retribution for the "ills" of the flesh, and censorship of the vocabulary. Sex was sought to be made morally acceptable and technically useful. In short, sex was to be administered. With the 18th century, sex became a police matter, thus moving beyond the religious one of the 17th century. The government became interested in birth rates, fertility levels, and frequency of sexual relations because it was now assumed that the wealth and prosperity of the nation depended upon these. Bedtime in schools, sleeping arrangements was monitored. Medical reports, clinical cases and reform methods became a part of the school system. A movement toward heterosexual monogamy becomes evident here. The sexuality of children, criminals, lunatics and homosexuals came under scrutiny. Four operations of power emerged:

(1) The sexuality of children was subordinated. The adults were called upon to monitor the child's "solitary habits."

(2) An incorporation of "perversions" and specifications. The homosexual was now a species, a symbol of disorder.

(3) Constant checks and examinations were encouraged and practised. This was the "medicalisation" of "sexuality" in an attempt to locate the origins of perversion.

(4) Modern society encouraged the compartmentalisation of sexualities. Sex was to be restricted to certain ages, relationships, times, and spaces. Age (adults), practice (heterosexuality, monogamy), relationships (conjugal), space (the bedroom) became the correlates of procedures of power. Anything "outside" these were classifiable as perversion and illness that required and necessitated correction.

Two great procedures for producing the truth about sex were developed:

(1) *Ars Erotica*: in China, Japan, India and Arab-Moslem societies. Truth was believed to be produced from pleasure itself. Pleasure was considered not in relation to any absolute laws of permitted and forbidden, but in relation to itself. Knowledge about it must remain hidden not due to fear of infamy, but because, by tradition, it would lose its effectiveness by being revealed.

(2) *Scientia sexualis*: the confession was linked to power and truth. Interrogation, inquest were modes to discover truth. A whole discourse of what is right thus began to evolve, and was supported by the scientific studies. Sexuality, for instance, was now a subject of scientific inquiry, something that had to be interpreted by a team of experts—which automatically granted the experts authority and power over the subjects (individuals of inquiry and investigation). These constituted what Foucault terms the *medical, psychiatric* and *pedagogical* discourses of sex.

Four strategic unities and four sexual subjects emerged due to the development of specific mechanisms of power and knowledge centred on sexuality:

Strategic Unities	**Sexual Objects**
(1) Hysterisation of women's' bodies	Hysterical Women
(2) Pedagogisation of children's sex	Masturbating Child
(3) Socialisation of procreation	Malthusian Couple
(4) Psychiatrisation of perverse pleasure	Perverse adult

In (1), the female body was analysed (a) as saturated with sexuality, (b) therefore it was made the subject of medical practice, and (c) placed in social contexts of the family, the life of the children. The "nervous mother" is the most visible form of hysterisation.

In (2), children were defined as "preliminary" sexual beings. Adults—parents, teachers, families, and doctors—therefore had to take charge of this potentially dangerous sexuality.

In (3), social and economic measures were brought to bear on the fertility of couples. This was the "responsibilisation" of the couple with regard to the social body, i.e. their duties as parents, reproducing couples in terms of the social fabric as a whole.

In (4), psychiatrisation of perverse pleasure, here sexual instinct was isolated as a separate biological and psychical instinct. Each of these four stages thus produced the four sexual objects listed above.

Foucault's work thus suggests a "*genealogical or archaeological analysis*"—that examines the formation of discourses and the constituting processes of desire. Foucault's critical practice thus argues for an interrogation of the will-to-truth, and to restore discourse to its status as an *event*. To this end, Foucault in his essay "The Order of Discourse" outlines certain methodological principles:

(1) A principle of *reversal or subversion*. Reversing the systems of figures and systems, which are normally seen as the *sources* of discourses in the history of ideas.
(2) A principle of *discontinuity*. The discourses must be treated as discontinuous practices, and must be put in opposition to the unity of a work.
(3) The principle of *specificity*. We must imagine that discourse can be resolved into a play of already existing significations (processes of meaning-production).
(4) A principle of *exteriority*. The analysis of the external conditions or structures of possibility for a discourse which produces its (the discourse's) appearance and fixes its limits.

Genealogy is the Foucauldian attempt to reconstruct the origins and development of discourses by demonstrating their "rootedness" in a field of forces/powers. It sees the origins of things in relation to and in contest with other things. Thus genealogy is less textual than deconstruction because it pays attention to the economic and political practices that utilised, imbedded and articulated subjects and power. For Foucault the history of the rules of formation is more important than the formation itself. That is to say, the disciplines *around* texts (literary, legal, scientific, medical) are themselves *part of the problem* that needs genealogical analysis for their role in power relations. Thus Foucault's work to uncover the context of the discourse is through the excavation of the unconscious intertext, the archive.

IV Relationship with Other Disciplines

Deconstructive thought has been enormously influential in a number of other disciplines. We have already noted the Lacanian and Deleuze-Guattari extension of the poststructuralist thought. Gayatri Spivak has yoked deconstruction with Marxism and feminism, and more recently postcolonialism, to develop extraordinarily powerful critiques of patriarchy, class relations, the issue of democracy and the welfare state (best seen in her dialogue with David Plotke in *Radical Democracy*). French feminists such as Luce Irigaray, Helene Cixous and Julia Kristeva have also adopted techniques and modes of reading from poststructuralism. Ernesto Laclau and Chantal Mouffe in *Hegemony and Socialist Strategy* have employed poststructuralist concerns in their analysis of family and civic spheres of power relations. In architecture the work of GHR Tillotson (notably in his *Paradigms of Indian Architecture*, see especially Tillotson's Introduction to the volume) shows signs of poststructuralist influence. The work of Michel Foucault has inspired a range of theoretical readings of the discourses of science, medicine, history, geography, sexuality and gender. Edward Said, the acknowledged initiator of postcolonialism, owes a great deal to Foucault. In a sense there is no "post"-poststructuralism, since newer approaches like postcolonialism and New Historicism owe much to poststructuralist thought.

Poststructuralism and deconstruction thus sought to destabilise traditional unities of the text and the subject. With their turn towards the inherent instabilities within language and the intensely self-conscious critical practice, deconstruction reworked traditional critical studies.

Further Reading

Arac, Jonathan et al, ed. *The Yale Critics: Deconstruction in America.* Minneapolis: University of Minnesota Press, 1983.

Culler, Jonathan. *On Deconstruction: Theory and Criticism after Structuralism.* London: Routledge and Kegan Paul, 1983.

Norris, Christopher. *Derrida.* London: Fontana, 1987.

______. *Deconstruction: Theory and Practice.* London: Methuen, 1982.

Chapter Three

Psychoanalytic Criticism

If psychoanalysis begins with Sigmund Freud, psychoanalytic criticism also finds its earliest expression in Freud's readings of *Hamlet* (1899) and Dostoevsky (1908). Psychoanalytic criticism seeks to uncover the "latent" content of a narrative by teasing out fantasies, fears and desires that are presumed to be the informing "subtext" of any work of art. Evidently such a criticism is "psycho-biographical," locating in the artefact the author's neurosis. Language, images, literary themes are seen as expressing indirectly the author's mental landscape.

I Background and Origins

Sigmund Freud's extraordinary work on dreams, hysteria, sexuality and civilisation form the basis of psychoanalytic criticism. For many decades after Freud, his followers like Ernest Jones and Marie Bonaparte followed Freudian theory to read texts. In the 1960s, the advent of the French thinker Jacques Lacan changed psychoanalysis irrevocably. Lacan, while advocating a "return to Freud," recast Freudian theory in a linguistic framework influenced by Saussure and Emile Benveniste. Lacan's work, which moves from structuralism to a definite poststructural phase, was followed by the philosophical orientation of psychoanalysis in the writings of Gilles Deleuze and Felix Guattari. Other critics such as Harold Bloom, Lionel Trilling and Norman Holland have also adopted Freud at various stages in their work. First, let us survey the Freudian scene.

Freud's work, *as relevant to literary criticism*, may be read under various heads: dreams, sexuality, art, and civilisation.

(1) Freud's main discovery was the role of the *unconscious* in human lives. Freud identified three "levels" of personality:
   (a) the ego—which is consciousness
   (b) the super-ego—which is the conscience

(c) the id—which is the unconscious

The unconscious is the part of the mind, which is beyond the consciousness. This unconscious has, in spite of its "pushed away" existence, a major role in human lives and actions. Unadmitted and inexpressible desires, unresolved conflicts, traumatic pasts and inarticulate fears constitute it. This unconscious therefore contains those elements that cannot be expressed in civilised society. They are "repressed" or "sublimated." Repression is the Freudian term for the "forgetting" or ignoring of these fundamental fantasies and fears. Civilisation is built upon a repressive mechanism. Sublimation entails the conversion of these elements into socially acceptable forms, such as art. Sublimation is thus the disguised escape-mechanism, an alternative to the "madness" of the unconscious. In art the artist's repressed fantasies are given an outlet through the *expressed fantasies* of the artefact. Or, the unconscious may express itself through jokes, puns, and sudden unexpected errors. These are the famous *Freudian slips*.

(2) The libido is the energy drive of sexual desire. For Freud, the libido has three stages: the *oral*, the *anal* and the *phallic*. The oral stage is the first phase, and is associated with the drive to incorporate/ingest objects into the body. The anal stage marks the recognition of the anus as an erotogenic zone. The child derives pleasure from expulsion and removal. The child acquires a psychological tool: where pleasure and anger at others is expressed through the retention/withholding of faeces or the expulsion/granting of the same. The phallic stage organises the pleasure zone around the genitals. Thus the libido is here centred and circumscribed by the child's own body. The child takes an erotic delight in his/her own body: autoeroticism. The libido is part of the life instinct, what Freud termed "*eros*." In opposition to this pleasure drive of eros, Freud postulated the *thanatos*, or the death instinct.

(3) In people who are not artists, the unconscious finds expression in dreams. The dream has two levels: the *manifest content*—which is the dream retained in the memory. The dream, after analysis, reveals a totally different "material," the *latent dream content* and the actual unconscious. Dreams, which thus help un-

wittingly, express the unconscious, are *wish-fulfilments*—they fulfil in dreams what cannot be possibly fulfilled in real life.

(4) The dream work has many mechanisms.

(a) Condensation occurs when a number of disparate elements and images coalesce in a dream. Two or three experiences or impressions are put together and the common element in them draws them into one image. This is a method of superimposition and results in "composite figures"—where one person's face has another's name associated with it in the dream.

(b) Displacement occurs when the psychical intensity passes over from the thoughts and images to which it properly belongs onto another. To phrase it differently, dream displacement shifts the emphasis of meaning from one object to another. Thus aggression, desire, hate, fear are shifted from one object to another in our dreams. Displacement therefore prevents us from identifying actual objects of our unconscious desires/fears because we cannot recognise them anymore. By distorting the dream-thoughts, displacement enables repression because it prevents revelation of disagreeable thoughts.

(c) Transformation is the process by which thoughts are transformed into situations and "dramatised."

(5) The child—always male in Freud (female sexuality was a "dark continent," in Freud's notorious phrase)—passes through the Oedipal stage. Here the boy, as a result of his fixation and separation from the mother's body, recognises in her the first object of his sexual desire. The recognition of this desire is simultaneous with his recognition of the father as a potential rival for the mother's love. Under the *castration threat* of/from the father, which is more perceived/imagined than real (invoked by the boy when he sees the "castrated" female-genitals) the child represses the Oedipal desire. This is the child's turn from the pleasure principle to the "*reality principle*," and his insertion into the "symbolic order" of manhood. The Oedipal complex is thus the point at which the human subject is constituted in society, when he accepts the rules of "civilised behaviour." The "super-ego"

takes shape as his conscience. The father now comes to symbolise all authority, oppression, denial and threat.

(6) What Freud did was therefore to question the ideal of the unified, homogeneous human subject. By revealing that the human is also constituted by the unknown, uncontrollable unconscious, and suggesting that a part of the human lies submerged under repressive sanctions, Freud posited the "split" subject.

(7) During psychoanalysis, the analyst seeks to uncover the unconscious, by interpreting the dreams narrated to him/her by the analysand (patient). The analyst peels away the manifest content of the dream to reveal their latent content. At this point the analysand shifts the object of his psychical troubles, such as his father, onto the analyst. This re-enacts the childhood situation where the analyst is perceived as the same threatening figure. This stage is the famous "transference" one, and helps the analyst unravel the patient's secrets.

(8) For Freud, and for psychoanalysts like Mikkel Borch-Jacobsen and Rene Girard, what triggers desire is not an object but the impulse to identify with the desire of another. Desire is mimetic, and mimesis (imitation) is the matrix of desire. This is illustrated by Borch-Jacobsen in *The Freudian Subject* thus: "I want what my brother, my model, my idol wants—and I want it in his place."

(9) The final goal of all life is death for Freud. It marks and desires the return to a blissful state of pure energy. The clash between eros and thanatos is the fundamental battle of life. Finally the ego, thus far threatened by the conscience-keeper, the superego, and the accumulated frustrations of the id, breaks free.

This is essentially the Freud adopted by psychoanalytic critics.

II Assumptions and General Methods

Psychoanalytic critics follow a general scheme in their analysis of literary texts. The focus is primarily the individual consciousness—of the author or the character—rather than social conditions.

(1) They assume that all texts have an *explicit* content and a hidden one. These correspond to the author's conscious and uncon-

scious respectively. The task of the critic is to unravel these two strands.

(2) They locate in texts images of the libidinal evolution (oral, anal, genital). The role of the body and its "libidinal economy" is seen as all pervasive in the development of the human subject/character.

(3) They locate the Oedipal figures of authority and oppression in the work. They then read the story in terms of the son-father encounter, as mediated by the son's desire for the mother. The son's embattled position vis-a-vis the father, the rivalry between the two, incestuous relations, become subjects of analysis. Thus love is never a mere relationship between two people but a contest between three, where the third is present as a "psychic obstacle" (Maud Ellman's term).

(4) Slips, word games, unguarded sexual symbols (phallic ones such as the gun or the tower, or images of the womb such as caves and hollows) are seen as symptomatic of the author's or character's psychic fantasies/fears. Neurosis and sublimation, repression and dream-states are all read into a text's imagery. Sleep, vampirism, symbols of penetration and conquest, feminisation are frequently analysed as masking deeper anxieties of sexuality, rape and trauma and mother-fixation in texts.

Moving on to a survey of psychoanalytic critics, we shall look at the work of Ernest Jones, Marie Bonaparte, Norman Holland, Norman O. Brown, Jacques Lacan, Shoshana Felman and Deleuze-Guattari. It must be mentioned here that thinkers like Holland and Felman have also been read/classified under other categories of critical theory (in this case Reader-Response and Feminism respectively). Harold Bloom (see section on American deconstruction above) has also demonstrated a considerable Freudian legacy in his work on the anxiety of influence of poetic fathers. Also, I have not included thinkers who have followed and developed Freudian thought but who are not directly concerned with, or influenced, literary theory. Among such thinkers are Erich Fromm, Herbert Marcuse, Melanie Klein, Joel Hovel, Christopher Lasch and developments like ego-psychology or object relations theory.

III Key Thinkers and Concepts

Ernest Jones: Jones, better known for his massive *The Life and Work of Sigmund Freud* (the first full biography, 1957), wrote on dreams, war, religion, vampirism and such diverse subjects. In his first major essay, "The Theory of Symbolism" (1916) Jones connected dream symbols to "primary process" ideas rooted in the repressed unconscious feelings and representations about the body, sexuality. Here the unconscious is the reservoir of images common to all humans and "come out," as it were, during moments of stress, dreams or artistic creativity. Based on the above argument, Jones develops a list of 100 commonly symbolised concepts. In his reading of *Hamlet*, in *Hamlet and Oedipus* (1948), Jones develops Freud's theory of the Oedipal nature of Hamlet's dilemma. Jones argues that Hamlet is ambivalent in his attitude towards his mother (a departure from Freud, who argued that Oedipal motivation was behind Hamlet's procrastination in killing Claudius). Jones argues that Hamlet hesitates because of his wish to kill his mother, which ruins his attempts to kill his uncle. The question for Hamlet, according to Jones, is whether the betrayed man wants to kill the rival lover or the lady.

Marie Bonaparte: She is best known for her massive study of Edgar Allan Poe, widely regarded as the prototypical psychoanalytic reading of any author. An exercise in psychobiography, Bonaparte's work tried to link events in Poe's life to his literary writing. This is done by tracing/reading images and symbols in Poe's tales to certain specific repressed and unconscious fears. Bonaparte treats Poe as an artist who translates his unconscious fears and fantasies into literary images. Bonaparte argues that the death of Poe's mother when he was two years old was his most traumatic experience, and his entire artistic career was an attempt to resurrect the mother. Analysing landscape, characters, symbols in Poe, Bonaparte's uncovers the "maternal image" in tales like "The Black Cat," where the image is disguised and split between the house, the wife and the cat itself. Images of caverns, hollows, and crypts, and of burial alive in tales like "The Cask of Amontillado," "The Premature Burial" are seen as artistic renderings of Poe's fixation with the maternal body and as representing his unconscious desire to return to the womb. Bonaparte's work is now treated as a classic in psychobiography.

Norman Holland: He is one of the more important reader-response theorists. He is here treated as a psychoanalytic critic for his adaptation of Freudianism in developing a theory of reading in works like *The Dynamics of Literary Response* and *Psychoanalysis and Shakespeare*. Holland's foundational theory of literature is this: that readers read to sublimate and transform their unconscious fantasies. The text is enjoyable precisely because it helps us transform our fantasies and fears into something socially acceptable and individually bearable. In later works like *Five Readers Reading*, Holland rejected his earlier idea that the text was a sum total of core fantasies. Instead, he argued here, a text was a "prompter" which generates a series of "recursions" in which the readers are located. Holland argues that critics must admit and recognise their own anxieties, defences and socio-political biases in reading texts. Holland argues that the individual ego adapts to social conditions. It is therefore possible to uncover an "essence" of individual identity by analysing their responses to texts. The readers adapt their identities through the process of interpretation and discover this essence of themselves.

Norman Brown: His works like *Life against Death* (1959) and *Love's Body* (1966) present a mixture of Freud and thinkers like Nietzsche, Emerson and Wilhelm Reich. Brown accepted Freud's controversial argument in *Civilisation and its Discontents* that the human species suffers from a universal neurosis, and that all human institutions and cultures rely upon subjugation of the instincts (repression). Human life was thus based on an illusion, and sublimation of desires. The genitalisation of sexuality, and the enforced social codes are all repressive mechanisms. Even the logic of order and sequentiality are, for Brown, repressive (he therefore adopts a "free association" kind of style in his writing, where ideas are juxtaposed with no apparent sequence). For Brown the only solution to this terrifying problem was available in Freud's notion of the clash between Eros and Thanatos, the pleasure and death instincts. Brown turns to Christian gnosticism, the Cabala, Taoism, Blake and the mystic traditions of the world to suggest that the two drives may be subsumed as the drive for unity of the self and the Other (Freud's "oceanic feeling"). Once this unity is achieved, argues Brown, repression ceases to have any effect upon the individual. Poetry is the dramatisation of the horror of sublimation and repression. Brown here links Freud and Protestantism in his reading of the scatological poetry of Jonathan Swift to argue that the link between money and excrement suggests a world based on the death instinct. This is symbolised, for Brown, in the concept of "filthy lucre" in literature.

Brown traces the unity of self and Other through psychological, historical, and social stages. The movement that Brown suggests (in the drive towards unity) is from the separateness from the mother's body, through repression of political society, intellectual rebellion, the achievement of freedom and finally, nothingness. Evidently Brown is arguing along the lines of the mystic tradition of "inner" journey or quest. For Brown, every writer seeks this unity in a movement towards some ultimate "word."

Jacques Lacan: He is certainly the most influential psychoanalytic thinker since Freud. Lacan's works available in *Ecrits, The Four Fundamental Concepts of Psychoanalysis* and *The Seminars of Jacques Lacan*, suggested a "return to Freud" in a new form—with insights from linguistics. Lacan's theories require extensive elaboration, partly because of his highly dense writing and partly due to his contribution to and influence on later psychoanalytic and post-structuralist thought.

(1) Lacan argues that the child's notion and sense of the self emerges in its reference to an Other. Before the emergence of the self, the child lives in the realm of the *Imaginary*. Here there is no distinction between the I and the Other. There is no centre ("me"). In the pre-Oedipal stage the child has a *symbiotic* relationship with the mother, and does not distinguish between the mother's body and itself.

(2) The "*mirror stage*" is the origin of a fundamental alienation in the child's sense of the self. The child, who is uncoordinated and unintegrated, sees in its mirror image a self which *it would like to be*, an ideal self, well co-ordinated and unified. This is a *misperception*, an illusion, according to Lacan. The child now identifies itself, *imaginatively,* with images and objects. The illusion of a unified self-hood is thus built up.

(3) In terms of language, the child is unaffected by difference in the Imaginary, it is the pre-linguistic and the pre-Oedipal stage. What he sees in the mirror is himself: the signifier (child) and the signified (the mirror image) are not separated. In the Imaginary, the self and the objects-in-the-world are interchangeable: they are the self itself. This is the *metaphoric* stage: where one object can be easily *replaced* by another. (One recalls that Jakobson suggested the metaphoric and metonymic poles of language. Here Lacan equates the Jakobsonian metaphor with Freudian *condensation,* where one may substitute one sign/object for the other. Metonymy is *displacement* because it is relational, and shifts from one object to another).

(4) The belief of the child (of a unified self) is what Lacan terms the "Desire of the Mother," which suggests two things.

   (i) The child imagines itself to be the desire of the mother, that is it (the child) *is all that the mother desires*. Desire here is the metonym for *what is desired.* The child satisfies the mother's lack, it will complete her desire.

   (ii) The Desire of the Mother is also the child's desire *for* the mother. She is the first object of desire because she was instrumental in satisfying its first lacks and needs. Both these desires therefore keep the child in the Imaginary state.

(5) With the mirror stage, the child enters the language system. The figure of the father, prohibitions and laws also enter the child's world. The father is, in Lacanian terms, the *Law*. Social taboos are instilled in the child in the prohibition of incest. The child discovers that it is separate from the mother, and is a part of a whole network—of family and society—in which it is expected and pre-ordained to play a specific part. It discovers that identity is based on difference—its *difference from others*.

(6) Further, the child has to repress his desire for the mother, and the desire is now consigned to the unconscious. This new order is the *Symbolic*. In its entry into the Symbolic, the child is made aware of sexual difference, the recognition of the phallus and gender roles. This awareness accomplishes the child's socialisation. The child has thus discovered that it cannot have a direct access to the body of the mother.

(7) Language in the Symbolic Order which suggests the identity of "I" and "mother" is thus based on the *separation and absence of the mother.* She is *mother* in language, but is not part of *I*. Instead of the signifier *I* being interchangeable with the signifier *mother* (as happens in the Imaginary Order where objects are the self and self is objects, including the inseparability of I and *mother*), the child recognises that the signifier *I* merely refers/relates to and is *different from* other signifiers in a language relation. The signifier *I* is related to other signifiers: *mother, father* and so on, in an endless chain. Thus the Imaginary's *metaphoric condensation* where one could replace any signifier *by* another now gives way to the Symbolic *metonymic displacement* from one signifier *to* another. Language thus assigns gender roles and gender-oriented desire.

(8) The *Real* is the field of experience (life) over which the Imaginary and the Symbolic seek control. The Real is the site where all significations and actions finally orient. In literature the realist text represents the Symbolic with its patriarchal order and insistence on unity, laws and organisation. The anti-realist, modernist text represents the Imaginary because here language moves beyond itself, and is transgressive of order, sequentiality and logic.

(9) Unconscious desire mistakes one appearance for another similar to it, and therefore substitutes one with the other. Or desire may shift from one thing, say A, to another—B which is found/associated with A. B is now discovered as being more appropriate for desire. This movement from one signifier A to another B represents a lack.

(10) For Lacan the lack is *desire*, and desire seeks to *fill* the lack, but can never do so. This is so because desire is the desire for a final meaning, a filling up of the lack of a true signified. If all signifiers refer to other signifiers endlessly and metonymically, it follows that the desire for an end-signified is impossible to fill. Language will always be a "sliding of the signified beneath the signifier." Signifieds that fill desire are always inaccessible (like the mother), perpetually distanced from the signifier (I), and are therefore *repressed*. Meaning, then, always escapes us.

It is merely temporary and symbolises the slipperiness of repressed desire, signifieds, and identities.

(11) The repressed desire is the *unconscious*, which, in seeking an end to the chain of signification, only effects metonymic shifts from signifier to signifier. The unconscious is therefore structured like a language: consisting of the play of difference, of the relational shifts from signifier to signifier.

(12) The self and human subjectivity are linguistic constructs for Lacan. The three important facets of his argument may be summed up thus:

(i) In the mirror stage the child creates the "I." However, Lacan points out the pronoun "I" is an unstable and empty entity: it takes meaning only from the context of its utterance. Thus the "I" can shift from one place to another, from one time to another.

(ii) Language always refers to something not present in the sign. This is to say that language always operates by *absence*. Symbolisation is, for Lacan, predicated upon the object-as-absence. Desire is always, like language, concerned with absence.

(iii) The human subject lives under the illusion that desire/meaning will finally reach the end-signified, that desire will be fulfilled. However, language and desire perpetually postpone this end-signified. All signifiers, as noted above, merely refer to other signifiers.

(13) Lacan's notion of the Unconscious derives from Freud, especially the suggestion that this unconscious has a structure, it is a self. Lacan does not accept the idea that the unconscious is merely instinct. For him the subject does not own the unconscious: the unconscious is the Other of and within the subject. Arguing that negation is merely the taking into account of the repressed, Lacan suggests that whatever is *negated* in a sentence (for example, "I may appear to be insulting, but I really do not wish to insult you" actually implies "I want to insult you") is the unconscious material. Simply put, the unconscious is experienced as the "discourse of the Other."

Shoshana Felman: She is one of the most important post-Lacanian psychoanalysts. Felman's work is situated at the interface of post-modernism, cultural criticism and psychoanalysis. For our purposes the following ideas from Felman's work are of great import.

(1) Adapting the ideas of the speech-act theorist, J.L. Austin, Felman reworks the notion of the *performative* and the *constative*. The performative is the rhetorical enactment, a pure doing in the act of speech itself. For instance "I now pronounce you man and wife" or "I promise" are performatives because they perform the action referred to in the phrase—they do not carry any information. A constative speech act merely states things, and is used for conveying information.

(2) For Felman, Lacan's singular contribution has been to suggest that the performative and the constative are engaged in a perpetual dialogism (see Bakhtin in Chapter One). The human subject is constantly a battleground for the conscious and the unconscious. The two inform and undermine each other. This is the double writing of the self, of what is *enacted* (performed, as in a performative) beyond and outside what can be *known* (as in the constative speech act of information) at any moment.

(3) Felman's interest in pedagogy has also made innovative use of Lacan. Following Lacan, Felman argues that a teacher should teach in relation to the student's unconscious or "unmeant knowledge." This unmeant is the resistance to knowledge, where its laps and gaps are unconscious in origin. The teacher must address the unconscious Other. To this end she suggests a performative enactment of reading the unconscious text by recognising the resistances, absences and unmeant knowledge. Felman's readings focus on the rhetorical dimensions of hiddenness by paying attention to the rhetorical strategies of a text.

Nancy Chodorow: Chodorow is studied under both psychoanalysis and feminism. In two important works, *The Reproduction of Mothering* (1978) and *Feminism and Psychoanalytic Theory* (1989), Chodorow combines the object relations theories of Melanie Klein with contemporary gender concerns.

(1) Chodorow argues that mothers experience their daughters as their "doubles." This is what she calls "*narcissistic object-*

attachment." The mother sees the daughter simply as an extension of her own life.

(2) This means that the daughters find it difficult to form their own identities. They are brought up with a strong capacity for empathy and intimacy but they cannot achieve their desire for autonomy.

(3) For Chodorow, the "core gender identity" of women—narcissism, lack of self-control, weak ego-boundaries—proceeds from their inability to discover separateness.

(4) Desperate, the daughter turns to the father. The father represents the outside world. Here the daughter becomes aware of the social privileges of the phallus.

(5) For boys, masculine identity is also achieved through this relationship with the mother. However, in this case, the mother recognises gender differences and encourages the boy to *discover* separateness. This is because the mothers experience their sons as separate from themselves (note the difference from the relationship with the daughters). This is what Chodorow terms "*anaclitic object-attachment.*"

(6) The "association" with the father in the Oedipal stage is handled differently by boys and girls. Girls, caught in the narcissistic relationship with the mother, develop emotionally through relationships, nurture and care. Boys discover themselves through separation and independence. Though fathers represent the outside world for Chodorow, they have only nominal roles to play. As Chodorow puts it in *Feminism and Psychoanalytic Theory*, paternal authority is the "last-ditch escape from maternal omnipotence."

Deleuze and Guattari: The two are unusual subjects for this study because their work has attempted to reveal the bourgeois ideology imbedded in the apparent "radicalism" of psychoanalysis. They therefore focus on the institutionalisation of psychoanalysis in works like *Anti-Oedipus* (1977) and *A Thousand Plateaus* (1987). The concerns and targets of Deleuze and Guattari may be summarised as follows:

(a) To reveal that repression and castration are fundamental instruments of psychoanalysis itself.

(b) To reject the static model of the unconscious.

(c) To expose the psychoanalytic "situating" of discourse within the oppressive constraints of the Oedipal narrative.

Their arguments may be summed up thus.

(1) Deleuze and Guattari reject the idea of repression and castration as blanket conceptions. They argue that the castration idea (castration is the threat which is supposed to inform the unconscious) implies that there is only one sex—the masculine, in relation to which the woman is defined as the lack (see chapter on Feminism especially section on Irigaray for an elaboration of this idea in the feminist context).

(2) In contrast to this *molar* concept of repression and castration, they suggest a "molecular" model of the unconscious, where the unconscious knows nothing about castration. Castration for them is an ideological construct; it is not a unifying concept.

(3) The unconscious, for Deleuze and Guattari, produce multiplicities and flows with (in their famous definition) "n sexes . . . a hundred thousand." This leads them to argue that even for Freud the unconscious was associated with static *representation* rather than *production* of myth, tragedy and dreams. This means that finally, the unconscious is linked to the family and other such ideological structures of Western civilisation.

(4) Oedipus is not to be perceived as merely an ideological interpretation of psychological functions. For Deleuze and Guattari, Oedipus is the very hegemonic and *limiting* system of Western culture. They therefore propose a *post-Oedipal* world. This would be world without the "genital economy" that will produce a "*body without organs*" (BWO), full of flows and excesses. Instead of the dichotomous model of all Western culture (symbolised in the tree model of knowledge, life, heredity. The tree divides dichotomously, suggesting a binarism and linearity) they propose a "*rhizome*."

(5) The rhizome is a-linear, multiple, spread out, all proliferating and without boundaries, centres/margins or limits. This is what Deleuze terms a "horizontality" of thought. Rejecting the "father principle" or the principle of the origin-as-identity, Deleuze and Guattari argue that there is no distinction between the indi-

vidual and the collective. Traditionally the individual has always been associated with desire and the collective with the law. Deleuze and Guattari instead propose a "social desire." This suggests that desire is always in movement, always constituted by different elements depending upon the situation. This, they suggest, is machine-like rather than a drama (of Oedipal representation). Desire is not lack, which suggests negativity. It is affirmative in its state of movement and change. Thus the BWO is constantly in the process of formation, deformation and reformation. The BWO is itself rhizomatic, which loses a point/channel of desire (deterritorialisation) only to start off along a new path like a rhizome's, spread (*reterritorialisation*).

IV Relationship with Other Disciplines

Psychoanalytic criticism has moved into film studies in the work of Deleuze and Guattari and Shoshana Felman. Lacan has been adopted by numerous influential feminists thinkers such as Luce Irigaray, Jacqueline Rose, Elizabeth Grosz (whose current work coalesces psychoanalysis with gender studies, urban sociology and geography), Judith Butler, Juliet Mitchell and others. Freud's work has influenced social theorists such as Marcuse and Fromm. Elizabeth Wright, Maud Ellman, Harold Bloom and numerous critics have adapted various aspects of psychoanalytic thought for literary exegesis to produce brilliant readings. Though psychoanalytic criticism has become the subject of much ridicule for its "eromania," critics have found it useful in debating texts. A case in point would be the never-ending debate over the Derridean and Lacanian readings of Edgar Allan Poe's "The Purloined Letter."

Further Reading

Ellman, Maud. *Psychoanalytic Literary Criticism.* London and New York: Longman, 1994.

Elliott, Anthony. *Psychoanalytic Theory: An Introduction.* Oxford: Blackwell, 1994.

Lemaire, Anika. *Jacques Lacan.* Trans. David Macey. London: Routledge, 1970.

Wollheim, Richard. *Freud.* London: Fontana, 1971.

Wright, Elizabeth. *Psychoanalytic Criticism: Theory in Practice.* London: Methuen, 1984.

Chapter Four

Feminism

Feminist literary criticism is essentially linked to the political movement for equality of the sexes and end to discrimination against women. Feminist criticism seeks to uncover the ideology of patriarchal society in works of art. It reads literary texts for their representations of women, and argues that these representations mask socio-political oppression of the category of women by justifying this oppression and naturalising it. For feminists, the text is a battleground where actual power relations between men and women are played out.

I Background and Origins

Writers like Mary Wollstonecraft in *A Vindication of the Rights of Women* (1792), male authors like J.S. Mill in *The Subjection of Women* (1869) and Friedrich Engels in *The Origin of the Family* (1884) wrote of the need to rethink the role of women and social oppression against them. In the early twentieth century, Olive Schreiner, Virginia Woolf and later Simone de Beauvior have written on the gender questions from the perspective of and oriented towards issues like education, marriage, economics, sexuality and morals.

With the 1960s, the Women's Movement became a major political force. While the movement took various issues for the gender-debate (including science, politics, economics, culture, epistemology) literary critics influenced by the movement undertook a whole new project. This included re-reading the canon of English literature to expose the patriarchal ideology that informed the construction of the canon in the first place, and which made male-centred writing possible. The influences were many: philosophy, psychoanalysis, linguistics, Marxism and others. Feminist thinkers borrowed and adapted numerous such modes of critical thought to frame new theoretical positions.

II General Assumptions and Methods

The feminist critics are informed by certain assumptions and follow certain modes of analysis. The analysis varies according to the ideological/philosophical position espoused by the thinker, yet certain common features are discernible.

(1) They assume that literary texts operate on the lines of power struggle: that between men and women. The text naturalises the oppression of women through its stereotypical representation of women as weak/vulnerable, seductress, obstacle, sexual object of the male's desire, a procreating device and so on.

(2) They argue that literary texts reproduce social biases that see the woman as only the "Other" of the male. Religion, social conditions and cultural traditions perceive the woman as an adjunct to the male. This means that the woman's identity is never separate but is subsumed under that of the male.

(3) The woman is typecast as "Mother Nature," thus reducing her to the perpetually giving, all-forgiving nature that never demands anything, is willing to suffer anything for her Son. Religious doctrines aid these representations. Language makes it appear permanent and "natural" through the use of patriarchal terms like Mother Earth, Mother Nature.

(4) *Sex* is biological while *gender* is socially constructed. There is no necessary link between gender and biological sex. Masculinity and femininity are essentially coercive categories that straitjacket men and women. In Simone de Beauvoir's famous statement, a woman is not born: she becomes, is made a woman. This is to say that the socialisation of woman renders her a woman with certain apparently "inherent" qualities—weakness, feeble-mindedness, patience and so on. All these help patriarchal males to argue that women need to be confined to the home (they are not strong to "go out" into the world), be protected and controlled. Her sexuality and desires are made and treated as subservient to that of the male's. Thus the feminists suggest that inequality of sexes does not have a biological basis or origin, it

originates in the cultural constructions of gender difference. *Gendering* is a practice of power, where masculinity is always associated with authority.

(5) There is a relationship between gender dualism, sexuality and sexual orientation. Sexuality is the product of cultural processes and forces: we are not born gay, lesbian or heterosexual. The discourse of sexuality, which privileges/enforces a "*compulsory heterosexuality*" (as the poet Adrienne Rich terms it. See chapter on Lesbian and Gay Theory) creates conditions of legitimacy and illegitimacy where heterosexuality alone is legitimate. This becomes the social norm, and reinforces the division between the genders by positing that sexual desire may "prevail" only between men and women.

(6) Disciplines such as psychoanalysis or philosophy (which, feminists point out, were built upon male thought and "discoveries") helps retain the hierarchy of male/female. These disciplines must be studied to expose their ideological biases.

(7) There is the need for a canon of women's writing.
   (a) Since literature, criticism and departments/syllabi have relied upon male texts for understanding and "revealing" the condition of women, all they have actually done is reinforce patriarchal ideology. They have also helped subtly disseminate this ideology through their self-created status as "representative" or "authoritarian" texts
   (b) A woman's text will suggest an alternative picture of the conditions, desires, psychology of the woman.

(8) In terms of language and epistemology, the feminists seek to formulate either a gender-neutral language which will reject patriarchal terms like *his*tory and *man*kind, or a specifically female language (see Irigaray and Cixous below) which will help create an alternative epistemology itself—one based on female subjectivity, identity and experience. This would also suggest a new historiography itself, where the voice of the silenced subaltern-woman will provide an alternative history.

(9) Feminist criticism is political in its scope. It demonstrates the link between the economic conditions, work-place conditions and political hegemony that influence, inform and create gender

oppression, inequalities and exploitative mechanisms against the women.

(10) Feminists in the 1980s and 90s also move beyond the essentialising tendencies of early feminism by delineating local, racial, and region specific gender oppression. While the early feminists sought a common platform for all women irrespective of racial or regional differences (based on the common denominator of oppression), the later feminists argued for different approaches to suit these specific conditions. Here feminism moves away from the Eurocentric and heterosexual biases of early feminism and develops into Black feminism, "Third World" or postcolonial feminism, and lesbian critical theory (see chapters on Black and Gay/Lesbian Theory below).

We can now survey the development of feminist thought in the twentieth century. The strands and thinkers in feminism discussed here are early feminism (Woolf, Beauvoir, Kate Millett), psychoanalytic feminism (Juliet Mitchell, Luce Irigaray, Helene Cixous), political feminism (Pauline Johnson, Carole Pateman), socialist and Marxist feminism (Eli Zaretsky, Michele Barrett) and poststructuralist feminism (Irigaray, Cixous). Nancy Chodorow, also a psychoanalytic feminist, is discussed in chapter three, under psychoanalytic theory. Lesbian feminism figures in the chapter on lesbian and gay theory. There are overlaps, since feminism is perhaps the most interdisciplinary and plural of approaches. Most of the thinkers mentioned above borrow from and adapt theories from linguistics, psychoanalysis, philosophy and poststructuralism. Thinkers like Spivak and strands such as ecofeminism will figure in the chapters on postcolonialism and ecocriticism respectively.

III Key Concepts and Thinkers

Virginia Woolf: Woolf in *A Room of One's Own* (1929) and *Three Guineas* (1938) has analysed the gender biases and oppressive structures in pedagogic practices to meditate upon the woman's question.

(1) Gender oppression and patriarchal university institutions prevent the female researcher from discovering or interpreting as a

woman. They deny access to woman's texts, and suggest that the male's version/vision of the woman is the true one.

(2) Language itself is gendered, so that when the woman takes to writing she is forced to use the masculine tongue. The male novelists have already decided on form and structure of literary language—a language that privileges order, tight diction, linearity and pattern. This is not suitable for the woman novelist, who requires a "freer" language. Woolf detects a sense of bitterness in women novelists such as George Eliot, Charlotte Bronte and Jane Austen for this reason: they are unhappy with the language they are forced to use.

(3) Economic independence and a separate space are crucial to the woman. Further Woolf analyses the different "culture" of males.

(4) It is the male sex which has fought wars and killed people.

(5) Women see things differently. Being "outside" enables the woman to look at the institutions of power, all of which are based on the male's need to pander to his ego. Without denigrating women, even leaders like Mussolini and Napoleon could not have survived as "heroes." If the nineteenth century feminist fought against the patriarchal state, the contemporary feminists fight against the fascist one.

(6) To prevent fascism one needs to build colleges based on the women's value systems. This college will do away with war-related research and advocate a humanistic ethic.

(7) Women must enter positions of power. Yet they must retain their feminine value system. This value system derives from what Woolf calls "the four great teachers of educated men—poverty, chastity, derision and freedom from unreal loyalties."

(8) Woolf advocates the establishment of an "Outsiders' Society" (her term for separatist cultural and social institutions). This will encourage the development of a women's ethic that is holistic, anti-war, anti-fascist and life-affirming. This ethic can eventually become the basis for a whole new public morality, according to Woolf.

Simone de Beauvoir: Her *The Second Sex* (1949) seeks to understand the relegation of the woman into a "second sex."

(1) De Beauvoir argues that the terms "man" and "woman" are not value free. The man is positive, the standard one. By implication the woman is negative, the Other/variation of the standard and second.

(2) The woman thus has no value or identity by herself—she is defined in relation to the man. More precisely, she is defined as *what man is not*. De Beauvoir argues that the concept of "Othering" is crucial to the construction of human identity. *I* define myself as different from *you* or *not-I*. The *not-I* is the "Other" of me. Individual, racial, national identities are based upon this essential notion of their difference from the Other. Similarly, the male defines himself in terms of his Other—the woman. In Beauvoir's words "[woman] is defined and differentiated with reference to man and not he with reference to her. . . . He is the Subject, he is the Absolute—she is the Other."

(3) This results in a situation where the Other/woman is an emptiness which is granted a value depending on what the dominant and dominating group requires at the moment. The man is able to construct himself in terms of his *difference* from the not-man (the woman). That is, different from the not-man possessing qualities which are in negative opposition to the man's. Thus the woman is emotional where the male is reasoning, she is weak where the male is strong, and so on. In all these the male is able to articulate his maleness (associated with virility, reasoning, scientific logic, strength) as positive qualities.

(4) Woman, for de Beauvoir, becomes mythicised, the subject of male dreams, and idealisations. Cultures all over the world and through history have therefore projected certain qualities into/onto the woman, depending on the masculine need of the moment. Beauvoir writes: "the categories in which men think of the world are established from their point of view, as absolute. . . . A mystery for man, woman is considered to be mysterious in essence." Thus the woman becomes associated with life, fragility, purity, beauty, goodness, "nature" on certain occasions. On other occasions, she is evil, seductress/temptress, corrupter, death.

(5) De Beauvoir argues that such a representation enables the man to bestow woman with his fears as well as his desires, his loves

and his hatreds. This is the "double and deceptive image [of the woman]." "A woman is not born, but rather becomes, a woman," as Beauvoir phrased it.

(6) The woman is thus "naturalised" with the qualities that are granted her. She is never able to be other than this image given her. Male versions of femininity are deemed as the definitive versions—there is no female truth except what the *male construes it to be*. This is, unfortunately, deeply assimilated into/by the woman too. Ironically, the woman herself sees men's visions of feminine as authentic too. This is what de Beauvoir describes famously as "[women] still dream through the dreams of men." What is needed then is for women to start *reading as women*.

Kate Millett: Millett's *Sexual Politics* (1969), situated at the crossroads of literary and cultural criticism and political theory, launched a major criticism of canonical male authors like Lawrence, Norman Mailer and Henry Miller.

(1) Focusing on the man-woman relationships between characters in the works of these novelists, Millett demonstrated that sexual relationships controlled by the males reinforced gender oppression.

(2) For Millett sexuality becomes a tool through which stereotyping of the female—as prostitutes, virgins, unchaste women, or sexual anorexics—achieves patriarchal domination. Millett defined sexual politics as "the arrangements whereby one group of persons is controlled by another." For Millett these arrangements that controlled sexual relationships extended into the domain of ideology, biology, socio-cultural institutions like family, religion and education and psychology.

(3) Violence and coercion are used to sustain these images/ stereotypes so that the male's control over sexuality is never loosened. The hypermasculine "machismo" image of the male characters in these novelists, for Millett, is produced out of a fear of a "second sexual revolution."

(4) Millett also devotes a lot of space to uncovering the "phallocentrism" in the work of Freud. Freud was, for Millett, instrumental in suggesting masculine sexuality as *the* sexuality, and

thus reinforcing patriarchal domination. The biological determinism of Freud that led him to see women as suffering from a fundamental "lack" (and the resultant penis envy) was simply a continuation of the Western idea (since Aristotle) of the woman being "incomplete." Instead, argues Millett, it might be possible that the girl child, with her "childish narcissism" takes "*her own body as norm*." Millett's accusations against Freud were to be very influential among later feminists.

Juliet Mitchell: Writing in the sixties and seventies, Mitchell's work in *Woman's Estate* (1971), Mitchell argued that woman's oppression was linked to FOUR essential social structures: production, reproduction, sexuality and socialisation. Mitchell sought to combine a critique of socialist thought and psychoanalysis for feminist theory in what was one of the earliest attempts to make feminism interdisciplinary, and overtly political (especially in its reliance upon Marxism). In *Psychoanalysis and Feminism* (1974), and her collaborative (co-edited) work with Jacqueline Rose in *Feminine Sexuality* (1982), Mitchell responded to the accusations levelled by Kate Millett against Freud.

(1) Mitchell, here influenced by Lacanian thought, argues that to abandon Freud would be detrimental to the feminist cause, especially since Freud's work was a *critique* and analysis of patriarchal society. Defending the Freudian theory of castration, Mitchell suggests that fantasy rather than fact determines gender.

(2) The unconscious is the "domain . . . of the reproduction of culture or ideology." The exchange of women in marriage as a mode of relationship in primitive societies actually renders women as *objects* to unite society. In Mitchell's words, women's identities are determined by their "cultural utilisation as exchange objects."

(3) Since the female is supposed to be anxious over her "lack" (of the male organ) and the male is anxious about losing it through castration, Mitchell argues that the castration is only symbolic, never realised. Definitions of masculinity and femininity are constituted through the symbolic, where man is the self-

determining, autonomous agent and the woman is the lacking Other.

(4) Gender is thus a cultural construct, one created as a fantasy in children to explain the unpleasant discoveries of genital differences. It rejects the sexual distinction by presupposing and fictionalising that the sexes were once one (i.e. before castration). This *socially conditioned fantasy*, rather than an instinctually constructed one institutes the gender divide. Man sees and believes himself to be a unified whole as a result. This makes the feminine at once knowable and the guarantor of fantasy.

(5) This is itself the result of late capitalism where there is the split between the private and the public, and the idealisation of male-centred family life.

Elaine Showalter: Showalter's work has pioneered work on creating a woman-centred literary history. Along with Nina Baym's *Woman's Fiction* (1978), Showalter's *The New Feminist Criticism* (1985) and *Speaking of Gender (*1989) have argued for a specifically "female framework for the analysis of women's literature."

(1) Calling for new models based on the woman's experience rather than a blind addiction to and adaptation of masculine theories and models, Showalter launched the search for "*gynocriticism*" (her term).

(2) Gynocriticism should, in Showalter's description, look at "the history, styles, themes, genres, and structures of writing by women; the psychodynamics of female creativity; the trajectory of the individual or collective female career; and the evolution or laws of a female literary tradition." Citing Irving Howe's famous praise of Hardy's *The Mayor of Casterbridge* as an example of "phallic criticism" that ignores the woman reader's reaction to Henchard's deed of selling his wife and child, Showalter argues that Howe's criticism is built on the *stereotype* of the nagging wife, while simultaneously suggesting the constricting conditions of domesticity *upon the male*. It is this kind of criticism that reinforces patriarchal structures of power, argues Showalter. The 1970s have been marked by a shift of critical attention from such evidently patriarchal *androtexts* to "*gynotexts*" (texts by women).

(3) In her seminal *A Literature of Their Own* (1977), Showalter analyses the mechanisms through which the women writers were assiduously kept out of the literary canon during the nineteenth century. The criticism of the time was almost entirely patriarchal in its opinions, rejecting women's texts as limited in range, superfluous and trivial. Showalter detects a double bind on the woman writer of the age: in the first place she was limited to certain themes in her writings by the prevalent male critical opinion. This opinion stated: "the woman's novel deals with domestic problems, children, clothing fashions and food." This means that the male literary establishment decided the themes for her. Secondly, this same male establishment attacked the woman novelist's work as inconsequential precisely because she wrote only of home, fashion and food! Showalter comments: "to their contemporaries, nineteenth century women writers were women first, artists second." Rejecting the practice of identifying a "tradition" only in terms of great figures, Showalter lists 213 women authors in her appendix.

(4) Showalter identifies three major phases in the development of women's writing. These three phases are predominantly responses of women authors to the socio-cultural contexts which were patriarchal through and through.

(i) The *Feminine* phase, 1840-1880. Here women writers imitated the male writer's modes. Worse, they assimilated, accepted and finally perpetuated through their work the patriarchal aesthetic and social values. Showalter points out that the women writers of the nineteenth century adopted masculine names or emphasised their marital status. The examples are of George Eliot, Mrs. Gaskell, Mrs. Oliphant and others. There was an "all-inclusive female realism" used by these authors for "exploration of the daily lives and values of women within the family and community" as well as a mode of symbolic fiction to "dramatise the inner life."

(ii) The *Feminist* phase begins in the 1880s-1890s and extends to around the 1920s. This phase is characterised by Showalter as a protest phase, where women authors rebelled against prevalent patriarchal attitudes. The authors rebelled against the Victorian sexual stereotypes and began to explore the woman's position in terms of work, class and the family. This phase is marked by the demand for autonomy on the part of women and the initiation of an "all-out war between the sexes."

(iii) The *Female* phase which follows the feminist in the twentieth century is marked by the woman writer's search for her own voice and identity as opposed to the identity "granted" here by patriarchy. Showalter perceives the post-1960s as a heightened Female phase. Here there is the "double legacy of feminine self-hatred and feminist withdrawal." More importantly, it polarised sexuality, and perceived sexuality as the possible source of creativity. Showalter detects Freudian and Marxist influences in authors of the female phase.

Ellen Moers: Moers' *Literary Women* (1976) was, along with Gilbert and Gubar's (see below), one of the early attempts to uncover the female literary tradition. Reading a range of authors like George Eliot, Harriet Beecher Stowe, Emily Dickinson and Elizabeth Barrett Browning, Moers presents an interactional relational model of female literary history. Moers' work explores the influence of women writers on each other. This ability and need to listen to other voices is, for Moers, a special feature of literary women. This results in the commonality of certain images, all of which are, in some form or the other, symbolic representations of the female body.

Moers' work focuses on the practical and living history of women writers from the eighteenth to the twentieth centuries. Attempting to unravel the unique experiences of women, Moers reads much archival and manuscript sources. The tradition of women writers are discussed under the traditional genres and categories such as Gothic, The Epic Age and Realism. Moving onto a discussion of literary feminism, Moers detects a heroic structure for the female voice, one that she terms "*heroinism*." Heroinism includes as its constitutive features traditional ones such as loving, caring and "radical" ones such as education.

Sandra Gilbert and Susan Gubar: Like Showalter, Gilbert and Gubar have analysed the nineteenth century for the position of the woman novelist in *The Madwoman in the Attic* (1979), the 2-volume *No Man's Land* (1987-89) and their edition of *The Norton Anthology of Literature by Women* (1985). Their interest, like Showalter, is in the material conditions of the woman writer's creativity. Hence their reading of authors like Austen, the Brontes, Mary Shelley, George Eliot and Emily Dickinson in *Madwoman* is mainly an analysis of the social conditions of authors' lives, the literary canon and the archives. The early nineteenth century women writers were working from within a male vision of creativity. Women had to negotiate with the male fantasies of the female, which were either of the submissive female-as-angel or the dangerous female-as-monster. These fantasies were literary models for women authors. Gilbert and Gubar argue that the madwoman image in most fiction by the woman author represented her (the author's) double, the "schizophrenia of authorship" and the anxiety/rage of creation. Beneath the surface of the conformist woman's text, Gilbert and Gubar detect a "true" woman's story. Women's texts, argue Gilbert and Gubar, construct techniques of evasion and concealment. Women writers responding to early authors present characters who resort to subterfuge to win the battles. By the projection of rebellious impulses into mad/monstrous women, the female authors of the nineteenth century "dramatise their own self-division, their desire to both accept the structures of patriarchal society and to reject them." Bertha Rochester represents for them the symbol of confinement *and* revolt.

The women move out of the attic—to which they have been confined like Bertha Rochester in *Jane Eyre*—to wage a battle with men. Studying the works of male authors the essays in *No Man's Land* (volume one: *The War of the Words*) presents the battle in figures of erotic duels, the impotent man, plots where men defeat hypersexual women and so on. In volume two, *Sexchanges*, the model of battle is extended to consider sexchanges. Gilbert and Gubar write: "the sexes battle because sex roles change, but when the sexes battle, sex itself (that is eroticism) changes." These changes include the rebellion against the feminisation of the American woman in World War I, lesbianism and transvestism.

Thus Gilbert and Gubar suggest two theoretical models to chart the female tradition.

(1) The "*anxiety of authorship*": deriving from Freud's notion of the Oedipus complex. If women (argue Gilbert and Gubar) follow a female resolution of the Oedipus complex, the father/male literary canon becomes the object of female desire and the pre-Oedipal desire for the mother/female literary canon is abandoned. Twentieth century women authors have the option of the "*affiliation complex*" which allows them to adopt literary *mothers*, now that a female literary tradition has been established, and thereby escape the father's anxiety of influence. Traditionally in Freudian theory, the girl-child upon discovering that her mother is castrated turns away from the mother and towards the father as the source of power and authority. This was easier for the nineteenth century woman authors. The twentieth century is more complex. If the female author tries a *normative*, that is rule-bound, resolution of the Oedipus complex, it may lead to anxiety of having usurped paternal primacy and therefore fear of male retribution and vengeance. A *non-normative resolution* may help a "*masculinist complex*" which grants autonomy, maternal relation with female/mother predecessor authors and the creative option of male mimicry. However, Gilbert and Gubar suggest that such identification with the mother/precursor author is not free from anxiety—this time it is fear of castration at the hands of the *mother*. They write: "we suspect that the love women writers send forward into the past is, in patriarchal culture, inexorably contaminated by mingled feelings of rivalry and anxiety."

(2) *Fantasies* figure prominently in the theories of Gilbert and Gubar. These may be *linguistic fantasies* or *fantasy identifications*. Feminist and linguistic fantasies grant a primary role to the mother rather than the father in the process of language acquisition. Women fantasise not about a revision of women's language but a revision of the woman's *relation to language*. They argue that the use of the sentence as definitive, the acquisition of a priestly language which resists the vernacular and the "mother tongue" as modes of retaining male authority over language. Woman authors now seek fantasies in identifications

with alternative figures, myths and metaphors: Sappho, Aphrodite, and transvestism.

Eli Zaretsky: Her *Capitalism, the Family and Personal Life* (1976), along with the work of Juliet Mitchell in *Woman's Estate* (1974) and the writings of Zillah Eisenstein, is an important text in the *socialist-feminist* tradition. A brief sketch of the central concerns of *socialist feminism* is in order before we move on to Zaretsky.

Socialist feminism looks at the following areas.

(i) The issue of domestic labour and its role in capitalist economy. The woman's labour in the house is much more integrated with her life than for the male. Her economic dependency is an important factor, since it deprives her of any political control.

(ii) The relationship women have with the modes of production as wage earners. Here the "double duty" of women becomes clear: as wage earners in the public sphere, but as unpaid labourers in the private/household one.

(iii) The role of the family in ideological socialisation (private and public, the role of the mother, moral values and so on).

(iv) The question of ideology and consciousness.

Zaretsky's work shows a concern with all the four issues mentioned above.

(1) Zaretsky argues that capitalism produced a massive spilt between the public and private spheres. Material production was split between commodity production in the public/socialised sphere and private labour performed by women at home. As a result "work" and "life" were separated.

(2) The transformation of workers into commodities (what Zaretsky terms "Proletarianisation" split off the external world from the inner world of feeling.

(3) The only sphere of subjective resistance was therefore the home. The family became the "utopian retreat," away from the industrial set up.

(4) Housewives had the responsibility of maintaining the emotional and psychological realm of personal relations. For the women, within the family, "work" and "life" had collapsed into one another. Housewives' labour remained essentially unalienated, but

was given the job of preservation of human values (which was considered impossible in the public sphere).

Michele Le Doeuff: A philosopher by profession and training Le Doeuff's *The Philosophical Imaginary* (1989) argued that philosophy has a specific imaginary level intrinsic to itself. This imaginary level sets the conditions of what can be constructed as rationality within it. For Le Doeuff, images such as islands, fog, stormy seas in philosophical texts are not merely metaphorical. These images function to close off the text, making it self-contained. Images in philosophy are explained within philosophy's meta-discourse (discourse about itself) in two ways: (1) as the mark of the return of a primitive or child-like form of thought. (2) as possessing an intuitive self-evident clarity which communicates the thoughts of the speaker/philosopher to the reader/listener. These images are perceived as means of communication to an uncultivated reader. But for Le Doeuff, the real effect of the image is hidden. Images help dogmatisation, positing the "that is the way it is" condition to forestall any counter argument. It is presumed that the good reader will bypass such illustrations. Images, then, are a means whereby philosophy can be unphilosophical by closing off the subject of discussion. This is almost the closure of philosophy itself.

Le Doeuff does not accept the Irigaray argument that the language of philosophy is masculinist (and therefore prevents the woman from speaking). Le Doeuff argues that reason and rationality are not inherently masculine. There are a plurality of rationalities, and not a single hegemonic one. There has been, Le Doeuff admits, a systemic structure which has prevented women from taking to philosophy. The reduction of woman to her sex has alienated her from philosophy (Le Doeuff's target here is Rousseau, who announced that abstract truths are not for women). To deconstruct the sexism of philosophy, Le Doeuff resorts to the very conditions of philosophy itself: its need for openness and dialogue, its self-reflexivity and self-questioning tradition. The historical practice of philosophy has misrecognised the role of images, has emphasised abstractedness, has rejected the true openness ("wandering") of thought, has treated the woman as the Other, and has been rigid in its style and method. Women have always been seen as *devotees* of great male philosophers, rarely as independent thinkers. What distinguishes a man is his independence as person and thinker. But women like Simone de Beauvoir use the male's text to address women's question. Thus *The Second Sex* adapts Sartrean existentialism to address the issue of morality. De Beauvoir, for Le Doeuff with her own twist to Sartrean philosophy stops being a devotee. For Le Doeuff philosophy is a liberating force. Philosophy offers a model of autonomy and independence of thought.

Carole Pateman: Pateman's work has been in the realm of political theory. Pateman argues that for political theory to become more democratic it must develop a truly general theory of the political. This must necessarily avoid the trap of disqualifying certain categories of persons from being political subjects. Rereading Locke, Hobbes, Rousseau and Marx, Pateman's work has focussed on two particular issues:

(a) The issue of legitimate political obligation: Pateman believes that a convincing explanation for political authority based on consent is absent in political theory. That is if we ask why any individual should obey the law, political theory can give no answer.

(b) The nature of political society, and the distinction between the private and public spheres: The definition of the political almost entirely in terms of the public sphere/civil society has affected the political rights of women. The domestic sphere, reproduction, mothering, kinship, emotional bonds are seen as the woman's domain, in the area of particular and local interests. The public sphere is thus the site of reason, rationality, autonomy and creativity. This system therefore makes the entry of the woman into the public sphere extraordinarily difficult.

(1) Pateman argues that the woman's "domestication" implies that she cannot participate in the public sphere with any great efficacy. The public sphere and the political require rationality and objectivity. The woman by being (represented) irrational and emotional cannot therefore undertake such an office. The "free and equal" individual, the subject of liberal political theory is thus only the *man*.

(2) Pateman further argues that political theory continues to read canonical texts which do not account for the woman's role in the social and political life. The transition from tradition to modernity as seen in political theory can be equated with the opposition between the public and private spheres. The public society and body politic revolves around the male individual who is constructed through the separation of civil society from women. Thus to grant citizenship to women is to suggest that the woman assumes a male identity. The only means of entry into the public sphere for the woman is to *imitate* men: for they cannot be different and citizens at the same time. This means that women must first reject their bodies.

(3) Evidently what is required is a new approach to the idea of the politic. Pateman argues that since the woman did not consent to the Social Contract, the Contract has not been fully realised. Likewise in marriage, women cannot be said to have given their consent for an unequal power relation. The problem is to understand how a private/individual sphere (such as marriage) which is not subject to the law but which has unequal relations and the subjection/silencing of one "side," can be retained in a truly democratic society. The private-public dichotomy must be therefore rethought to discover a new political theory.

Luce Irigaray: In her works like *Speculum of the Other Woman* (translated 1985) and *This Sex Which is Not One* (1987), Irigaray has argued that the woman has been constructed as the specular Other of man in all Western discourses. Combining psychoanalysis, philosophy and linguistics, Irigaray's work has been enormously influential in poststructuralist feminist thought. Irigaray's rejection of the male symbolic order in order to highlight difference has been regarded as the "radical feminist" phase of the feminist movement.

(1) The speculum is the curved mirror (one turned back on itself) of feminine self-examination. This is opposed to the flat mirror which privileges the relation of man with other men but excludes the feminine. Psychoanalysis has always inscribed masculine ideology. Irigaray seeks to uncover a feminine order of meaning so that a sexual identity of the woman may be constructed.

(2) She therefore argues against the "logic of sameness" operating within all discourse. This logic means that two specificites—of man and woman—are consistently merged into one: "man is the measure of all things." Turning to Freud, Irigaray shows how Freud's theory of sexuality is basically premised on one sex—the male. There is the male and there is the absence or lack—the female. The male is the paradigm of all sexuality—physical changes (Freud, Irigaray points out speaks of the "lack" in the females, but never speaks of the degeneration of breasts in the males, which should also be construed a "lack") and sexual pleasure—and sexuality is *a priori* male for Freud. Irigaray notes: "female sexuality has always been conceptualised on the basis of masculine parameters."

(3) Irigaray traces the logic of sameness right back to Plato. She argues that the logic of sameness collapses the two specificities as follows: into one and its negative-man and not-man, A and not-A (or A-minus). This means that instead of two separate autonomous entities A, B we have one positive (A) and its negative. The second term/identity is only what the first is not. All difference between the sexes is eradicated through this means. This is why Irigaray suggests that the *flat* mirror reflects back to the male, indicates only the fullness of male identity. This also means that it becomes impossible for the woman to represent herself. She is always, writes Irigaray, "off-stage, off-side, beyond representation, beyond selfhood." This logic is also indicative of the privileging (a) of the male organ and (b) of the unitary notion of truth, where the patriarchal truth is *the only* truth. Irigaray has set the stage for the articulation of the autonomous feminine subject, the thus-far effaced B of discourse.

(4) Irigaray suggests a specifically feminine writing practice. Proceeding from the assumption that a different order of meaning is necessary to construct a positive representation of the feminine, Irigaray searches out new linguistic modes of expressing the feminine self. The Lacanian idea that language is phallic, Irigaray argues, implies a dangerous situation. For the woman to speak, she must speak *like a man*, or else to break away from

the social/symbolic. If women are to have their own identity, they must subvert the phallic version of the symbolic. She sees writing as going through the looking glass into a world of woman's self-representation.

(5) Irigaray therefore adopts a slippery kind of writing herself. Puns, word plays, syntactic experiments and new arrangements, fragmentation become the modes of feminine writing that breaks the stranglehold of masculine rigidified and rule bound language. Reading and writing then must favour the images and metaphors of fluidity, dynamism, polysemy and plurality (all feminine) rather than those of unity, monologism, stability and fixity.

(6) She associates the metaphor of the specular mirror with this feminine representation. The curved surface of the speculum produces a deformed image which reverses the reflections of masculine discourse. Irigaray writes: then "the specular surface [will be] found not the void of nothingness but the dazzle of multifaceted speleology. A scintillating and incandescent concavity." This curved surface represents the inner specificity of the female body. Women need to first represent themselves to themselves in order to constitute themselves as social beings *who can form positive relationships with one another.*

(7) Rejecting the primacy of sight in psychoanalysis, Irigaray returns to the pre-Oedipal stage where the sense of touch rules the mother-child relation. In addition, Irigaray rejects the focus on genitals as the erogenous zone in classical psychoanalysis. Arguing that the woman's body is multiplicity itself, Irigaray suggests that female sexuality is also multiple in its erogenous zones. It is now necessary to see female sexuality as not a lack but as "two lips" which are evidently different from the unitariness of the male organ. The lips are "continually interchanging" and touching, they are "neither identifiable nor separable from one another . . . these two are always joined in an embrace." Fluidity, multiplicity and the primacy of touch inform Irigaray's writing. Lacanian psychoanalysis which privileges metaphor (considered semi-solid) over metonymy (considered fluid) has resulted in the neglect of the feminine sexuality. Feminine sexu-

ality which is fluid is always ignored in favour of the solidity of the phallus.

(8) Foregrounding the mother-daughter relationship, Irigaray argues that the woman's inability to represent herself is due to the undermining of the mother-daughter bond by and in the Symbolic Order. Motherhood is allowed only a small space, denied economic or social status and separated from the very aspect of sexuality. Creativity is a male domain, motherhood is restricted to the nurture and care of the child. The daughter in the patriarchal system must separate from the mother in order to gain her own identity. The daughter is thus "exiled" from her first identity and history.

(9) Irigaray argues that this condition must be rectified by the invention of a new language that redefines motherhood in explicitly sexual terms. Such a language will allow the mother and daughter separate identities but retain their bond. In her search for the equivalent of the mother-daughter bond, Irigaray has resurrected those aspects of Western culture that symbolise specifically feminine conditions: witchcraft, sorcery and the divine feminine. These have been repressed in the masculine symbolic order, argues Irigaray. There is not even a feminine god, she points out. The feminine god has to be the god of becoming, the god of fluidity, of porous boundaries, and of the very elements (air, fire, water and earth). The quest for such a feminine god is thus the search for an alternative point of reference other than the patriarchal one.

Helene Cixous: Cixous' work has been influenced by Derridean deconstruction. Essays such as "The Laugh of the Medusa," "Sorties," *"Coming to Writing" and Other Essays* (1991), *Readings* and *The Newly Born Woman* (with Catherine Clement, translation in 1986) are her attempts to discover a writing that is fluid, transgressive and beyond binary systems of logic. Cixous has also written fiction and plays.

(1) Analysing Western discourse, Cixous discovers binary oppositions at work everywhere. The binary hierarchy is always a relationship of violence, and the feminine term, is always killed. And since logocentrism attributes all origins to the phallus,

creativity and life is also assumed to be male. This principle of exclusion is summed up by Cixous thus: "Intention: desire, authority—examine them and you are led right back . . . to the father. It is not possible not to notice that there is no place whatsoever for women in the calculations."

(2) Patriarchy is maintained by the exchange of women as *possessions* from father to husbands in order to gain something. The male gains authority, power, virility and pleasure in this economy based on *property* and exchange. The feminine economy is based not on the property and exclusion but on the *gift*. The woman, writes Cixous, does not try to "recover her expenses." She is able to "depropriate herself without self-interest . . . endless body, without end." Writing is also structure by a "sexual opposition," one that favoured the male and reduced writing "to his laws."

(3) Exclusion and linearity, the characteristics of male writing, created a hierarchy of sexual difference within language and discourse. The exclusion of women from writing is due to the fact that Western history of writing is synonymous with the separation of the body from the text, of the privileging of reasoning over feeling. The need is thus for a woman's writing, one that will be a flow of "luminous torrents," excess, never-ending and open, without hierarchy, repressive logic or control.

(4) In her search for the *ecriture feminine*—a feminine writing practice—Cixous suggests that such a feminine writing can never be "theorised enclosed, coded." This writing can help escape (what she terms a "sortie") to an "elsewhere" beyond the oppressive identities of binarisms. In "The Laugh of the Medusa," which is one of Cixous' best read essays, Cixous demonstrates what the *ecriture feminine* can be. A celebratory and ecstatic tone is visible in this writing which ranges in style from the poetic to the densely theoretical, the use of slang and colloquialisms to the use of high rhetoric. This is what Cixous described as "flying in language and making it fly," since "for centuries we've been able to possess anything only by flying; we've lived in flight, stealing away." Puns, declamations, fragmented syntax and associative word play are very often the sta-

ple of Cixous' writing. Here *creative and academic/theoretical discourse cannot be distinguished, for to separate the two would be to put into place a binary opposition.* The writing celebrates excesses, flows and creative extravagance, and (like Irigaray) emphasises the sense of touch. Cixous refers to even male authors like Joyce and Jean Genet as writing this kind of *ecriture feminine*.

(5) A feminine text is, for Cixous, never anything other than subversive. The emphasis on word-play, on fragmentation and slipperiness, of the economy of rhythm and sound and many-voiced discourse seeks to undermine the unitariness of phallocentric writing that represses fluidity and the flow of desire in favour of order and "system." The subversiveness of *ecriture feminine* is the rejection of such a repressive binary logic—of man/woman, theoretical/creative, nature/culture, and inside/outside—and therefore of the *reality* the logic represents. The stories need to be retold without the oppressive logic of patriarchal society.

(6) Femininity is plenitude, excess. In order to deconstruct the logic of the symbolic order one needs to return to the pre-Oedipal. This would mean a return to the early stage of *bisexuality*. Bisexuality, for Cixous, is the means to collapse the unitary sexual identity, which "doesn't annul differences, but stirs them up." It also, therefore rejects any sexual essentialism, leading to the argument that there is no "pure" male or female sex: each is the Other.

Michele Barrett: Writing under the influence of Marx and cultural materialism, Barrett in *Women's Oppression Today* (1988) argues that a feminist analysis of "culture" is imperative today. Barrett's engagements with aesthetics and subjectivity have proved to be the cutting edge of Marxist feminism. In her famous 1980 lecture "Feminism and the Definition of Cultural Politics," Barrett identified three main issues for a materialist feminism.

(1) The indeterminacy of literary and aesthetic meaning: Artistic meaning depends upon who is reading, and the actual process of reading. This however does not mean that there is the anarchy of interpretation. For Barrett every work has a "dominant or preferred reading" that limits the possibilities. Barrett argues that

literary texts are dramatic performances that are marked by inner contradictions which cannot be easily traced to authorial lives or intentions.

(2) The relationship between women's art and feminist art: Women's art is not necessarily feminist. However, feminist political interests are also not necessarily served by the recovery of a female literary tradition.

(3) The problem of judging aesthetic value and pleasure: Questions the feminist rejection of aesthetic value and pleasure. The assumption that value judgements have to be made becomes problematic because values are inevitably the values of the dominant classes.

Barrett argues that feminist critics lay an undue emphasis on the work's *content*, while ignoring the role of the *reader* in producing/ reproducing meanings that may be phallocentric. She argues that there is no intrinsic merit in modernist/avant-garde forms, and the pleasures from soap operas and such politically "regressive" art forms must not be ignored. Barrett writes: cultural politics, and feminist art, are important precisely because we are not helpless victims of oppressive ideology. We take some responsibility for the cultural meaning of gender and it is up to us all to change it."

Pauline Johnson: Johnson has sought to resituate feminism within the humanist tradition. Arguing against the anti-humanism of contemporary feminism, Johnson's *Feminism as Radical Humanism* (1994) argues that feminism must see itself as "the interpreter of the cultural ideals of modern humanism." To this end Johnson suggests that humanism must be interpreted as the "value idea of autonomous self-constituted personality." Radical humanism understands humanism as an historical project born of conscious value choices. It defends the ideals of modern humanism as contingent. Radical humanism, for Johnson, detects a tension between the universalising character of modern humanist ideals and the particularist terms in which these claims (to universality) are made. Contemporary feminism sees itself as a principled commitment to difference, plurality and to freedom from all imposed integrations. Radical humanist feminism recognises that contemporary feminism is itself an articulation of an emancipatory social movement. This movement presumes a "turn away" from "natural" categories (male and female, for instance). It sees itself as a necessarily particular and inchoate reworking of the cultural ideals of modern humanism. Johnson rejects feminism's belief that a refusal to enter into any communicative relation with the phallocentric world/values/system amount to "heroics." She rejects the idea of the "rebellious feminine" which believes that the refusal to enter into any communicative relation with the phallocentric system/thoughts/world is a "heroics." Johnson argues that we need to ask question of the difference of feminine identities in humanist terms: of the value ideals of humanism such as the moral autonomy of the individual and the notion of authentic self-realisation.

IV Relationship with Other Disciplines

Feminism has an "academic arm" in women's studies. The rise of women's studies as a discipline has been crucial in the development of cultural theory. Catherine Simpson in 1986 outlined three major goals for women's studies: (1) teaching the subject of women properly (2) ending sex discrimination in education at all levels (3) integrating feminist activism and feminist thought. This suggests that pedagogy, epistemology, methodology, and content (canon) are all part of feminist studies. The project to recover women's texts has been a major contribution of feminist literary research. Sandra Gilbert and Susan Gubar suggested that curriculum revision involve a four-stage process:

(1) Critique—analysis of women's representations, absences and sexist biases in the disciplines.
(2) Recovery—refocusing women's historical experience and their role in the production of culture. Thus an alternative action may be formed through such a recovery.
(3) Reconceptualisation—of paradigms, theories and methods. There is the need for new categories itself to study development, technology, economics and culture.
(4) Reassessment—focuses on gender relations seeking a *beyond* the binary set up of male/female.

These approaches have resulted in feminist readings of science in the work of Donna Harraway (*Simians, Cyborgs and Women,*

1991). Deconstruction and postcolonialism have adapted feminist thought (and vice versa) in Gayatri Spivak (*In Other Worlds*, 1987; *The Postcolonial Critic*, 1990) and Rajeshwari Sunder Rajan (*Real and Imagined Women*, 1993). The work of Bell Hooks in *Ain't I a Woman* (1981) and *Yearning* (1990) reorients feminism into addressing the issue of race and gender, especially in the case of black women. Jacqueline Rose and Elizabeth Grosz have focused on sexuality and gender issues in *Sexuality in the Field of Vision* (1986) and *Jacques Lacan: A Feminist Introduction* (1990) respectively. The assimilation of film studies to feminism has resulted in theoretical works like Annette Kuhn's *Women's Pictures* (1982) and Teresa de Lauretis' *Alice Doesn't: Feminism, Semiotics and Cinema* (1984) among others. Geography and urban sociology has also come under feminist scrutiny in the work of Doreen Massey (*Space, Place and Gender*, 1994). The problem of applying European or American feminism to the "Third World" has also become an area of intense public debate, as works like Chilla Bulbeck's *Re-Orienting Western Feminisms: Women's Diversity in a Postcolonial World* (1998) demonstrate. In India the recovery of women's texts in Susie Tharu and K. Lalitha's seminal *Women's Writing in India* (1991), environmentalism, development and feminism in the work of Vandana Shiva (*Staying Alive*, 1988), are disciplines that have adapted insights from feminism, poststructuralism, and critical theory to address specifically local issues. Feminism has thus been the most eclectic and radical thought/activism of the contemporary world.

Further Reading

Donovan, Josephine. *Feminist Theory: The Intellectual Traditions of American Feminism*. New York: Frederick Ungar, 1985.

Jacobus, Mary. *Reading Women: Essays in Feminist Criticism*. London: Methuen, 1986.

Mohanty, Chandra Talpade et al, ed. *Third World Women and the Politics of Feminism*. Bloomington: Indiana University Press, 1991.

Moi, Toril. *Sexual/Textual Politics: Feminist Literary Theory*. London and New York: Methuen, 1985.

Ruthven, K.K. *Feminist Literary Studies: An Introduction*. Cambridge: Cambridge University Press, 1990.

Chapter Five

Marxism

Marxism has undoubtedly been the most influential intellectual "movement" in the history of ideas. Its influence has been visible in fields as diverse as history, cultural studies, economics, psychoanalysis, geography, sociology, and political theory and literary/cultural theory. Though Marxism cannot be termed a "literary theory," the work of Terry Eagleton, Fredric Jameson, Raymond Williams in literary studies are located within a Marxist framework.

I Background and Origins

Marxist theory begins in the massive work of Karl Marx and Friedrich Engels in the 19th century. These writings are mainly in the discipline of economics and politics. However, the Marx-Engels analysis of society and the conditions of production generally spilled over into an analysis of culture. And this is the significance of Marx to later Marxist critics. Their writings on literature and art constitute two volumes in the collected works.

Karl Marx and Friedrich Engels: Their oeuvre is too large to even begin to be summarised. However, we shall look at the salient and relevant features of Marxist thought as culled from the writings of Marx and Engels.

(1) They developed their critique of capitalism in terms of the relationship between man and the material world.

(2) The capitalist mode of production justified and naturalised itself through certain patterns of thought. These patterns circulated through the entire society and replicate the unequal relations of labour. This means that the unequal *economic* relations of the factory or the feudal economy (say, that between the factory owner and the factory labourer) are carried over into the *social* realm. The *economic base* influences the *social superstructure.*

The social institutions such as education, culture, religion are superstructures that replicate the inequality of the economic base. The oppressed classes, however, believe this order of inequality as "natural" or "preordained," and do not even recognise that they are oppressed. This system of thought that helps implement, reinforce, legitimise and naturalise inequality and oppression is termed *ideology*. It refers to the writings, speeches, beliefs and opinions that assert the "naturalness" and necessity of such practices of inequality. The ideology is therefore the "ruling ideas" of the dominant class, it is essentially an instrument of power.

(3) Ideology prevents the recognition of oppression by the oppressed. Thus it is a "*false consciousness*," a mode of misrecognising the true nature of our lives and social roles. For Marxists ideology is the all-encompassing and invisible presence: there is no escaping it.

(4) Ideology is sustained and reproduced through *cultural* forms such as art. All imaginative production is social production. The social is the matrix within which all other terms are fleshed and shaped (Eagleton). An author *unconsciously* replicates the dominant ideology in his/her works and thus "spreads" it among the readers. Both authors and readers thus come to be assimilated into the dominant ideology. Thus, in Marx and Engels, the cultural spheres are understood within internally self-transforming networks of social relations. Consciousness, form, taste, literary history and tradition are all explained as embedded in these relations.

(5) Nothing in social life can be seen in isolation. All social phenomena are *related* to others. For example the cultural and familial life of a factory worker is related to the employer-employee class relations. Morality, consciousness, ethics, literary tastes are all embedded in the network of social relations. These relations are dynamic, in a constant process of transformation. The Marxist view of dialectics: that conflict, antagonism, contradiction is necessary condition for attaining truth and social change. There is a *dialectical* process—of thesis and antithesis meeting, negation and synthesis at work.

(6) The good life of an individual is one of active *self-realisation*. This is the full and free actualisation and externalisation of the powers and abilities of the individual. The ideal of self-realisation is not fulfilled in a society which *coerces* people to develop socially valuable talents at the expense of those they *want* to develop. Material scarcity also forces people to develop talents that they themselves do not prefer. In a communist society (argues Marx), there will be no material scarcity to constrain self-realisation. In capitalism, individuals are caught between unintelligible psychological forces that shape their desires and social forces that restrain fulfilment of these desires.

(7) Under capitalism, labour is *dominated* by capital. This occurs in two stages: (a) the capitalist exploits the worker through his ownership of the means of production but does not extend the domination to the process of production. (b) Here the capitalist moves into the process of production. In the factory system, the worker is reduced to an appendage of the machine, he works under coercive supervision. He loses all autonomy and personal satisfaction from his work. The industrial worker is *alienated* from the objects he helps create (the products of his labour). He is "deskilled," made to perform fragmented and repetitive tasks but never grasps the *entire sequence of production* of which he is a part. Workers are also bereft of their full humanity, and are thought of as "hands." They are merely depersonalised objects. Alienation adds to exploitation—a belief on the part of the workers that the capitalist has a legitimate claim on the surplus by virtue of his ownership of the means of production.

(8) Methodological individualism: the view that all institutions, behavioural patterns and social processes can be explained in terms of individuals only—in their actions, properties and relations.

(9) The capitalist economy creates illusions about itself. The workers are under the illusion that they are free and unexploited, that the capitalist has a legitimate right to the surplus, and that the commodities, money, and capital have properties and powers of their own. This is fetishism, where properties are assigned to objects. Money is fetishised, in the idea that money is inherently

productive. Capital fetishism is the belief that capital has the inherent power to produce, and that this productive power is *not* the result of labour.

(10) *Historical materialism*: This is the Marxist conception of history, a general theory of the structure and dynamics of any mode of production and a theory of the historical sequence of the mode of production. This is an analysis of the sequence of the modes of production (feudalism-capitalism-communism) and the class struggle that marks each stage. This class struggle at every stage is between social groups defined by their relation to the organisation of labour. The sequence of the modes of production is as follows:

Asiatic mode → Slavery → Serfdom → Capitalism

(11) *Class*: These are the basic units in social conflict. The definition of class is based on property, exploitation, market behaviour and domination. Most frequently, class membership is defined by the ownership or lack of ownership of the means of production. The working class is made up of those who sell their labour power, the capitalist class of those that purchase labour power. *Class-consciousness* is the awareness of the members of a class that they have a common situation and common interests. Class struggle may range from hidden manipulation to overt conflict, from direct confrontation to complex alliances between two or more classes.

(12) *Mediation*: Mediation seeks to understand the method by which institutions and practices shape class formation. That is what connects the ideal with the real, between theory and practice? How can structures promote class struggle? Lenin suggests that the Party mediates between the intellectuals and the working class. Georges Lukacs with his concept of *reification* and Antonio Gramsci's notion of *hegemony* suggest two modes of mediation in Marxist theory (see Lukacs and Gramsci below)

II Assumptions and General Methods

(1) Literature and culture must be understood in relation to the economic conditions of the age. There is a definite correlation between the socio-economic conditions and the kind of cultural

and aesthetic works produced. Literature and art can be fully understood only in relation to ideology, class and economic substructure.

(2) Truth is institutionally created. Language itself is socially constructed.

(3) Art is a commodity, and shares with other commodities an entry into material conditions of production. Artistic production can be seen as a branch of production in general.

(4) Literature is the refracted site of class struggle. Thus literature may be the arm of political revolution.

(5) Art should express what is typical about a class or historical condition (Engels): this is the *typicality* of art. However, art does have a "relative autonomy," that art may sometimes transcend its ideological roots, and that the superstructure (art/culture) is determined by economic conditions only in the "last instance."

(6) Art and literature seeks, in general, to implement the ideology of the ruling class. Thus "tradition," "values" which literary texts recommend as "standards" are always the tradition and values that the ruling class seeks to impose upon society for its own benefit.

(7) Marxist criticism seeks to locate the ideologies implicit in a text. Traditional criticism moves in the realm of consciousness and subjectivity, while ignoring the social conditions that shape this consciousness and being.

(8) The absences and silences in a text are places where the real history is embedded. That is, the absences link a text to the history from which it is produced, it effaces instances of class struggle, exploitation and the true dynamics of history. A Marxist reading seeks to uncover the hidden/repressed subtext of texts. These subtexts are then related to actual *material-historical* conditions such as class struggle, the transition of economy (say, feudal to capitalist).

(9) Authors are not just geniuses, they write in social contexts. Both their choice of *form* (genre, style) and *content* are influenced by the author's class position. The Marxist critic relates the context of the work to the author's own class position. It is presumed

that the class-consciousness and prejudices of the author seep into her/his work unconsciously, but can be made visible through a close reading.

(10) Moving from individual texts to genres and forms, a Marxist critic will seek to explain the development of genre in terms of the changing class relations and social conditions of the age. Thus the rise of courtly love poetry and the Renaissance drama is explained in the context of the citification of England, the development of the market economy, the system of patronage by kings. The novel's rise is linked to the rise of the middle class. The sonnet and the iambic pentameter developed, as are literary symbols of the desire for social stability, order and decorum. Later Marxist criticism also paid attention to the role of the reader in the development of genres/themes in art. Thus the New Historicists and cultural materialists (see chapter below) discuss the role of readership in the development of the dime or penny novel, the institutionalisation of criticism (constituted exclusively by males) that prevented women's texts from being made part of the canon and so on.

We can now move on to the major thinkers in the Marxist critical tradition. The classical Marxists include Georges Plekhanov, Leon Trotsky, V.I. Lenin. In the twentieth century Georges Lukacs and Antonio Gramsci were the early influences. The work of Lucien Goldman, the structuralist Marxism of Louis Althusser, the writings of Theodore Adorno, Walter Benjamin, the British Marxists—Raymond Williams and Terry Eagleton—and the American thinker Fredric Jameson will figure in the following discussion. The Frankfurt School and Critical Theory are discussed in the note at the conclusion of the chapter.

III Key Concepts and Thinkers

Leon Trotsky: In his *The Revolution Betrayed* (1937) and his best known *Literature and Revolution* (1924), Trotsky argued that the Party can offer leadership only in certain areas. He wrote, "the domain of art is not one in which the party is called upon to command. It can and must protect and help it, but it can only lead it indirectly." However, Trotsky does not envisage complete freedom of art and artist. He suggests the need for a "watchful revolutionary censorship, and a broad and flexible in the field of art." He recommends a clear set of limits to this mechanism of censorship. While arguing for the complete freedom of all art, Trotsky believes that all true art is revolutionary in nature. Trotsky also argues that the proletariat cannot construct a new culture without assimilating the older ones. There is always the need for a continuity of creative tradition. As the proletariat dissolves into the socialist community, it will cease to be the proletariat. Thus a "proletariat culture" will eventually be replaced by a human culture. Art has its own laws of development, there is no organic link between art and class interests. Creativity inevitably lags behind the spirit of a class and is not subject to conscious influence. Trotsky praises Dante, Shakespeare and Goethe as great authors precisely because they were able to "transcend" their class positions.

Lenin: In his "Party Organisation and Party Literature" (1905), Lenin argues that literature must become a part of the common cause of the proletariat. He does not support the then prevalent idea that art must be controlled, and suggests that freedom of expression must be complete and unfettered. Yet, like Trotsky, Lenin argues that the Party should be empowered to control writing written under its banner, i.e. the freedom of expression cannot be fully applied to Party literature. Lenin argues that the writer only believes (falsely) that he is free. He is actually trapped in the "bourgeois-shopkeeper literary relations." Thus, for Lenin, art is circumscribed in the commercial and material transaction, like all commodities. Therefore literature cannot be "an individual undertaking." In his analysis of Tolstoy, Lenin argues that Tolstoy's attack on capitalism and his advocacy of non-violent resistance to evil symbolises the contradictory conditions of revolutionary peasantry. Assailing Tolstoy's "revolutionary flabbiness," Lenin still praises them as socialist in tone. Lenin suggests that not only is artistic creativity the product of class conditions, all interpretations are also conducted within the parameters of class interests. The Party is the vanguard of the revolution, it mediates between the intellectuals and the working classes.

Georges Plekhanov: Plekhanov is better known as the founder of the Russian Social Democratic Party. Rejecting the Aesthetic

Movement's idea of "art for art's sake," Plekhanov argues that such a tendency is symptomatic of the artist's alienation from his socio-cultural environment. Art which seeks to promote the social good arises when there is a mingling of the artist's artistic interests with members of general society. Human beings may pursue art simply for the sake of pleasure.

Antonio Gramsci: Gramsci has been a major influence on literary theory especially after the English translation of his Prison Note-books appeared in 1971. Gramsci adopted certain fundamental categories for his analysis of culture and society: hegemony, ideology and the division between state and civil society.

For Gramsci, culture is neither a simple reflection of the economic base nor a separate entity. Instead he argues that the relationship between the base and superstructure is one of reciprocity. This means that Gramsci rejects the passive role of the "reflected" culture for that of an active dynamic condition. Gramsci levels three "isms" against traditional Marxist theory:

(a) Instrumentalism: since traditional Marxism regards the state as an instrument of a dominant class, and thereby denies the state any autonomy of its own. The Marxist notion of the "inevitable stages of history" gave rise to political passivity, according to Gramsci.

(b) Reductionism: the concept of politics as a superstructure, an "epiphenomenon" derived from an economic base. This smothers the role of the state in society.

(c) Catastrophism: the assumption that relations between bourgeois and the proletariat will increasingly polarise as the inevitable consequence of the capitalist crisis. This makes the need/idea of intervention unnecessary.

(1) Ideology: Gramsci's notion of ideology suggests that "men acquire consciousness of structural conflicts on the level of ideologies." That is revolutions are facilitated by shifts in the economic structure *and* their outcomes are decided on the level of ideologies. Ideology is thus the *site* of class conflict for Gramsci. To understand the implications of the Gramscian notion of ideology, one must read it with his idea of hegemony.

(2) Gramsci redefines ideology by emphasising the institutional and cultural bases of ideology. Ideology may be of any form: political propaganda, sermons, folklore, and popular songs. Ideology is not false consciousness, simply because for Gramsci popular songs and superstitions are themselves *material forces*. Ideology is an object of interpretation. The purpose of a "*philosophy of praxis*" is to uncover the roots of the development of the current ideologies. It must treat class conflict as much at the level of ideas as at the level of economic areas. This is better understood in Gramsci's idea of the *historical bloc*.

(3) Hegemony: Dominant classes maintain their position not only though acts of *coercion* but also through *symbolic action* which renews and recreates the social order. Hegemony is the *nexus of material and ideological instruments through which the dominant classes maintain their power*. Hegemony thus *mediates* between the ruling ideas and the subjects. The hegemony of the ruling/dominant class is maintained through coercion and consent. The material sphere is a "structure" that is allied with a superstructure of ideas. These ideas are institutionalised in the *civil society*: the law courts, the bureaucracy, the religious and educational systems. The coercive apparatus is the *state* with its army and police apparatuses. A more subtle form of control is to employ intellectuals to naturalise the present (oppressive order). The ruled must be made to accept things as they are, i.e. accept and *consent* to oppression of their own volition because they are convinced of the legitimacy of the order. Gramsci is also certain that there will be a decisive change in man's consciousness (Gramsci does not explain how, though). Gramsci writes: "the school as a positive educative function, and the courts as a repressive and negative education function, are the most important State activities in the implementation of ideologies."

(4) Gramsci argued that "intellectuals" are people in whom the philosophical instinct is better developed than in others. There are two kinds of intellectuals: (a) the *organic* type are those who are needed by the new class to develop a new social order (b) *traditional* intellectuals are those who remain tied to an earlier historical period. Both types help construct a cultural-social

unity that forms the basis of a "*historical bloc*." A historical bloc represents a unification of various groups with differing interests, but who remain united under the leadership of the party. The party thus has a cultural function too. The political party is the first cell for the development of hegemony, the mechanism which carries out in civil society the same function as the state carries out in political society.

(5) Literature participates in the struggle for hegemony in society. It may help *counter* oppressive hegemony by suggesting and popularising new ones. The organic intellectuals play an important part here.

Christopher Caudwell: Caudwell was not a literary critic by profession, he wrote on physics, aerodynamics, and literary history. Caudwell argues that there is a central illusion that persists precisely because it arises from the defining class position of the bourgeois. The illusion, which Caudwell terms the "*bourgeois illusion*," takes on different forms in different ages. These forms are projected into the works of art. The artist's technique is a way of elaborating and realising these forms.

The bourgeois sees human freedom in the absence of social ties. When capitalism arrives he is still not free, but trapped by the laws of the market. At every stage in the development of the economy a new form of the *consciousness* of unfreedom, and a new form of the *aspiration* of freedom occurs. In art, this aspiration is in the form of fantasies. Thus, in the Elizabethan age, the Renaissance Prince is the phantasm. Caudwell argues that it is practically necessary to have a world of phantasm in order to embody the emotional and intellectual sources of collective action. The world of any one work of art exists to construct some possible self in the individual auditor or the collective audience. Art "changes the emotional content of his consciousness so that he can react more subtly and deeply to the world. . . . It makes possible new levels of conscious sympathy, understanding and affection among men, matching the new levels of material organisation achieved by material production."

Georges Lukacs: In his early *Theory of the Novel* (1916, translated 1971) Lukacs considers literary form as an expression of a world-view or ideology that originates in economic or cultural relations, and the writer's experience of these conditions. Literary form acts as the communication device between the writer and the public, with some scope for misreading. For Lukacs the genre is the essential unit of literary discourse. Lukacs' later and more important works are *History and Class Consciousness* (1923, translated 1971) and *The Historical Novel* (1962).

(1) In *History and Class Consciousness*, Lukacs argued that the proletarian revolution was imminent in "the agenda of world history."

(2) Reification is the relation between people that takes on the character of a *thing* and attains a "phantom objectivity." This is Lukacs' advance on the traditional Marxist notion of *mediation*. Lukacs argues that commodity exchange and its structural effects influence the outer and inner life of society. The transformation of human properties relations and actions into properties, relations and actions of objects (man-produced things) makes them independent. These objects are then seen as *independent of man* and actually guide his life. Human beings are in turn converted into things, and do not behave like humans, but as *things*.

(3) He argued that theory must dismantle the false consciousness of people to produce a revolutionary practice. Theory would then become a material force capable of transforming society.

(4) On realism: Lukacs argues that literature provides a critical understanding of underlying social and historical processes by revealing the *contradictions* of the age. Lukacs attacked the stream of consciousness technique and the modernist mode of the novel. Castigating authors like Beckett, Faulkner and Joyce for narrowing the fullness of history into the bleak inner history of absurd existences, Lukacs argues that modernist fiction failed to perceive human existence as a part of a *dynamic historical environment*. He argued that Thomas Mann, Tolstoy, Balzac and Walter Scott must be emulated because they portray society critically, in their portrayal of the tension between characters and the social conflicts of the ages. Lukacs thus recommended a *critical realism* as the best mode for a novel. By merely reflecting reality, the novel simply creates a "mental structure" transposed into words. What is needed is that the novel should

conduct the reader "towards a more concrete insight into reality." The artist does not impose an abstract order upon the world, but rather presents the reader with an image of the richness of life from which emerges the sense of order. Realist fictions measure the real against an ideal that is "always and never there in reality," so that they reveal the deficiencies of the prevalent ideologies. The goal of artistic reflection is a picture of reality in which there is a unity of essence and appearance, individual case and general principle. The "concrete artistic embodiment" of particularity is the typical—the reproduction of *typical* features of the people, feelings, thoughts and objects *and* also of the *system of relations* into which these typifications are inserted. The text, for Lukacs possesses its own autonomy only insofar as it establishes a correct correspondence with the immanent meaningfulness of historical life. The work of art is subordinated to a purposeful design located outside of art. The author is merely the medium through which the laws of history come to expression.

(5) Ideology manifests itself in various ways in all stages of life. Lukacs showed that there was a correspondence between the "economic forms of society," the "cultural forms," the "forms of expression" and its literary forms (an idea adopted by the Frankfurt School).

(6) Objectification of all aspects of production, its alienation from producers, the reification of social relations, the quantification and depersonalisation of culture, and the rational calculation of the bureaucracy create systems of relations that seem to operate by their own laws. Individuals are subjects of these systems.

(7) Knowledge of objective reality is possible, but only if it goes beyond the reflection of immediate reality. Mere mimesis is not enough, it must go beyond to the "genesis, the creation of the object." The subject has an active role in constructing the knowledge of the real world and in transforming objective circumstances.

(8) Creative intellectual work is the only means to overcome alienation from themselves, from their world and from other people.

(9) The critic's role is not merely to reveal the "real meaning" of a literary work. The critic must use literature to ask ultimate questions about life.

Lucien Goldman: Goldman in *The Hidden God* (1964) and other works rejected the idea that texts are creations of individual genius. He argued that they are based upon "*trans-individual mental structures*" belonging to particular groups or classes. These "world-views" are perpetually being constructed and dissolved by social groups, as they adjust their mental image of the world to the changing reality before them. Goldman focuses on the "*homology*" (homology is a similarity of *structure* between social and cultural phenomena of different orders, though they may *appear* different) between the structure of the modern novel and the structure of the market economy. For instance, the post-1945 period was marked by the reduction of value to commodity value and the domination of the human world by a world of objects (Lukacs' reification). This is reflected in the depersonalised world of Alain Robbe-Grillet's and Kafka's fictions. The central object of sociological enquiry is the *significant structure*, which is always a mental one. The tragic vision is one such example of the significant structure for Goldman. Goldman rejects the static structure of French structuralism, and elaborates a "*genetic structuralism.*" Goldman argues that a transindividual subject (TS) produces the significant structure. This TS may be a class (proletariat or bourgeois), or even a more restricted group. That is, a "world view," a set of aspirations, ideas and feelings may be elaborated by a whole social class. A collective Subject (the TS of Goldman) thus produces the worldview, and this may find expression in a major literary or philosophical text. The TS is the true subject of history. The situation of the TS will contain certain *objective possibilities* which may not be visible to the individuals belonging to it. We therefore have to distinguish between the *actual* consciousness of the individual and the *possible consciousness* (here Goldman comes close to the "imputed consciousness" of Lukacs). Great writers articulate the possible consciousness of such a TS. The great writer therefore helps us grasp the meaning of the fundamental social conditions of our lives.

Louis Althusser: Althusser's "structuralist Marxism" has been a major influence on twentieth century Marxists, especially those like Raymond Williams and Terry Eagleton.

(1) Althusser argued against the idea that individuals are in any way prior to social conditions.

(2) The "*social formation*" (Althusser prefers social formation to social system) is a *decentred* structure with no overall unity or governing principle. Society is a structured whole consisting of *relatively autonomous levels*—legal, cultural, political—whose mode of articulation is determined only *in the last instance* by the economy. This concept of the decentred structure enables Althusser to reject the economic determinism of classical Marxist thought—for Althusser argues that social formation cannot be reduced to an "essence" of economic conditions (base) which is "reflected" in the superstructure.

(3) Marx's concept of the mode of production cannot be read off from the level of consciousness or ideology. As a structured phenomenon it can exist only in an *overdetermined* way throughout the social formation in question. Here Althusser borrows a term from Freud—that of "*overdetermination.*" Overdetermination is the effect that arises from a variety of sometimes-contradictory causes acting together rather than from a single factor. That is, there is no simple causal link between the economy and the superstructure, but rather a "structural causality" of the whole structure. In certain ages the economy determines what level is decisive in a particular society. Thus in a feudal society, politics rather than economics may be the dominant level. Thus Althusser is able to modify the simplistic base-superstructure equation in classical Marxism. Thus through "overdetermination," the reality of the economic level or the mode of production is not *directly* expressed in ideology or consciousness. It is *dispersed* through the social formation.

(4) Ideology: Althusser's concept of ideology is crucial for later Marxists. Ideology represents in its necessarily imaginary distortion not the *existing relations* of production, but the *imaginary relationship of individuals to the relations of production.* Ideology therefore provides the framework in which people live

their relationship to the social reality in which they are located. It is the representation of the imaginary relationship of individuals to their real conditions of existence. Ideology *interpellates* the individuals as *subjects* of the system. It gives them the identity necessary to the functioning of the existing state of affairs, while making them feel *as if they are free agents*. It encourages subjects to feel as if they are independent of the social formation. Ideology is a system with its own logic and proper rigor. Ideology itself exists by constituting concrete subjects *as subjects*. It is a system of *representations* (images, myths, ideas or concepts), endowed with an existence and a historical role at the heart of given society. Thus Althusser suggests that ideas are material because "they are material actions inserted into material practices governed by material rituals which are themselves defined by the material ideological apparatuses from which derive the ideas of the subject." Ideology for Althusser pre-exists the individual. When the concrete individual arrives, a predetermined set of roles are already available into which the individual is interpellated (a subject-position). Ideology is thus our whole lived experience.

(5) Ideological State Apparatuses: Every economic system seeks to reproduce its conditions of production. The modern capitalist state achieves this through two apparatuses.
   (i) Ideology always has a material practice, and is embodied in an apparatus that has a *material* existence. State power is maintained through *Repressive State Apparatuses* (RSAs) like the police, the army, law courts and prisons that operate through actual or threats of *coercive* force/violence.
   (ii) Power is also maintained through the actual *consent* of the subjects. This is achieved through *Ideological State Apparatuses* (ISAs) of State control: the political groups, the media, the education system, the church and art. The ISAs thus work through ideology. These apparatuses instil a set of ideas, an ideology surreptitiously and convince the subjects that they have chosen. (See the similarity to Gramsci's notion of hegemony above.)

For Althusser, Christianity is an ideology because it inserts concrete individuals as subjects/children of God. Here God is the Absolute Subject in the Centre *around* which individual subjects are arranged in a "mirror connection." This connection works in two ways: (a) *specularly*—when the subject is subjected to the Centre/Absolute Subject/God, and (b) *doubly specular*—when it guarantees that the position is really about them (subjects) and Him (God). This simply means that the concrete individual is both subject *of/to* God, and contemplates himself *as the double of/in the Absolute Subject.*

(6) Art is located somewhere between ideology and scientific knowledge. Art makes us see in a distanced way "the ideology from which it *originates*, and from which it *detaches* itself as art and to which it *alludes*." Art achieves a "*retreat*" from every ideology that feeds it. In this way, a major literary work can *transcend* the ideology of a writer.

E.P. Thompson: Thompson's greatest and best-known work is *The Making of the English Working Class* (1963, and never out of print since). A historian by disciplinary affiliation, Thompson has also written on Blake, William Morris, and the history of religious belief and manners.

(1) Thompson argued that class is a relationship and not a thing. An individual becomes a member of a class by playing a social role. Thompson argued that class was not an automatic response to economic change but was a dynamic and interactive creation between social groups. How the individual got to be in this social role and how the particular social organisation got to be there are historical questions. He rejected the idea that the economic base simply determined the superstructure. Rather, Thompson's focus was on culture and consciousness as important factors in the making of the working class.

(2) Thompson's monumental work began with the assumption that between 1780-1832 most English working class people felt an identity of interests between themselves and against their rulers and employers. Thompson charts the history of events (in part one of the book) leading upto the Jacobin agitation of the 1790s, the grouping of workers during the industrial revolution and

their relationship with the Methodist church (part two), leading upto the plebeian radicalism through Luddism.

(3) An example of Thompson's enquiry would be his historical data on the famous wife-selling scene in Hardy's *The Mayor of Casterbridge*. Thompson in an essay "The Sale of Wives" (included in his book, *Customs in Common*, 1991) demonstrated that Hardy may have been referring to an unofficial and highly ritualised minority form of divorce that existed and continued within plebeian community against the rules and codes laid down by churches.

(4) Writing on the riots and crowds in England he suggests that these were not futile or spontaneous reactions to hunger. Thompson argued that these were attitudes formed within a context of customary expectations and that their actions were a realistic form of direct action within the political system of eighteenth century England.

(5) Thompson's project may best be described as "history from below." The Marxist orientation and the emphasis on the cultural and social interactions as producing and determining the class was summed up by Thompson thus: "The making of the working class is a fact of politics and culture as much as of economic history. It was not the spontaneous generation of the factory system. The industrial revolution was imposed not upon raw material, but upon the freeborn Englishman—and the freeborn Englishman as Paine had left him or as the Methodists had moulded him. The factory hand or stockinger was also the inheritor of Bunyan, of remembered village rights, of notions of equality before the law, of craft traditions. He was the object of massive religious indoctrination and the creator of political tradition. The working class made itself as much as it was made."

Raymond Williams: Since the 1960s Williams has been synonymous with Leftist writings from the English academy, joined later by Terry Eagleton. Williams' *The Country and the City*, *Keywords*, *Culture and Society, 1780-1950*, *Marxism and Literature*, *Problems in Materialism and Culture*, and numerous other works revolutionised literary criticism, and helped found the discipline of culture studies. Redefining certain "keywords" in terms of the changes in their use, and the class distinctions, exclusionism that they evoked, Williams shifted the basis of criticism from a purely textual exercise (as it used to be in the heyday of New Criticism, and even structuralism) to the material world.

(1) Williams argued that the key moments which should be of interest to Marxism are (a) the emphasis on language as activity (b) emphasis on the history of language. Williams stresses the connection and interaction between social and historical processes and language. Active meanings and values are embodied within language, and, in turn, the changing patterns and meanings in language exert a social force. The changes and conflicts of a whole way of life are deeply implicated in that culture's systems of learning and communication.

(2) The opponents of Marxism see it as reductive and deterministic. Williams argues that within Marxism the only objective conditions are and can only be the result of human actions in the material world. The real distinction can only be between historical objectivity (the conditions into which at any particular point in time men find themselves born, the accessible conditions into which they enter) and abstract objectivity (where the determining process is independent of their will because they cannot control, they can only try and understand it and modify their actions accordingly).

(3) "Society" or "historical events" cannot be categorically abstracted from "individuals" and "individual wills." Such a separation leads to an alienated "objectivist society" working unconsciously. The individual or genotype then become positive extra-social forces.

(4) *Determination* is not the same as "predestination" of theology. In Marx, it means the setting of limit and exerting of pressure which originates in *man's own activities*. *Overdetermination* is the recognition of multiple forces rather than the isolated forces of modes or techniques of production. The social and political order, which maintains a capitalist market, like the social and political struggles that created it, is necessarily a material production. If the real world is material, it can be seen in its constitutive forms. Any reflection of these will be of material real-

ity. Thus the mind of the artists must be seen as "materially conditioned."

(5) *Hegemony*: the whole social process may be related to specific distributions of power and influence. The sense of an ideology is applied to the actual consciousness of both the dominant and subordinated classes. The dominant class has this ideology in pure and simple forms. A subordinated class has nothing but this ideology in its consciousness, or rather, the ideology *imposed* upon its consciousness. Hegemony constitutes a sense of reality for most people in society, it saturates their very consciousness.

(6) We have to reject the aesthetic both as a separate abstract dimension and as a separate abstract function. We need to grasp the specific and variable intentions and the specific and variable responses that have been grouped as the "aesthetic." Arguments of "value" are in the variable encounter of intention and response in *specific situations*.

(7) Marxist cultural theory has two basic propositions:
  (a) the determining base and determined superstructure
  (b) social being determines consciousness
  Superstructure is ideology and culture, which imitates the reality of the economic base.

(8) However, sometimes direct connections cannot be found between the base and superstructure. For instance, there are cultural practices that have no visible material cause. In order to explain this, Williams developed the notion of "*lags*." There are "lags" in time, which causes the distancing of some aspects of culture (say, philosophy) from economic activities. There is also mediation between the base and superstructure, but not a direct reflection. There are "*homologous*" structures in the superstructure, which can be made visible only after analysis.

(9) The base should now be regarded as a *process* and not a static object. The base is not merely the basic industry, but should also refer to men producing themselves (reproduction in real life) and primary production (material production). *Totality* refers to the totality of base and superstructure, that is the entire realm of social practices. The traditional base-superstructure

model, for Williams excludes the facts of social intention. Art and thought which have all along been thought of as "natural" and universal actually ratify the dominant ideology. Neither the notion of literature as "above" material conditions nor as truly reflecting them is relevant, argue Williams. The "theory of culture" is the "study of relationships between elements in a whole way of life." We need to look at "a felt sense of the quality of life at a particular place and time: a sense of the ways in which particular activities combined into a way of thinking and living." This particular sense of place and the particular community of experience, a structured social experience, is what Williams famously termed "*structure of feeling*."

(10) Ideology is incorporated through educational institutions and the family. A selective tradition is passed off as *the tradition*. From the archives of the past certain meanings and images are chosen for emphasis, and established as the *standard* or *the tradition*. The present notion of "culture" therefore emerges only around the time of the industrial revolution, as a *critique* of mechanisation and industrialisation, and to mark a distinction between the illiterate, "uncultured" factory worker and the aesthetically inclined, upper class "cultured" gentleman.

(11) However, there are always alternative opinions and attitudes that undermine (or try to undermine) this. Williams proposes a three-tier model here:

(a) Oppositional culture: or alternative culture that resists dominant culture.

(b) Residual culture: which is of some previous culture or social formation. Some of the dominant culture also survives through this residual culture.

(c) Emergent culture: where new values are being suggested. No dominant culture or mode of production exhausts all human possibilities. Some new ideas may be incorporated by dominant ideology, or else discarded. What the dominant class discards may be accepted by the rising/new classes. Or, these subcultures may decode dominant meanings in their own way, and incorporate them into their own style.

(12) All contemporary literary theory is a theory of consumption, especially symbolised in terms like "taste" and "sensibility" (terms frequently used to describe criteria for criticism). The New Criticism helped project the artefact as an autonomous object/text and ignored the productive practices. Art is a practice. We have to discover the nature of a practice and then its conditions. We have to look for the processes of transformation or mediation that the components have gone through. We should compare art and society with the whole complex of human actions and feelings. Culture, for instance, must be analysed in terms of class, industry, democracy and art. Culture/art must be treated as social uses of the material means of production. The focus is on "the social organisation of culture, as a realised signifying system, embedded in a whole range of activities, relations and institutions, of which only some are manifestly 'cultural' ."

(13) Thus *conceptual terms* like creativity, culture, individual, society and the *institutions/instituted forms* such as literacy, the press, education, standardisation of the language, the conventions of drama and fiction, must be situated within networks of active social relations that bestow meaning to these terms. Tradition, according to Williams, is always a selective tradition passed of as "the tradition." This is always being re-made, with a continuous selection and re-selection, re-interpretation. All this is what constitutes critical activity.

(14) Williams argued that we are living through a "*long revolution*" that is simultaneously economic, political and cultural. This revolution transforms people and institutions as it transforms nature, forms of democratic self-governance and the modes of communication and education.

(15) Williams summed up the function of Marxist theory thus: "I believe that the system of meanings and values which a capitalist society has generated must be defeated in general and in detail by the most sustained kinds of intellectual and educational work. This is a cultural process which I have called a "long revolution . . . a genuine struggle which was part of the necessary battles of democracy and of economic victory for the or-

ganised working class. Anything as deep as dominant structure of feeling is only changed by active new experience . . . the task of a successful socialist movement will be one of feeling quite as much as one of fact and organisation."

Fredric Jameson: One of the most influential thinkers in the Marxist critical tradition, Jameson's work in *Marxism and Form* (1971), *The Prison-House of Language* (1972), *The Political Unconscious* (1981) and *Postmodernism, Or The Cultural Logic of Late Capitalism* (1991) has been provocative, brilliant, controversial, and notoriously inaccessible. Adapting ideas from psychoanalysis, structuralism and Marxism, Jameson has sought to rework classical Marxism to suit newer paradigms in cultural studies (films, painting, literary texts, magical narratives, Palestinian liberation and Marxist pedagogy) through his "*dialectical criticism*." Jameson proceeds from the traditional Marxist assumption that individual literary texts cannot be isolated for analysis, since they are part of a larger historical situation.

(1) There are no pre-set categories to apply to literature. Dialectical criticism seeks to unmask the inner form of a genre or body of texts. It works inward to the level where literary form is deeply related to the concrete. It analyses categories and methods. Since categories articulate historical content, they must be read in terms of the historical content from which they emerge. Dialectical criticism involves:
   - (a) analysis of categories and procedures while simultaneously performing close, concrete and specific studies
   - (b) relational and historical thinking which contextualises/historicises the object of study in its historical environment
   - (c) utopian thinking which compares existing realities with future alternatives and finds utopian hope in literature, philosophy and such cultural texts
   - (d) totalising thinking to provide a systematic framework for cultural studies.

(2) Jameson believes that narrative is an essential "*epistemological category*," reality presents itself to the human mind only in the form of stories.

(3) All ideologies are "*strategies of containment*" which allow society to provide an explanation of itself which suppresses the underlying contradictions of History. It is history itself that imposes this strategy of repression. The "*not-said*" is *repressed* history.

(4) Jameson takes his notion of the "*political unconscious*" from Freud's concept of repression. The function of ideology is to repress "revolution." The oppressors need this political unconscious. Paradoxically, the oppressed need this too: for they would find life intolerable if the revolution were not repressed! These cultural narratives are therefore to be seen as "transformational," which "transform social and political anxieties and fantasies, which must then have an effective presence in the cultural text to be subsequently repressed or managed." These buried narratives and social experiences are to be teased out through sophisticated literary analysis. Criticism needs to "detect the traces of [an] uninterrupted narrative . . . restoring to the surface of the text the repressed and buried reality of [a] fundamental history, [in which] the doctrine of the political unconscious finds its function and necessity."

(5) Jameson accepts Althusser's view of social totality as a "decentred structure," with various levels developing in "relative autonomy" at different time scales (feudal and capitalist time scales coexisting). This is the heterogeneous History, mirrored in the heterogeneity of texts. Thus Jameson argues that the heterogeneity of texts can be understood only as it relates to the heterogeneity *outside* the text. His own work has been characterised by a shift (in Jameson's own words) "from an interest in the multiple dimensions and levels of a text to the multiple interweaving of an only fitfully readable narrative . . . from the attempt to talk about the sentence . . . to the attempt to talk about modes of production." That is, there is a shift in emphasis from the dimension of a text to the ways in which texts are inserted into historical sequences, to demonstrate how history enters and helps *constitute* texts.

(6) Jameson argues that there have been three fundamental moments in capitalism, each of which has had corresponding cul-

tural form. Thus *market capitalism* had *realism*, *imperialism* had *modernism*, and the present stage of *multinational capitalism* has *postmodernism*.

(7) Interpretation, for Jameson, is essentially an allegorical act. This consists in rewriting a given text in terms of a particular interpretative "master code." Local interpretative systems valorise a particular master code; these valorisations are historically explicable. Jameson suggests that the interpretative progression has three concentric frameworks:

   (a) Construction of the text within the *horizon of political history*. The individual object is conceived as a strategic act within a political arena.

   (b) Covers the extended tensions of the *class struggle*. The object of analysis is "reconstituted in the form of the great collective and class discourses of which a text is little more than an individual; utterance or parole. This object is the *ideologeme*—which Jameson defines as the "smallest intelligible unit of the essentially antagonistic collective discourses of social classes."

   (c) History, now conceived of as the *sequence of modes of production* (Asiatic mode to serfdom to feudalism to capitalism) and the succession and destiny of the various human and social formations. Texts are read in terms of "the ideology of form," that is the symbolic messages transmitted to us by the co-existence of various sign systems which are themselves traces or anticipations of past/future modes of production. The text is thus analysed in terms of the economic mode of production and of the choice of genre as symbolic of the same.

(8) In his controversial comments on the literature of the so-called "Third World," Jameson suggested that all narratives from the "Third World" must be taken as "national allegories." Jameson writes: " a certain nationalism is fundamental in the third world. Thus the telling of the individual story or experience is the 'laborious' telling of the experience of the collective itself, and is hence an allegory."

Jameson's views on postmodernism will be further elaborated in the chapter on postmodernism.

Terry Eagleton: Eagleton's numerous writings are wide-ranging and difficult to summarise. His Marxist works like *Criticism and Ideology* (1976), *Marxism and Literary Criticism* (1976), *Ideology* (1991), *The Function of Criticism* (1994), *The Ideology of the Aesthetic* (1990) and his popular *Literary Theory: An Introduction* (1983) have been extremely influential.

(1) In his essay on Marxist literary criticism in Hilda Schiff's (ed.) *Contemporary Approaches to English Studies*, Eagleton argues that the intention of Marxist criticism is not to discuss the insights of, say, stylistic, psychoanalytic or even straight empiricist criticism but to establish a hierarchy among these alternative methods, and in doing so, constitute itself as that hierarchy's determining base.

(2) All imaginative production is social production. Literature designates a privileged order of values defined and realised within certain institutional discourses. The social is the matrix within which all other terms are fleshed and shaped. Eagleton argues that Marxist critics have tried to discover the synchrony of structure, thus enabling a deciphering of the outline of an informing structure of social consciousness in the aesthetics of the text itself.

(3) A text "presses up" against the frontiers of what can be said, thus exposing the ideological frontiers and allowing the critic to identify them. This means that a text in *saying* one thing, reveals other possibilities which it is ideologically *prohibited* from realising. Thus the absences or silences in a text tie it to the history from which it is produced. Texts, in Eagleton's view, do not *reflect* historical reality, they work on ideology to convey an *effect of the real*. Ideology is thus defined by Eagleton as the systems of representations (aesthetic, religious, judicial) that shape the individual's mental picture of lived experience. *The meanings and perceptions of/in a text are a reworking of ideology's own working of reality.* That is to say, a text works at reality at *two* removes.

(4) We are not attending to the words on the page if we fail to grasp them as the cryptic but revelatory signs of a real history. A work's sensitivity to the "typical" developing dynamics of its history is a major constituent of its aesthetic worth. But this sensitivity may be locked in productive conflict with the conscious ideological stance of the author.

(5) We need a dialectical criticism (see Jameson above) conscious of its historical roots and relations, and so capable of interrogating the limits of other critical methods which substitute their own "synthetic totalities" (such as myth, genre) for the founding totality of history itself. That is, against the traditional critical modes which replace the actual dynamics and contradictions of history with its all-encompassing categories like myth or genre, Marxist criticism reveals the fractured bases of tradition, form, and aesthetics. A practice of "reading against the grain" is necessary to produce a "revolutionary criticism" which connects with the practical activity of the truly mass and truly revolutionary movement. Eagleton sums up the aims and agenda of Marxist criticism beautifully when he writes: "the problem-solving process of the text is never merely a matter of its reference outward to certain pre-existing ideological cruxes. It is, rather, a matter of the 'ideological' presenting itself in the form of the 'aesthetic' and vice versa." Marxist criticism then seeks to understand the "ideological significance whereby certain historical texts are severed from their social formations, defined as 'literary', bound and ranked together to constitute a series of 'literary traditions' and interrogated to yield a set of ideologically presupposed responses."

(6) Eagleton adapts the notion of the "*public sphere*" from Jurgen Habermas. The public sphere is the realm of social institutions like clubs, journals, coffee-houses, and periodicals in which private individuals assemble for the free equal exchange of ideas and reasonable discourse. They thus weld themselves together into a relatively cohesive body whose deliberations may assume the form of a powerful political force.

(7) In his seminal *The Function of Criticism*, Eagleton argues that the modern concept of literary criticism is closely tied to the rise

of the liberal, bourgeois public sphere in the eighteenth century. Literary discussion becomes an arena to pave the way for political discussion in the middle classes.

(8) Culture is the negation of all particular forms in the name of the totality. This totality is thus a void because it is no more than a totality of negated, silenced and marginalised moments.

(9) Criticism in the Victorian age achieved security by committing, in Eagleton's terms, "political suicide." The moment of criticism's institutionalisation is also the moment of its demise as a socially active force. The role of the contemporary critic is to resist the domination of the late capitalist mode by reconnecting the symbolic to the political. We need to engage with those repressed needs, interests and desires which may then (finally) emerge as cultural forms with their own collective force. If modern criticism was born of a struggle against the Absolutist State, its future should now be defined as a struggle against the bourgeois state. It must break with its "ideological prehistory" and become a "science." Eagleton phrases it thus: "The guarantor of a scientific criticism is the science of ideological formations."

(10) Such a scientific criticism would focus on the general mode of production and the literary mode of production, a general ideology, an aesthetic ideology and an authorial ideology. All these interact in complex ways that change through time. Individual authors are seen as the bearers of such categories. The history of literature may be derived from these interactions.

(11) Eagleton accepts the potential of deconstruction and post-structuralism to undermine absolute forms of knowledge and all certainties. However, deconstruction for Eagleton denies "objectivity" and the material interests.

Walter Benjamin: Benjamin's *Illuminations* (1968), his essays on translation and aesthetics attempted to formulate a whole new notion of "critique."

(1) Critique, for Benjamin, means that nothing can simply be taken as "given." Any text or artefact demands something more, exceeds itself, in a movement that structures literature, culture and history. Critique was immanent to art itself; critique is art's nec-

essary supplement. There would be, simply put, no art without critique because art is *critical* from the very beginning.

(2) Benjamin distinguished between critique and commentary. The former is concerned with "truth content," the latter with "subject matter."

(3) Translation is a mode of critique to the extent that it resists imitating the original and instead reveals what remains incomplete in the original. Benjamin rejects the idea of language as a mere tool for communication and representation as a bourgeois concept. He thus rejects the traditional mode of thinking about language in terms of *ends* and *means* (transmission of information) in favour of understanding the sheer materiality of language, historical survival and violence that makes possible culture politics and economics.

(4) No poem must be seen as *intended* for the reader. The text must be the centre of attention. Here the difference between the original and the translated must be taken into account. The original must not be hermetically sealed off from subsequent translations by appealing to the virtue of its "purity." One cannot translate literally, but only by "touching it [the original] lightly." A literal translation "demolished the theory of the reproduction of meaning and is a direct threat to comprehensibility." Non-literal fragments of a translation can reproduce the whole of the original. *The principle of the reproduction of meaning is in the word itself: the principle of translation/reproduction is original, not the object reproduced.* The text has an "afterlife" which propels it into history via tradition/translation. The "reproduction of meaning" is the translation of the poetic element of the work: reproduction is part of the work. What allows the story told by the storyteller to be reproduced is not the content of what is told. Rather it is the story in the memory which is important. A story is what allows the content to be retained in memory. Story is the element of transmission (what Benjamin terms "tradition"), and transmission is the "afterlife." The story, which always presupposes a community, turns the listener into a storyteller. Benjamin writes: "the cardinal point for the unaffected listener is to assure himself of the possibility of reproducing the story."

(5) In his famous essay "The Work of Art in the Age of Mechanical Reproduction" Benjamin argued that modern technical innovations such as the television, the radio and the cinema have altered the status of the "work of art." Where it was initially restricted to the bourgeois elite for being "unique," the reproduction of art objects by photography or radio transmission means that they are actually designed for *reproducibility*. Their "authenticity" was thus lost with their reproducibility: the difference between "original" and "copy" ceased to make sense with the multiple photographs. This divorced art from "ritual" and opened it to the realm of politics by bringing the art-object closer to the mass audience. In order to wrest new technology from the bourgeois, it was necessary for the socialist writers/artists to become *producers* in their own artistic spheres. Here *technique* plays an important role, because in a field such as photography, technique is not incidental to the art, but *an essential part of the art*. Benjamin lauds the democratic potential of the reproduction of "classical" works of art. The reversibility in the effect of art world produced and the new concept of "originality" are of prime concern for Benjamin here.

(6) Benjamin rejects the idea that revolutionary art is achieved by attending to the correct subject matter. The artists must revolutionise the *artistic forces of production* of his time. With the possibility of reproduction a work of art can receive meaning from different contexts. A new form of creativity may be inaugurated just when people think that reproduction has deadened and degraded the art-object (this is a concept developed by the postmodern theorist Gregory Ulmer).

V Relationship with Other Disciplines

Marxism has been the most influential thought in the history of ideas. Historians such as E.P. Thompson, sociologists such as Herbert Marcuse, Max Weber and Jurgen Habermas have variously grappled with Marxist thought. Raymond Williams and his followers in cultural studies—specifically Stuart Hall and others—have benefited from their adaptation of Marx. Environmentalism in the writings of Ariel Salleh and others have discovered the "emancipatory discourse" of Marxism useful for their purpose. The feminist movement has perhaps been the best deployment of Marxist thought in the work of Michele Barrett, Gayatri Spivak and others. Pierre Macherey's work on literary production is cast in a Marxist framework. Postcolonial theory, especially from the developing nations (most notably in the work of Aijaz Ahmed and Homi Bhabha have retained the materialist framework for their analysis. Jacques Derrida in *Specters of Marx* specifically, and controversially, claims a Marxist legacy for deconstruction, especially in deconstruction's stress on continued interrogation, self-critique and the irreducibility of emancipatory potential and notion of justice.

Critical Theory and the Frankfurt School: A Note: The Frankfurt School of Sociologists initially meant the work of Theodore Adorno and Max Horkheimer. The work of Jurgen Habermas after the Adorno generation has helped establish "critical theory" as a whole disciplinary field today. It is interdisciplinary in scope and has influenced much work in cultural studies. Critical theory looks at philosophy's genesis in the tradition of philosophising. Critical Theory argues that authentic philosophy is negative. It denies that all philosophy originates in class. The negation of philosophy is visible in two areas: (i) philosophy's denial of historical circumstances (ii) its criticism of the present.

Raymond Geuss in *The Idea of a Critical Theory* (1981) sums up the salient features of critical theories:

(1) Aim at enabling subjects and agents to understand their true interests
(2) Are inherently emancipatory
(3) Are forms of knowledge
(4) Are reflective in nature

Critical Theory postulates a failure in Reason itself (the project of the Enlightenment, with its valorisation of Reason). In fact the Frankfurt School sees an utterly rationalised world as a failure precisely because Reason has conquered the world. There is also a crisis in the unconsciousness of the rational process. This means that Reason does not know itself and therefore lapses into its opposite.

There is a cultural crisis:

(1) Crisis of the work of art itself—untenable and completely dependent on technology
(2) Culture itself becomes affirmative and mediocre. A denial, rather than a constituting of consciousness occurs.
(3) Crisis of institutions—a bureaucratic structure of the "culture industry."

The term "culture industry" is associated with Adorno and Horkheimer. The idea here is that the Marxist notion of "commodity production" could be applied to the production of symbolic ("aesthetic") goods. The culture industry also used "alienated labour," pursued profit, utilised technology, and was primarily concerned about "producing customers." These were, therefore, exactly like any other industry. Adorno and Horkheimer summed it up thus: "The stronger the position of the culture industry, the more summarily it can deal with consumers' needs, producing them, controlling them, disciplining them, and even withdrawing amusement." The effect is a *manipulation of desire*. The Frankfurt School was delineating the outline of mass culture where the qualities of cultural goods were the effect of technology and production system. Here the difference between, say, an item of furniture and a music album breaks down: both have been produced in the same way. At a different level, the analysis of the culture industry is the analysis of the organisation of cultural production. Public broadcasting, state policies; legislation also become part of the culture industry.

Further Reading

Eagleton, Terry. *Marxism and Literary Criticism*. London: Methuen, 1976.

Eagleton, Terry. *The Function of Criticism: From The Spectator to Post-Structuralism*. London: Verso, 1994.

Hall, Stuart, et al, ed. *Culture, Media, Language*. London: Hutchinson, 1980.

Hawkes, David. *Ideology*. London: Routledge, 1996.

Held, David. *Introduction to Critical Theory: Horkheimer to Habermas*. Chicago: University of Chicago Press, 1989.

Mulhern, Francis, ed. *Contemporary Marxist Criticism*. London: Longman, 1992.

Williams, Raymond. *Marxism and Literature*. Oxford: Oxford University Press, 1977.

Chapter Six

The New Historicism and Cultural Materialism

Proceeding from the poststructuralist assumption that reality, history, subjectivity and identity are *textualised*, the New Historicists practise an extremely close reading of texts. The New Historicism may be defined as a simultaneous reading of *literary and non-literary texts*, and demonstrating how a work of art may be read and interpreted on terms of its context of other texts, such as those from economics, legal tracts and medical records. This is so because the work of art is embedded in specific material conditions and relationships of power—the context of the text. The New Historicism thus *foregrounds the background.* All texts are simply texts, there is no privileged work of art. Stephen Greenblatt has termed it a "poetics of culture." The New Historicists and the cultural materialists may together be termed "materialist critics," where the label invokes a specific Marxist influence.

Cultural materialism, closely linked to New Historicism, was popularised by Jonathan Dollimore and Alan Sinfield. Focusing on the *political nature/ideologies and contexts of texts*, the cultural materialists read texts firmly within a political critical practice. Culture is now taken to include forms as diverse (and thus far ignored or marginalised) as television soap operas and popular music. Cultural materialism assumes that just as the socio-political and economic contexts shaped literary and non-literary texts (for instance, the kind of class readership that helped the formation of the "dime novel"), these texts helped form socio-cultural conditions (such as the adventure fiction of Defoe and later Rider Haggard that inspired colonial enterprise). There is no cogent "grouping" of the materialist critics, and therefore one cannot organise the chapter around "schools" of thinkers.

I Background and Origins

New theories of historiography, anthropology and ethnography have been extremely influential in the notion of "text" and "representation" in the New Historicism and cultural materialism. As such, it might be helpful to sum up some of the new approaches to history, historiography, ethnography here, for they form a link to poststructuralism and postmodernism. The work of Frank Ankersmit, Hayden White, and Richard Rorty (at a more distant level), in historiography and the notion of culture and ethnography in the writings of James Clifford, Clifford Geertz and others are important here.

Frank Ankersmit: Ankersmit's *Narrative Logic: A Semantic Analysis of the Historian's Language* (1983) was instrumental in the move towards a postmodern historiography. For Ankersmit, history is a set of individual statements that constitute texts. These statements, culled from various sources, are selected and combined by the historian from the many statements that s/he *could have made*. A certain "picture of the past" is thus fabricated. Thus Ankersmit posits two issues about historical statements:

(1) Individual statements refer to or describe a fragment of the past and can either be true or false

(2) Collectively, these statements define the picture of the past, which is simply an iconic impression.

While individual statements/facts can be verified against the source, the entire/whole picture cannot be. This is so because the *individual events do not make up a picture*: the historian *makes a picture out of them through selection, combination and explanation*. Therefore since history is at the level of the *whole* rather than individual statements, historiography is *invented*. The cause-effect, the relation of the event to the age are imagined and/or invented by the historian. Since history is a figurative, imagined and created account (story), one cannot perceive history as either *mimetic* ("true representation") or *empirical* (*factually* true). The events of the past are available only in these stories/narratives about the past: a *textualisation of history*.

Hayden White: White is indisputably the most important theorist of history after Jules Michelet. White's notion of history, available mainly in works like *Tropics of Discourse* (1978), *Metahistory* (1973), and *The Content of Form: Narrative Discourse and Historical Representation* (1987) may be summed up as follows. History is a verbal prose structure in the form of a narrative discourse the content of which is as much imagined/invented as found. In the construction of their historical narratives, historians inevitably combine known parts (facts) with imagined wholes. This means that there is a definite textualisation of historical "facts," and there is no empirical history possible outside the text. This is metahistory. White sums up his reading of history thus:

> The historical work has the following components: (1) chronicle, (2) story, (3) mode of emplotment (4) mode of argument and (5) mode of ideological implication. Both chronicle and story may be the "primitive elements" in the *historical account* but they are selected, arranged and combined in certain ways for certain audiences. This means that history writing is the mediation between the *historical record* (unprocessed), other *historical accounts* and the *audience*. Together they constitute the "*historical field*." We shall look at the 5 elements of the historical narrative in some detail.
>
> (1) Chronicle: It is the arrangement of events and people to be dealt with in the temporal order of occurrence. They are open-ended, without beginnings or ends. The chronicle begins when the chronicler begins.
>
> (2) Story: The arrangement of the events with a beginning, middle and end. Characterising the place and time of occurrence, the detailing of the importance of the event are features of the story. A "*hierarchy of significance*" is necessary here to show why certain events are more important for history to remember and so on. The transformation of the chronicle into a story is a fiction making: because the historian decides the hierarchy of significance (the important events) and the order of events (this resulted in that). The historian endows the events narrated with meaning and importance so that a comprehensible story emerges, especially

in the cause-effect pattern. They also indicate relationships between events and people through this method.

(3) Emplotment: This is the way a sequence of events is fashioned into a particular kind of story. To change a sequential story into a meaningful narrative, it must be emplotted. Since the events themselves are not organised into plot, emplotment is necessary in the retelling. For example, no set of events is intrinsically tragic, comic or farcical. Imposition of the structure of the story alone gives them this quality. There are four main modes of emplotment:
(a) Romance (b) Comedy (c) Tragedy (d) Satire

(4) Explanation: The historian must reveal that the random collection of events are integrated. This itself may take four modes:
   (a) Mechanistic: They may show this integration under the *cause-effect* relationship between events
   (b) Organistic: They show the relationship as the *whole-part* one, where the events are subsumed as various constituent parts under a general/whole event.
   (c) Formist: When the historian sorts out the various entities after identifying their class, with their specific attributes and labels and adequate *description*. Here depiction of the variety, of the uniqueness of the events becomes the main function of the historian.
   (d) *Contextualist*: They focus on the *background* to the particular events. They depict in great detail the historical period, the era and the movements in which the event took place.

(5) Ideology: White argues that the detection of "coherence" in the events is implicated in the ideology of the historian. He brings to his analysis the baggage of his theories of knowledge, the socio-cultural position from which he speaks. There is no a-ideological history.

History and Tropology: White argues that the organisation/ emplotment of the events requires a certain troping. Since the events cannot describe themselves the historian does so. White writes: "in the very act of identifying and describing the objects he finds [in the past] . . . constitutes their subjects as possible objects of narrative representation by the very language [he] uses to describe them." These descriptions are linguistic tropes, and are of four main types in history writing. The historian decides the trope he will use even before his narration, and thus pre-figures the narrative into certain forms.

(1) Metaphor: this is representational. This is used for a formist explanation.
(2) Metonymy: this is reductive. This is used for a mechanistic explanation. Here, the individual acts are seen as part of, as giving meaning to, and as standing in for the larger phenomena.
(3) Synecdoche: this is integrative. This is used for an organicist explanation. Here the apparently particular phenomena are seen or understood in terms of the whole, as expressing some totality. Each act is seen as expressing the general trend.
(4) Irony: this is negational. The skeptic historian may use this. It takes away the greatness and significance of the particular event.

In summary, the correlation between the modes of emplotment, explanation and ideology used by the historian may be charted as follows (after Keith Jenkins):

Mode of emplotment	**Mode of explanation**	**Mode of Ideology**
Romance	Formist	Anarchist
Comedy	Organicist	Conservative
Tragedy	Mechanistic	Radical
Satire	Contextualist	Liberal

Richard Rorty: A philosopher who has rethought the concept of truth and pragmatism, Rorty's influence on history writing has been enormous. Rorty's main ideas may be set out as follows.

(1) The notion of "Truth" (with a capital T) which seems/is accepted to be true because it corresponds with the "Real" is absurd. The notion of the *known particular* and the *imagined whole* breaks down. We can choose between the sentences but we cannot choose between whole vocabularies. We assume that the *sentence's* veracity (truth content) implies the veracity of the *world* it refers to. For instance, in history what is true at the

level of the *chronicle* (the facts of the events from evidential record) does not mean that the story/narrative built over and around them (using cause-effect relations, for example. See White above on the construction of the *story* of history) is true. Culture loses the habit of using certain words, and acquires the habit of using others.

(2) Truth is only the name given to whatever proves itself to be good, for assignable reasons, in the way of belief.

(3) There is no way of understanding the Real except through language. Language is not a transparent medium for representing the world. Language is the instrument to get us what we want, and what we *ought to want*.

Language is most creative when used *metaphorically*. The metaphorical creation of new words and concepts leads to the possibility of creating new worlds, alternative actualities. Metaphors expand the possibilities of our present world. In Rorty's famous example, metaphors like "Love is the only Law" which is initially absurd (at the level of language), becomes literally true. Our beliefs begin to accommodate this as true. We can thus use metaphors to erase the "longest lie" (of God, the transcendental signified, absolute truth). We need new metaphors so that there is never a final resting-place for thought. We can be free from the "certainist discourse." Unfamiliar ideas from the outside create tensions in us. These tensions are necessary to transcend our monolithic acculturation into the realm of plurality and multiplicity.

The New Ethnography: the new approach to ethnography is visible in the writings of the anthropologist Clifford Geertz, James Clifford, Stephen Tyler and others. The essential features of the new mode of ethnographic writing are summarised by Clifford in his well-known Introduction to the volume, *Writing Culture: The Poetics and Politics of Ethnography* (1982). These are as follows:

(1) Culture is now perceived as constituted by contested codes and representations.

(2) Science and politics are not distinct categories, but are inseparable from and inform each other.

(3) Academic and literary genres interpenetrate and influence each other.

(4) All cultural accounts are inventions and reconstructions rather than representations. In Clifford's oxymoronic phrase they are "true fictions." These silence certain voices and enable others to speak.

(5) Literary processes such as metaphor, figuration, narrative are features of the ethnographic text too. To convey a sense of "truth," the ethnographic text selects, combines and juxtaposes events in a certain order, lending them a certain "space," and using certain rhetorical ploys. These accounts are thus the result of contingencies of language, rhetoric, power and history. The ethnographic text thus has a *poetics* of composition and a politics: it is essentially narrative.

(6) Ethnography is a performance emplotted by certain stories. These stories describe real cultural events and add moral judgements, which always proceed from an ideological position. The ethnographic account is allegorical at the level of what it says (content) and the manner of saying it (narrative style). This means that the account is not a *representation* of cultural events, but a *story* about them. There is no way of separating the actual event from the allegorical. The data makes sense only when schematised, systematised and narrated. (See the parallels with Hayden White's distinction between *chronicle* and *story* above, and his argument that the events of history have to be ordered to make sense). Thus the ordering and systematising in ethnography is always ideological, as White argues about history. This leads us to the next point about ethnography.

(7) The method of production of the ethnographic text is also analysed now. "Who speaks for/about/to the native?" is implicated in further questions like "From what position is the ethnographer speaking? What institutional affiliations enable her/him to speak?"

(8) What are the excluded categories in such accounts? This is the important question for a new ethnography. The gender, race and national/ethnic voices are given adequate discursive roles in a new multi-voiced ethnographic practice. Thus the view of culture is of something which is "relational, an inscription of

communicative processes that exist, historically between subjects in relations of power."

(9) The role of "*thick descriptions*" (Geertz's phrase) is crucial to unravel the significatory processes of culture. Reading culture as a system of signs, anecdotes, trivial descriptions and marginal references play an important role in the overall narrative. These particularities reveal the construction of the cultural text through the motivating forces, codes and logic that control society.

The origins of the New Historicist criticism may be traced to 1980 when Stephen Greenblatt published his seminal *Renaissance Self-Fashioning: From More to Shakespeare*. Reading Renaissance humanism as closely linked to the colonial enterprise, Greenblatt argues that all these so-called *universally* humanist texts relied upon the marginalisation of a *part* of the universe—the native/colonised Other. Renaissance drama was seen by Greenblatt and the later New Historicists as influenced by, formed, and perhaps directly "drawn" from other texts such as penal, medical and colonial ones. Thus one discovers that the humanism of the age concealed a massive violence—of slavery, colonialism, sexual repression and penal torture. It is this covert political and ideological contradiction of "great" literary texts that New Historicism seeks to reveal.

Later texts in the New Historicist "tradition" followed Greenblatt in re-reading the entire Renaissance archive. The focus on the Renaissance was due to the fact that this age was the age of the great humanist "reform" of Western, especially European culture, and this age's influence has been enormous right down to the twentieth century. Also, the age has been well studied for its economic, social and cultural conditions, making documents available for re-reading by the New Historicists. An early text in the New Historicist mould, but which became popular after its reissue in 1987 (with an introduction by Jonathan Dollimore) was J.W. Lever's *The Tragedy of State* (originally published in 1971). The important texts that built up a whole New Historicist critical practice were John Drakakis' (ed.) *Alternative Shakespeares* (1985), Terence Hawkes' *That Shakespeherian Rag* (1985), Jonathan Dollimore and Alan Sinfield's (ed.) *Political Shakespeare* (1985) Marjorie Levinson's *Re-*

thinking Historicism (1989), Greenblatt's Shakespearean *Negotiations* (1988), and his book on the European discovery of America, *Marvelous Possessions* (1991). Levinson's book moved from Renaissance to the Romantic age, as did Cynthia Chase's *Romanticism* (1993). Aram Veeser's (ed.) *The New Historicism* (1989) brought together some of the most important essays in the field.

The work of the New Historicists and cultural materialists have been greatly influenced by the writings of the Marxist literary critic Raymond Williams. The term "cultural materialism" was used by Jonathan Dollimore and Alan Sinfield in *Political Shakespeare*, and is associated with British academia. The New Historicism is the American equivalent. Graham Holderness termed cultural materialism "a politicised form of historiography" where literary and non-literary texts were analysed in a political framework. The work of Michel Foucault on discourse (see chapter on poststructuralism and deconstruction above) was also a major influence on the cultural materialists. Books like Holderness' *Shakespeare's History* (1985) and the Terence Hawkes book mentioned above were instrumental in popularising this critical practice.

II Assumptions and General Methods

(1) The separation of the literary text from other forms of cultural production meant that art was seen as an autonomous and self-contained object. This notion was no more valid, and a careful *historicising of texts* was required to understand their implication with the forms/structures of power prevalent in that period. What was needed was an understanding of texts, literary and non-literary, as part of a whole *discourse*. All expressive acts are firmly grounded in specific material practices.

(2) Every approach to history must presuppose, in Hayden White's words, a version of the textualist theory of historical reality. The past is accessible to study only through its textualisation. All events have to be *first described* in order to be analysed. Thus the past is *first recorded as texts*, the analysis is of *these records* which supposedly represent the events themselves. History is a sequence of cultural systems of which both literature and social institutions are expressions. The relations between these cultural

systems and the institutions are symbiotic: *they influence each other.*

(3) To locate the extent of such a discursive context one needs to re-read Shakespeare alongside other thus far unread/ marginalised texts of the Elizabethan age such as colonial documents, travelogues and economic tracts. These other texts are not secondary for Greenblatt, in fact they "produce" Shakespeare. The literary and non-literary texts "circulate" and "negotiate" inseparably with(in) each other. Thus these critics "place texts in a material . . . context in order to show that canonical texts . . . are bound up with a repressive ideology, yet also provide scope for dissidence" (Scott Wilson's summary).

(4) Both New Historicism and cultural materialism show influences of poststructuralist thought in their interrogation of "standard truths," modes of knowledge, the inherently textual nature of reality, and the intertextual nature of all texts. In a sense, then, all theory after deconstruction, Derrida and Foucault is poststructuralist for its emphasis on forms and practices of knowledge rather than actual knowledge itself. New Historicism and cultural materialism, however, seeks to remedy the allegedly *apolitical* nature of poststructuralist thought (with its emphasis on language) by treating texts and language as political and cultural developments. Materialist analysis is therefore indisputably ideological.

(5) Cultural materialism accepted the assumptions of Marxist Criticism: notably that culture and cultural artefacts such as art cannot "transcend" the material conditions of production and the economic context of society. Though there may not be direct "base-superstructure" (see chapter on Marxist criticism) link, one cannot treat culture as independent of these conditions. There is a definite relation between human action and socio-economic formations. Literary criticism is inseparable from ideological values and biases.

(6) Ivo Kamps in his introduction to his (ed.) *Materialist Shakespeare* (1995) suggests that there are four commitments in materialist critical practice:

(a) to a patterned relationship between cultural forms (art) and social relations of production
(b) to the "relative autonomy" of the literary text
(c) a programme of rigorous and concrete historical research
(d) an ideological critique.

(7) In the introductory remarks to their (ed.) *Political Shakespeare*, Jonathan Dollimore and Alan Sinfield summarise the critical method of the cultural materialists. They pay attention to:
(a) Historical context: to question the apparent timelessness of literary texts. One needs to look at the specific conditions in which certain texts were *produced* and *received*. Thus issues of the poor laws, the agricultural practices and the trial of dissenters/blasphemers are part of the history of Renaissance texts.
(b) Theoretical Method: The emphasis on textual history, and the textualisation of history involves reading across disciplines under the assumption that all texts are intertexts.
(c) Political commitment: All readings are to be politically oriented. This means that issues that have not been addressed by traditional critics such as the effacement of women, the racist overtones and the repression of non-heterosexual relationships must figure in the cultural materialist practice.
(d) Textual analysis: No generalisations are forwarded. All critiques are derived from extraordinarily close readings of texts, including marginal references, footnotes, apparent errors and so on. They carry to the logical extreme the Derridean notion of the textual nature of everything, and that there is nothing outside the text.

(8) The New Historicists admit that all critiques use the very tools they condemn. Any critical method is trapped in the very capitalist culture/economy it seeks to critique.

(9) They do not favour hypothetical constructs, preferring, instead, to point out amazing and frequently ignored coincidences between events and literary themes. Thus the link between the arrival of a mode of dress and a protest movement that smashed windows is explored (see Jane Marcus' essay in Veeser's book).

(10) They reject the "grand narratives" of history such as the Marxist one of the class struggle as the governing factor in all subjectivity, cultural artefacts and human relations. Instead the materialist critics argue that social and cultural events and literary texts are linked "messily," in a constant state of negotiation.

(11) It is assumed that the "possession" of social assets (prestige) is *equivalent* to the possession of currency. The exchanges of these invisible assets are frequently ignored because they are not convertible into liquid assets. Thus it is "symbolic capital" (see Bourdieu below). Greenblatt thus argues that the economic-noneconomic distinction is untenable. Even the most noncommercial act such as art, self-sacrifice provides symbolic profit (as prestige, fame) which can be encashed and capitalised upon. The materialist critic would therefore focus on how a text effaces such social and symbolic transactions which are also relations of power.

(12) The approach of the materialist critic is by necessity interdisciplinary. Since the work of art is grounded in the socio-political and economic contexts, one cannot read it without understanding how these contexts have shaped the choice of genre/themes/structure of the author's work. There are always surprising coincidences between the social context and the text. The text, in turn, has its influence, however small it is, on the context: another exchange and negotiation.

Differences between New Historicism and Cultural Materialism

(1) Hayden White suggests that the New Historicists are essentially *synchronic* in their approach. They look at a large number of almost *contemporary* texts (which are, of course, across diverse areas like popular culture, "classics," legal documents etc). They thus analyse the current "cultural system" *of that time*. Therefore, unlike the Marxists, the New Historicists while explaining *historical differences* do not explain *historical changes*. The cultural materialists focus more on *our times*, the historical *present*. Thus reading a historically distant text, the cultural materialist will connect it to, and comment upon, contemporary cultural systems (such as the present education system, national

identity, ethnic relations). Louis Montrose argues that this difference is because the British have a rigid class society and strong nationalist concerns. All meditations on the past tend to be inscribed within a concern with the national pride/identity and the collective consciousness. The diversity of the US, the tradition of radical politics and culture, finds this approach unnecessary: they simply cannot comprehend the "contemporary institutional force and social function of Shakespeare" (Walter Cohen's comment).

(2) The New Historicists argue that effective subversion of power structures by individuals is a myth. Greenblatt, in his early writings (*Shakespearean Negotiations*) argued that "we locate as 'subversive' in the past those things that are not subversive to ourselves, that pose no threat to order by which we live and allocate resources. Later, Greenblatt modified this position by suggesting that subversion may not be an overturning of hierarchies, but a corrosion of the principles by which authority is imposed. The cultural materialists argue that there *is* a limited role for the individual in contesting hegemony and oppression. A text's references to (other) conflicting and contestatory texts may be buried under the text of support and collaboration. Thus the cultural materialists focus on the *interventionary* role of the individual and the New Historicist on the manner in which the power structures *restrain* the individual.

(3) An accusation leveled by the cultural materialists against the New Historicists is that the latter eschew an *apolitical* reading of culture. In the latter's adoption of the poststructuralist idea of skepticism towards all certainty and knowledge, they run the risk of undermining any politically radical agenda in their own discourse, thus making the whole New Historicist enterprise ultimately a futile *textual* exercise. The New Historicists argue that they merely accept the dangers of asserting a monolithic, unquestionable truth and prefer, instead, to *indicate* alternative truths.

III Key Thinkers

Alan Sinfield, John Drakakis and Jonathan Dollimore's rereading of Shakespeare are well known examples of this approach.

Greenblatt, Louis Montrose, Terence Hawkes, Catherine Belsey have produced seminal essays on the Renaissance. Duncan Wu's monumental *Wordsworth's Reading* will undoubtedly pave the way for linking the famous poems to specific non-literary texts. The above thinkers and critics are well anthologised and have been at the forefront of the movement to produce a materialist literary historiography. Here the work of Greenblatt and Jonathan Goldberg, the central premises of Louis Montrose and the newer work of Valerie Traub and Douglas Bruster are summarised as samples of materialist criticism.

Stephen Greenblatt: Greenblatt's pathbreaking work on the Renaissance may well be said to have launched New Historicism. Greenblatt's arguments may be summed up as follows.

(1) The life of authors in the Renaissance was controlled by a number of institutions and authorities such as the church, the court, the Bible and the family. These powers were in conflict.

(2) The rival codes were cultural constructs, which the people used to understand their world and themselves. The powers, however, saw their customs as 'natural," and anything different as enemies and aliens. And, since the individuals were made subjects by the powers, their behaviour was formulated by the institutions with which they identified.

(3) Authors during the Renaissance reveal their complicated relationships with these institutions: complicitous or contestatory. Thomas More's work reveals his acceptance of the prevailing faith—the Catholic one—which resulted in his treatment of the Protestant one as alien and as a threat. Likewise Spenser articulates the anxieties about sexuality and its threat to the state.

(4) The invention of the printing press converted the simple book into a tool of power. They disciplined, suggested and fashioned norms of behaviour and the self—of obedience, faith in the religion and the king and so on. The book thus creates the identity of the Englishman. This is the link that Greenblatt uncovers between the literary text and the current socio-political conditions: each *produces* the other. The self is not autonomous and self-contained but constituted by social processes.

(5) These social practices which the characters in, say, Christopher Marlowe, seek to resist and subvert prove too strong (see point two under differences between New Historicism and cultural materialism above).

(6) In *Marvelous Possessions*, Greenblatt reads the early European encounter with the New World as the encounter fraught with the sense of wonder. Using anecdotes, which he considers as resisting the grand narrative of history, Greenblatt reads the accounts of the early arrivals on the American continent. He looks at: representations of the native; the tension between the marvel at the completely Other and the image of the sameness, and the related collapse of the same into the Other; the role of the native as the "go-between"; the use and abuse of language (especially the process of naming); the unequal exchanges (summed up wittily by Greenblatt as "I give you a glass bead, you give me a pearl worth half your tribe"!); the "appropriative mimesis" (imitation in the interest of acquisition); and the welding together of commodity conversion and spiritual conversion in the interest of colonialism.

Louis Montrose: Montrose is perhaps best known for his 1986 essay "The Poetics and Politics of Culture" in which he stated the aims and methods of New Historicism.

(1) One needs to rethink the framework of literary analysis by paying attention to the links between the text and the cultural system in which they are produced.

(2) Critics must problematise the formalist concept of literature as autonomous. The formation of canons has produced "enduring" texts that have perpetrated certain social, aesthetic, religious and moral values over centuries. This is the "gentle/manly" view of the discipline itself, and masks the violence, instability, and exploitation that went on during the time. Literature is thus not autonomous, but cleverly masks the differences and contradictions of the material conditions in which it is produced. In Montrose's famous formulation, we need to look at the "historicity of texts and the textuality of history." This suggests the New Historicist model of "a dynamic, unstable and reciprocal

relationship between the discursive and material domains" (Montrose).

(3) It calls for a reconsideration of the ways in which authors (like other individuals) interact with the social and linguistic system.

(4) On subjectivity: culture produces individuals who are endowed with subjectivity and the capacity of "agency." But it also imbeds them within social networks of power that creates codes of behaviour which ultimately overcomes the control of these same individuals.

(5) It is too early to say whether literature can offer or generate resistance. But the willingness to explore the political potential—interrogation of hegemony, resistance, counter-propaganda, and subversion—of writing is the characteristic of the New Historicism.

(6) Montrose argues that cultural poetics is not a theory or a systematic paradigm. Notions of textuality, ethnography and history, "thick descriptions" have influenced the New Historicists, especially in their shared emphasis on the discursive nature of all identity and reality.

Jonathan Goldberg: His best known work is *James I and the Politics of Literature* (1983). Goldberg focuses on the age of James I in terms of the political discourses of monarchical absolutism.

(1) Goldberg detects numerous contradictions in the rhetoric of James I.
    (a) The first contradiction is that while claiming to be the true heir to the lineage of British monarchy, he also, simultaneously, represents himself as self-originating.
    (b) James I refers to kingship as a performance in which the monarch's thoughts are revealed to the public. He then proceeds to argue that public display is opaque and misleading.

(2) Goldberg demonstrates how the literary and aesthetic works reproduce indirectly this royal authority. Goldberg argues that James I tries to *mystify* his body and prove his origins from a transcendental world/power. He tries to separate himself from his royal family lineage. With this move, argues Goldberg, James I is able to claim a spiritual origin to all life *and* to suggest his status as "above" common human and social laws.

(3) Goldberg suggests further that James I's mystification of his monarchical authority kept it as a private sphere from which his subjects were excluded. However, beneath the façade of the ideal heterosexual family, James I's homosexual orientation was discernible. The ideology of James' mystified body as "husband" to his "wifely kingdom," thus "masked the pleasures of the body."

(4) Renaissance texts adopted a similar rhetoric. Ben Jonson, for instance, refers to the royal patron as the source of their existence. Donne uses the metaphor of a strange disease in his body as a secret policy that governs a new kingdom. Thus in both cases, Goldberg demonstrates, the idea of the king's (or state's) secret and "sourceful" nature is replicated.

(5) In domestic portraits a similar strain is found. Goldberg's brilliant and virtuoso reading (an exemplar of the critical method) shows how the father in these portraits is modelled after the king—with the same air of authority and image of lineage. Yet he is shown distant and unaccountable as he gazes away from his family.

(6) Renaissance texts also replicate the second contradiction of James I's rhetoric. Reading Shakespeare's *Henry V* and George Chapman's *Bussy d'Ambois*, Goldberg argues that both plays have characters that use drama and the performative arts to *conceal* their aims and desires. Yet other texts play upon James I's notion of confusing and misleading theatricality to challenge the royal policies. Thus Jonson and Donne cleverly satirise the immorality of the court. They suggest that if the monarch is unaccountable and distant, then art cannot intentionally question the royalty. If accused of criticism of the royalty, the poet could always argue with the same rhetoric as James I: that his play/poem is misread, that their theatricality is misleading! Thus, Goldberg argues the resistance to power and the support of authority both use the same logic and rhetoric (which is, of course, restrained by the structures of power itself).

Valerie Traub: Her *Desire and Anxiety* (1992) analyses the erotic desire and the construction of male and female subjects in Shakespeare. Traub's work analyses the major strains in Shakespeare's representations of sexuality: the importance of female chastity; the disgust at sexual relations manifest in the equation between sexuality and disease; the fear and fascination for homoerotic desire; and the horrors of reproduction; the link of desire with patriarchal relations, their mediated representations and their role in "cultural fantasies." Traub's analysis focuses on the following:

(1) In tragedies like *Hamlet* and *Othello*, as well as in the romance, *The Winter's Tale*, women who are seen as erotically threatening are "monumentalised'. Their "warm" eroticism is transformed into "cold" and static forms: jewels, statues and corpses.

(2) Shakespeare's history plays perpetrate a repression of the fantasised female reproductive body, upon which the development of the "standard" male body depends. The female body is first constructed as the "grotesque" maternal *body* (Falstaff) and then displaced by the "classical" *body* (Katherine) which must be subjugated for Prince Hal to become monarch.

(3) There is a move from one "cultural polarity," virgin/whore, to another, virgin/mother. Thus the fantasy of female sexuality is perceived as a threat to the male subject.

(4) In *Troilus and Cressida*, the female body is the contaminant, and the venereal is the disease.

(5) There is a circulation of homoerotic desire in *As You Like It* and *Twelfth Night*. This homoerotic desire transgresses the logic of patriarchy. There is the subversion of heterosexuality in *As You Like It* and anxieties about homosexuality mingle with anxieties about female gender and reproduction in *Twelfth Night*.

Douglas Bruster: In *Drama and the Market in the Age of Shakespeare* (1992), Bruster seeks to link the developments in Jacobean drama to the changes in the market. There were three main modes through which the dramatists of the Renaissance tried to understand social change: linking the sexual with the economic, the urban and the rural, and the ancient with the modern. Bruster's arguments may be sketched as follows.

(1) The theatres emerged as a means of understanding the material foundations of urban England.

(2) Playwrights took to mythologising the realities of London's material "bases." The cuckold myth, the "objective inscription"

of identity in the Jacobean farces and comedies, the "staging" of London market through a version of the Troy tale (Shakespeare's *Troilus and Cressida*) are examples of this mythologising process.

(3) The playwrights achieved this through exploring the links between economic and sexual transactions. Identity was made into a reservoir of erotic potential. Identity was also ownership, and thus the property and the person became one.

(4) Writers used folk metaphors to understand this new reality. The cuckold came to symbolise profit: the man who "forgave" or even encouraged his wife's adultery for financial gain. The use of rural myths of the cuckoo, cony-catching, the bull and the stag formed a "portal trope" between the country and the city. Since the country was the site of natural struggle, these figures were used as metaphors to represent the bestial competitiveness and usury of urban life.

(5) London saw itself as the heir to ancient cities like Troy for an urban mythology. The social implications of a commercial culture was explored though this "history." The story of national conflict due to a theft inspired *Troilus and Cressida.*

Pierre Bourdieu: Though Bourdieu is not a literary critic his sociology of art and aesthetics has a strong resemblance to the New Historicist approach. Bourdieu in a series of works like *An Outline of a Theory of Practice* (1977), *Distinction* (1986), *The Field of Cultural Production* (1993) has sought to move beyond both the subjectivist and objectivist approaches in critical theory.

(1) For Bourdieu, objectivism refuses to acknowledge the role of consciousness, perception and conceptions that individuals make/have of the world. Subjectivism, on the other hand, ignores the social and material conditions that shape consciousness.

(2) He therefore seeks to develop a "*genetic structuralism*" (different from the one of Lucien Goldman. See section on Goldman in the chapter on Marxist criticism above) which combines an analysis of objective material practices with and analysis of the "genesis" within *individual* consciousness of the *socially con-*

structed mental structures (these mental structures generate actual practices by the individuals).

(3) In place of structures like "consciousness" and "subject," Bourdieu offers two concepts:

(a) Habitus: Bourdieu defines habitus as the system of "durable, transposable dispositions, *structured* structures predisposed to function as *structuring* structures." This is a "practical sense" that inclines agents to act and react in specific situations in a manner that is not always calculated and not simply a blind obedience to rules. The habitus instils/structures *dispositions* that last for the life of the individual (durable). They also generate practices in many different areas (transposable). The individual upon acquiring these dispositions may generate practices in fields as diverse as art, politics, sports, or family life. In each field, the individual thus *adapts* the practice and therefore the disposition is the "*structuring* structure."

(b) Field: Agents/individuals act in particular social conditions that embody specific social relations. A social formation is structured around hierarchically organised series of fields such as the educational, economic, political and cultural fields. Each field is a structured space with its own laws of functioning and its own relations of force. The relations between the positions occupied by the agents determine its structure. Thus a change in the position of the agents causes a change in the structure of the field.

(4) In any field the agents at various positions compete for control of "interests" and "resources" *specific to their field*. Bourdieu's argument is that these "interests" and "resources" are not always economic and material. For instance, in the field of cultural production the resources at stake are different.

(5) Bourdieu distinguishes between two kinds of capital.

(a) Symbolic capital: the accumulated prestige, celebrity, honour based on the interaction of *knowledge* and *recognition*.

(b) Cultural capital: the forms of cultural knowledge that equips the agent to appreciate and understand cultural relations or cultural artefacts. A work of art has meaning and value only to one who has the cultural competence/code into which the object of art is encoded. This cultural capital is acquired over years through pedagogy, the family, education, and institutions.

(6) Like other forms of capital even cultural capital is distributed unequally among social classes. These forms of capital may be exchanged for economic capital—an academic degree/capital helps acquire a job with economic returns. But the possession of one kind of capital does not imply the possession of the other.

(7) To enter a field, one needs to possess the habitus, which predisposes one to play the game: a minimum amount of skill, knowledge of the rules. Thus one "invests" a certain amount of symbolic/cultural capital in order to obtain certain "profits" from the game (say, a win).

(8) The specific economy of the cultural field is based on a kind of belief about the nature of the cultural work and its value. This belief is institutionalised (in, say, universities). Literature and art do not exist independently of the complex institutional network which authorise and legitimise them.

(9) One cannot seek the source of cultural productions in the productions themselves (which Bourdieu detects as the fault of the textual critics and discourse analysts). Neither is it possible to detect the source in external factors alone. What is required is a combination of the two approaches. One must therefore analyse the material production of the work and also the symbolic production. This is the analysis of the production of the value of the work. For Bourdieu, artistic mediators like publishers, critics, reviewers, agents and academies are producers of meaning and value. On the other hand, it is not adequate to simply pick authors out of the canon to understand how a genre has concretised certain beliefs and values (by which it judges later works for their symbolic capital). Such an analysis frequently focuses on the major works/authors. What is needed is the inclusion of the minor authors too. These minor authors had once functioned negatively, in opposition to the authors who are now canonised.

(10) We need to, suggests Bourdieu, focus on:

   (a) The position of the literary or artistic field within the field of power—the set of dominant power relations in society.
   (b) The structure of the literary field—the positions occupied by the agents competing for legitimacy and authority.
   (c) The genesis of the habitus of the producers.

(11) The field of cultural production is situated in a subordinate field within the field of power. In this field of power the possession of *economic capital* is the sign of legitimacy. But the field of cultural production, which possesses high symbolic capital, remains dominated because it does not possess much *economic capital*. Thus Bourdieu refers to the intellectual class as the "dominated."

(12) An opposition between two subfields structures the field of cultural production.
   (a) The field of *restricted* production—the field of high or serious art, the classics. Here the competition between agents is for symbolic capital—prestige, canonisation and celebrity status. Economic profit is usually minimal. The social apparatuses include galleries, exhibitions, centres for performing arts, reading sessions and so on. There is scope for experimentation here because the producer is not much affected by the rule of other fields such as economics (monetary gains).
   (b) The field of *large-scale* production—the field of mass or popular culture. This is sustained by an entire culture industry—the media, propaganda. It is based on appeal to the largest possible audience. But this makes experimentation less easy.

This is, of course, only a very brief introduction to Bourdieu's work. His analysis of strategies and trajectories, of the "gaze" that focuses on form rather than function, the appreciation of art are brilliant analyses that combine an "internal" and "external" method. For his grounding of cultural practices in the fields of power and power structures, Bourdieu's work parallels that of the New Historicists and cultural materialists.

IV Relationship with Other Disciplines

New Historicism's link with other disciplines has been explored in section one, which suggested the multi-disciplinary nature of this critical approach. Here I shall conclude by quickly sketching the rise of "Cultural Studies." This disciplinary area, which spills over into media studies, literary studies and popular culture, owes a great deal to the materialist critical practice.

Cultural Studies: A Note

Cultural studies grew out of the work of Raymond Williams (for elaboration of his work, see chapter on Marxist criticism above) notably in *Culture and Society: 1780-1950* (1958) and *That Long Revolution* (1961). In the 1970s and '80s cultural studies adapted structuralist and poststructuralist theories in their methodology. The establishment of the Centre for Contemporary Cultural Studies at the University of Birmingham in Britain and its activities under the directorship of Stuart Hall, the journal *Screen* and *Representations* (this latter in the US under the joint efforts of Stephen Greenblatt, Catherine Gallagher and others) helped the "arrival" of cultural studies as a major discipline. Let us survey the assumptions, informing ideas and points of critical scrutiny and emphasis in cultural studies.

(1) The roots of cultural studies are located in (as noted above) the work of Williams and Marxist thinkers such as E.P. Thompson. Their interests lay in the everyday life, the particularities of place and location, and ethnography. They saw Western Marxism as antidemocratic with an "enormous condescension" (Thompson's terms) towards the working class and their culture. Rejecting the elitism of French and German "high theory," they argued for an approach more oriented towards the material conditions and symbolic practices of working class lives. Rather than "macropolitical" frames of reference, what was needed (they argued) was a micropolitical analysis of culture.

(2) Cultural studies seeks to bridge theory and material culture. The cultural critic seeks to unravel (1) the *dominant* ideologies/ assumptions in a culture at the moment of production, (2) assumptions that are *residues* of a social condition that is on the

way out and (3) the *emergent* ideas that seem to be in a state of formation but have not fully concretised (for a detailed analysis of Williams' classification, see section on Williams in "Marxist Criticism"). The study of these three together can help understand the contradictions and complexities of literary works and other cultural artefacts. Thus cultural studies analyses the ideological effects of texts in terms of the "subjectification" (subject formation) of the reader/consumer.

(3) Cultural studies, as its most important contribution, eliminates the distinctions between high and low/mass/popular culture. It argues that this distinction is based on standardisation of aesthetic values that have been decided or framed by dominant classes and ideologies. Instead they argue that "there neither is nor can be a science of value. Value is something that must be *produced.* It is not an attribute of the text; it is rather something that is produced for the text" (Tony Bennett). Barbara Herrnstein Smith in *Contingencies of Value* (1988) goes so far as to suggest that not only are texts devoid of any value, they are also devoid of any intrinsic properties.

(4) Cultural studies seeks to identify forms of *cultural resistance* to and subversion of homogenising capitalism, class domination, bureaucracy and sexuality (the prejudice against homosexuality, for instance, where heterosexuality is deemed to be the "norm"). Thus they focus on "*subcultures*" (elaborated by Dick Hebdige in his 1979 book of the same title) like punk culture, working culture and gay/lesbian cultures that articulate resistance through the developments and adoption of distinct styles of dress, speech, music and social behaviour. The emphasis is thus on differences and local particularities that have been thus far ignored, subsumed, homogenised, even brutally denied/ suppressed under the prevailing dominant "high" culture. Culture studies is thus an attempt to discover counter-hegemonic cultures influenced, in the main, by Marxist views.

(5) Evaluation and selection of texts must be based not on their status as works of art (which is seen and defined in the high cultural sense), but for their role as performers of "subcultural work," as something that seeks to "redefine the social order"

(Jane P. Tompkins). Thus Tompkins argues that *The Scarlet Letter's* position in the canon of American literature is perhaps better suited to *Uncle Tom's Cabin*.

(6) Stuart Hall identifies "two paradigms" (the title of his famous 1980 essay) for cultural studies.

   (a) *Culturalist*: Based on the work of Raymond Williams, this approach sees the human subject as more or less free to create meanings for itself and rework social institutions. Thus it believes in the active interventionary role of the human agency. They focus on the actual reader rereading and reworking the text as an event in the socio-historical process.

   (b) *Structuralist*: Based on structuralist and poststructuralist theories, this approach sees the individual as determined ("interpellated," as Althusser put it. See Marxism and Althusser above) by and within social and ideological structures. The subject is thus an *effect* of these structures.

(7) Cultural studies is interdisciplinary, and uses ideas and methods from ethnography, media studies, film theory, anthropology, political theory, economics, history and sociology. It analyses films, cultural "products" like toys, dress and fashion, teenage and popular magazines, the advertising media, gender roles and sexuality, popular music, slang in speech as "alternative" cultures which destabilise and interrogate established texts, codes and standards.

Among the major areas and critics covered under term "cultural criticism/studies" are: film studies (Laura Mulvey, Colin MacCabe, Stephen Heath and Jacqueline Rose), modernity, nationality, identity and the politics of culture (Stuart Hall, Perry Anderson), popular and "subcultures" culture (Anthony Easthope, Dick Hebdige, Andrew Ross), literacy, literary canons/disciplines and culture (Richard Hoggart, Richard Ohmann). Others such as Lawrence Grosberg, Cary Nelson, Henry Louis Gates, Jr. Simon During, John Fiske, Diana Fuss, Alan Liu have also made important contributions to the area.

Further Reading

Dollimore, Jonathan and Alan Sinfield. *Political Shakespeare: New Essays in Cultural Materialism*. Manchester: Manchester University Press, 1994 (2nd edition).

Greenblatt, Stephen. *Shakespea rean Negotiations*. Oxford: Clarendon, 1990.

Miller, Toby and Robert Stam, ed. *A Companion to Film Theory*. Oxford: Blackwell, 1999.

Veeser, H. Aram, ed. *The New Historicism*. London: Routledge, 1989.

Wilson, Richard. *New Historicism and Renaissance Drama*. London: Longman, 1992.

Wilson, Scott. *Cultural Materialism: Theory and Practice*. Oxford: Blackwell, 1995.

Chapter Seven

Postcolonial Studies

The much-debated term "postcolonial" generally refers to writing/culture of nations/peoples/cultures who were once colonised by European powers. Postcolonial theory is an attempt to uncover the colonial ideologies implicit in European texts about the Other (in this case, native, non-European). It explores strategies of resistance and "independence" or a "counterdiscourse" in native texts against colonialism. The term "postcolonial literature" now replaces the traditional category of "Commonwealth literature" or "Third World literature." Postcolonial theory looks at: colonialism's strategies of representation of the native; the epistemological underpinnings of colonial projects; the "writing" of colonial histories; the feminisation, marginalisation and dehumanisation of the native; the rise of nationalist and/or nativist discourse; the psychological effects of colonialism on both the coloniser and the colonised; the role of apparatuses like education, English studies, historiography, art and architecture in the "execution" of the colonial project and the "transactive" or negotiatory structure of postcolonialism. Homi Bhabha defines postcolonial as "that form of social criticism that bears witness to those unequal and uneven processes of representation by which the historical experience of the once-colonised Third World comes to be framed in the West." No term in postcolonial studies is unproblematised. Meenakshi Mukherjee, Harish Trivedi among others "interrogate" the very idea of "postcolonialism." Aijaz Ahmed, arguing from a Marxist position, questions Saidian categories of Orientalist texts and Fredric Jameson's description of the "Third World" literature as "national allegory." The debates are extensive and cover an extraordinary range of issues.

I Background and Origins

Postcolonial theory may be said to have originated in the mid-twentieth century texts of Frantz Fanon, Aime Cesaire and Albert Memmi. Though studies of imperialism have been undertaken much earlier (notably in works like V.I. Lenin's *Imperialism: The Highest Stage of Capitalism*, 1916), it is with Fanon that studies in the psychological effects of colonialism really develop. Mannoni's work on the "psychology of colonialism" (1956) was a central text in this area. However, it is with Edward Said's phenomenally influential *Orientalism* (1978) and Bill Ashcroft et al's *The Empire Writes Back* (1989) that *postcolonial studies* (perhaps this is a better and more inclusive term than postcolonial "theory") becomes an institutional "enterprise." Today the field is vast, and ever expanding, including in its ambit and theoretical concerns, film and culture studies, language/religion, art and architecture, education systems and curricula, displacement, Diaspora and multiculturalism, feminism, historiography, nativism and fundamentalism, environmentalism, the "project" of modernity and development and, more recently, globalisation.

II Assumptions and General Methods

There are no specific "schools" in postcolonial theory (as an act of faith, the postcolonial would resist being subsumed under homogenising categories, which would delimit and define her/him), nor are there clear-cut methods of "postcolonial reading." The approaches, however, show some similarities and common concerns which we may summarise here.

(1) The term "postcolonial" (written, sometimes, with the hyphen as "post-colonial") indicates
   - (a) A temporal marker to suggest the age or period *after* colonisation, specifically the *decolonised* states. It therefore functions as a historical category that suggests a chronology—from the colonised to the decolonised or *post*colonial.
   - (b) a specific reading or analytical practice. Here it refers to the intellectual or theoretical practices that emerged in the academies where colonial texts were re-read for colonial

ideologies imbedded in them. In this sense, postcolonial refers to an oppositional analytic procedure.

(2) Postcolonialism/postcolonial theory after Edward Said analyses the European "construction" of the East/Orient as a discursive field called "Orientalism." The European colonial power "creates" the Orient as an epistemological category before dominating it militarily, politically and economically. That is, Europe first *produces* a category designated as the Other or the Orient through certain specific practices of knowledge acquisition and formation: philologic, literary, ethnographic, geographic and so on. This knowledge and representation relies upon a series of binary oppositions, all of which treat the native as the *negative/dark opposite of Europe*: civilised/barbaric, white/black, mature/immature, strong/weak, masculine/effeminate, rational/emotional, and progressive/primitive. Here the first term signifies the European, and the second (which stands for all the qualities rejected as inferior/or even bad by the West) always applies to the native. This knowledge now treated as an authentic survey/history/study is then used for "material" practices such as racial discrimination, political control, and economic exploitation. Said's argument thus adds a whole new dimension to the aphorism that "knowledge is power": here knowledge is colonisation.

(3) Adapting ideas from poststructuralism, postcolonial studies focuses on the discursive and linguistic construction of reality. This meant that representation of the native in Europe was hardly "innocent" or "true," but essentially an exercise that preceded more concrete alterations in the material reality of the native: the discourse that represented the native also ruled the native. This link between representation, epistemology and political practices becomes the subject of analysis in postcolonial studies. Thus the *conceptual foundations* of Western imperialism are unravelled for their complicity in actual political and economic practices.

(4) Ashcroft and others characterise writing emerging from the once-colonised nations as postcolonial. They identify three major characteristics of this postcolonial writing:

(a) The silencing and marginalisation of the post-colonial voice by the imperial centre
(b) The abrogation of the imperial centre within the text
(c) The active appropriation of the language and culture of that centre.

Ashcroft and others argue that postcolonial readings illustrate these common features of all postcolonial writing. They suggest a common thematic of these former colonies (including areas as distinct and diverse as Latin America, Asia and Africa).

(5) Postcolonial studies especially in the 1980s and 90s questioned the nationalist resistance to colonialism. They argued that the nationalist resistance and stress on "cultural independence" also relied on categories that were themselves European: specifically the idea of modernisation, development, the "nation-state" and democracy.

(6) Later developments added issues of ethnicity, displacement, gender, and race as categories for analysis. Thus the postcolonial arguments began to focus on how the nationalist project in colonial times and the decolonised nation-state replicated/ extended certain fundamental oppressive structures in class, gender and (in India) caste. The decolonised nation, argue the postcolonials, under the guise of homogenising, national stability, federalism, elide differences and perpetuate oppression of the marginalised—the women, the lower classes/castes. This, they argue, is essentially the same technique as that of colonialism. Under the rubric of postcolonial studies, we thus have an ongoing attempt to retrieve histories that have been silenced/erased by both colonial and nationalist powers. This is the subaltern studies project in India, which seeks to write the history of the subaltern as against/alternative (to) the history of the upper classes/castes, a "history from below."

(7) Other "resistance" struggles such as the Afro-American, the gay-lesbian and the environmental, now find increasing affinities with the postcolonial theoretical frameworks. The common denominator of oppression and marginalisation by certain self-imposed but questionable hierarchies (male, heterosexual,

white, Christian, human) links these apparently disparate groups.

(8) However, postcolonial studies is wary of uniting scattered positions under one umbrella. After the poststructuralist and postmodern distrust of essentialising, homogenising categories and master narratives (see chapter on postmodernism below), postcolonialism seeks to move beyond the universal into local, particular and singular conditions/concerns. That is, they focus on *local* sites of contests rather generalised categories of analysis. This is postcolonialism's emphasis on differences and particularities: such as the oppression of the tribal African woman in colonialism as compared to that experienced by the least literate 19th century woman in Bengal. It proceeds from the assumption that the experiences of these two are varied under the same conditions of colonialism, and therefore requires different parameters/approaches for analysis.

(9) Postcolonialism seeks to understand how oppression, resistance and adaptation have occurred during the colonial rule. This means that postcolonialism analyses specific strategies of power, domination, hegemony and oppression utilised by the coloniser in the colony. This includes a vast spectrum of issues: art and architecture, economics, political philosophy and their legal manifestations (courts, laws), psychological states, medical and other scientific apparatuses, the education system and civil codes, all of which embody, in some form or other, colonial ideology. That is, postcolonial studies uncovers the ideological *subtexts* of differences, Othering, discrimination and unequal power relations between the European and the native that are submerged in apparently innocent, universal or value-neutral texts of literature and culture.

(10) Postcolonialism also seeks to understand how the colonised reacted to, adapted and/or resisted this structure of domination. Thus, nativist/nationalist resistance and/or complicity, collaboration (unconscious or conscious) with colonisers, effects of colonialism (dehumanised, Westernised, schizophrenic, "hybridised," ultra-nationalist identities) are analysed.

(11) Postcolonial studies analyse representations and identity formations of the coloniser *and* the colonised in literary and cultural texts. Further, the adoption of postcolonial studies as a discipline in Western academies, the dangers of neo-colonialism and cultural imperialism in the age of global capital and information networks, the role of the nation-state in such a globalising context, the issues of multiculturalism are also addressed.

(12) Postcolonialism adopts tools from a wide range of disciplines. Psychoanalysis, feminism, poststructuralism and postmodernism, historiography, Foucauldian discourse analysis, cultural studies, anthropology, urban sociology, architectural studies, philosophy, reader-response theory and Marxism have all contributed to the theoretical rigour of postcolonial studies.

After a sketch of the basic assumptions and issues in postcolonial studies, we may now look at the principal thinkers in the area. The theorists discussed here include Frantz Fanon, Aime Cesaire, Albert Memmi, O. Mannoni, Ngugi wa Thiong'o, Edward Said, Gayatri Spivak, Aijaz Ahmad and Homi Bhabha. Later sections include discussion of the subaltern studies project and historiography, women and colonialism, the role of English studies, aesthetics and other discourses.

III Key Concepts and Thinkers

O. Mannoni: Mannoni's *Prospero and Caliban* was one of the earliest attempts to analyse the psychological processes of colonialism. Mannoni's arguments, now notorious for their essentialising schemata, may be summed up as follows:

(1) Mannoni argued that there were two kinds of European thought about other civilisations:

(a) they concluded that the non-civilised are non-civilisable

(b) they assume that all men are equally endowed with reason and refuse to see differences among them at all.

They ultimately conclude that the European way of thinking is the right one, that the mentality of the native is incomprehensible, and that the European mode of thinking must be *imposed* upon the rest of the world.

(2) Mannoni suggests that there is a difference in the "personality structure" of the races, which produces the differences in the civilisations. The European believes that the native is ready enough to *mimic* them, but never succeeds in *emulating* them.

(3) Mannoni argues that the personality of the colonial has certain inherent *latent* or repressed traits that colonial experience brings to surface and made *manifest* (note the parallel with Freud's latent and manifest dream content). Thus a colonial's personality develops solely in accordance with its own *inner* structure. A person free from complexes would not undergo change simply as a result of colonialism. Mannoni thus argues for a "*predestined colonial*." Mannoni argued that the European who comes out to the colony suffers from a "*psychologically inferior personality*" and the native a "*psychologically dependent one*." In order to get rid of this inferiority complex the European lords it over the native.

(4) The predestined colonial has a *misanthropic neurosis*, which suffers from "the lure of world without men" (in Mannoni's words). They have a pathological need for solitude, as symbolised in Defoe's Robinson Crusoe. The colonial countries, argues Mannoni, are the nearest approach possible to the archetype of the desert island.

(5) The native suffers from a "*dependency complex*." The European exploits this, and casts himself in the paternalistic role of the parent and master, and becomes the protector/provider to the child native. The personalised relationships allow the European complete control over the native. The native looks up to, and obeys the father-master. Feelings of hostility arise when these bonds of dependency are broken. The native feels that he has been abandoned, and so appears to the European to have no sense of gratitude. Dependence excludes gratitude. True gratitude implies a rejection of dependence and yet at the same time the preservation of an image of dependence based on free will. When the native feels he is inferior, he rectifies it by establishing a child-parent relationship with the European. Within this relationship, he no longer feels inferior. The threat of abandonment leads to a feeling of insecurity. The failure of dependence

by the European master seen as abandonment by native because he fears being "free." The child may experience betrayal by the parents, which is a projection of his own secret desire for independence for which he feels guilty. The colonialists live by the native's need for dependency. They in fact actively foster it by adopting a paternalistic attitude.

(6) Mannoni analysing the sexual aspects of racialism and colonialism sees the rapes allegedly perpetrated or threatened by the members of one race on those of the other are pure projections of the unconscious. He argues that the European's traditional fear of the rape of the Western woman by the oversexed native is simply an inversion of their own fantasies. Mannoni points out that it is always the *neighbour's* daughter/wife and not one's own who is the victim. Thus their desire for the white woman was subsumed and the guilt of their own fantasies shifted onto someone else (see section on women and colonialism below).

(7) Mannoni argues that the fact of belonging to a certain race is significant only so far as one is conscious of it. Such consciousness is not direct but acquired, and it is more quickly acquired the more often a man meets personalities different from his own.

(8) The natives, when Europeanised, impose one personality over another, thereby repressing the original. The repressed re-emerges when they go back. The hatred among "evolved" natives is because in them the process of civilisation has come to a halt and left incomplete. They have not become equal to the Europeans yet.

(9) A personality constructed in the European model is demoralised by a docile and inferior sexual partner. The native woman corresponds to an archetype of the collective unconscious—like Friday or Ariel. That native woman's personality is rarely externalised and only *reflects back to the European his own projection*. If a man lives in the midst of his own projections without truly admitting the independent will and existence of other people, he loses his own will and his own independence, while the ego inflates as it becomes empty.

(10) The white woman is constantly trying to impress upon the white man that there can be no comparison between herself and the native woman. Her tyranny towards the native male is due to her unconscious urge to control a male figure, an urge facilitated by the native's dependent personality.

Frantz Fanon: Fanon's *The Wretched of the Earth* (1963), *A Dying Colonialism* (1965) and *Black Skins, White Masks* (1967) were pioneer studies in the psychosocial aspects of colonialism.

(1) In a startlingly savage definition, Fanon indicates the psychological implications of colonialism when he writes in *Black Skins, White Masks*, of the soul of colonised where the death and burial of its local cultural originality have created an inferiority complex. Fanon argues here and in other works that colonialism drives the colonised to madness by rejecting any individuality-claims of the native. The native is annihilated, "objectified," and is made into something less than human, a nothingness. This was achieved by the emphasis on psychic difference, where the native's psyche was repeatedly represented, savaged, and "treated" as inferior. Fanon points out that the native is invariably mentioned in zoological terms—the "yellow man's reptilian motions," the stink of the native quarter, of foulness or bestiary. As Fanon puts it, "the settler paints the native as a sort of quintessence of evil, insensible to ethics, a negation of values." This was also accompanied by the description of the native as an animal—usually snakes, vermin, rodents and other less-liked animals. Such an assault reduced the native to a dehumanised object: the black man loses his identity. The universal category of "Man" now actually means "white man." In fact, the settler "ends his work of breaking in the native when the latter admits loudly and intelligibly the supremacy of the white man's values."

(2) Fanon reworks Lacanian theories to explain the complete dehumanisation of the native under colonialism. Fanon suggests that the black man is the Other for the white man. This Other is totally an alien, beyond his European self. Fanon suggests that for the black man the white man comes to symbolise power. He can see himself only as the black (mirror) image of the

white man. The white man is the master, and represents an object that is to be feared and desired. This is the power structure of the discourse of colour: the whiteness is complete, blackness is forever incomplete. The black therefore tries to be more like the (desirable) white man. He puts on "white masks," Fanon's symbol for both imitation and schizophrenia in the native. There is also the native's desire to "set himself up in the settler's place." However, the native never dreams of "becoming" the settler, but only "substituting" himself for the settler.

(3) The schizophrenia is also manifest in other areas. As Fanon points out in his discussion (in *A Dying Colonialism*), the native cannot talk to the Western doctor. The diffident native answers questions in monosyllables. He refuses to get himself hospitalised in the hospitals of the conquerors. Though the colonised finds the Western medicine effective, political, social and psychological reasons force the native to give his traditional medicine its due. Fanon writes: "accepting the (Western man's) medicine is demonstrating confidence in Western technique/science, swallowing it in one gulp is literally getting even with it."

(4) Further, Fanon argues that the white man comes to stand in for the father. The child cannot associate himself with others of his community or his family with a nation. In the colonial context, the black community and the nation are both controlled by the white man. The coloniser thus becomes the father, and the colonised is the child who has to obey the "law of the father" (for Lacan on the Law and father, see chapter on psychoanalytic theory above).

(5) The Church in the colonies is the white people's church. This church "does not call the native to God's ways but to the ways of the white man, the master, the oppressor."

(6) Fanon rejects Mannoni's idea that colonisation occurs (and is successful) because of the inherent "dependency complex" of the native which the coloniser exploits (see section on Mannoni above). Fanon argues that the dependency complex is not the *cause* but the *effect* of colonialism. It affects the colo-

nised's psyche through widespread changes in the native's culture.

(7) After years of unreality, of living among phantoms, the native discovers the only forces, which contend for his life—the forces of colonialism. He discovers reality and transforms it into the pattern of his customs, into the practice of violence and into his plan for freedom. When the native can't fight the colonisers, the violence turns against his own people, as a symbol, to work off their hatred. The development of violence among the colonised people will be proportionate to the violence exercised by the colonialists. Fanon argues that tribal feuds help relieve the tensions of the colonised. By using all his force in this, the native tries to persuade himself that colonisation does not exist, that his, and his tribe's history goes on as before. Fanon writes: "collective auto-destruction in a very concrete form is one way in which the native's muscular tension is set free." It is a "reactionary psychoses," where the mental pathology is the direct result of oppression.

(8) Fanon suggested a "national literature," perhaps a *negritude*, that would enable the development of a national consciousness. Fanon also attacks Western sympathies for and attempts to plead for negritude (such as Jean-Paul Sartre's). Fanon argues that such an attempt by the Westerner merely assimilated the Other into itself—which was again an imperialist gesture. Also, by suggesting and pleading for black solidarity and resistance, Sartre was denying the black any existential self-recognition, choice and identity in the movement. Once again this was a colonial move: harnessing black identities, cultures and power in order to create what the European considered "History."

(9) The native strengthens the inhibitions, which contain his aggressiveness by drawing on the myths. Myths and magic integrate the individual into the history of the district or the tribe. Likewise the ecstatic dances of the tribe/native are a means of exhausting the emotional sensibility. The circle of the dance is a permissive circle: it protects and permits. The coloniser, however, attributes the native's assertion of a distinct identity

and a concern with preserving some elements of his national ethos/existence to religious, magical and fanatical behaviour.

(10) Colonialism, argues Fanon, projects itself as self-born and the origin of everything. The colonised seeks to resist this move. Nationalist consciousness arises as a counter to this. This anti-colonial nationalism achieves solidarity between the disparate classes and groups of the colony. This may help prevent and overcome the cultural and psychological damage of colonialism. Thus an essentialising, pan-African solidarity (negritude) was necessary to escape the coloniser's full influence upon national culture and identity. In this period of decolonisation the colonised masses mock at the values of the white man. However, it must be mentioned that Fanon was also wary of the postcolonial national governments, which may end up being the bourgeois colonised nation-state.

(11) The birth of nationalist parties in colonised countries is contemporary with the formation of an intellectual elite engaged in trade. This elite attaches great importance to organisation. However, Fanon argues that the nationalist parties exhibit an elitism—they rarely direct their propaganda towards the country masses. In such a spontaneous nationalist movement the individual "stands aside in favour of the community." the progress of this nationalist spirit is charted thus by Fanon:

Tribalism in the colonial phase → regionalism in the national phase → federalism in the decolonised phase

(12) The native takes up arms because he is hungry, because he sees his social forms disintegrating and because the settler treats him like an animal. The native wants to be treated like a human. As the struggle goes on, the settlers' police forces behave more "humanly," and the native is addressed as "mister." The native is made to feel that things are changing. Whatever the native may gain through political or armed struggle is not the result of the kindliness of the settler, it simply shows that the settler cannot put off granting concessions any longer.

(13) In *A Dying Colonialism*, Fanon addresses the problem of women in colonialism. Fanon argues that the colonial administration's political doctrine (to destroy the structure of Algerian

society) was to conquer the women who were till then veiled and indoors-bound. It solemnly undertakes to *defend* this woman—pictured as humiliated, sequestered, cloistered. It (colonialism) describes the immense possibilities of woman, who, colonialism suggests has been "unfortunately" transformed by the Algerian man into an inert dehumanised object. In conquering the Algerian woman, there is aggressiveness—baring her secret, breaking her resistance: to bring her within the coloniser's reach, to make her a possible *object of possession*. With the Algerian woman, there is no progressive conquest: only straight-off, with the maximum of violence, rape and near-murder. Analysing the veil and colonialism, Fanon suggests that the Algerian woman's veil transforms her into a suspect for the Westerner. Since she can see without herself being seen, she is refusing to yield herself. The veil is transformed into "a technique of camouflage . . . a means of struggle." Hence the French colonial power's desire to unveil the Algerian woman. Her refusal to be seen by the colonial is interpreted as an act of resistance and invokes desire in the coloniser. He therefore seeks to unveil her, a metaphoric stripping and possession. Fanon argues that it is in this dynamic that the European's self-consciousness and identity itself is constituted: "when it [the colonial] encounters resistance from the other, self-consciousness undergoes the experience of desire . . . as soon as I desire I am asking to be considered."

Albert Memmi: Memmi's classic study *The Coloniser and the Colonised* (1965) analyses the psychology of colonialism and the effects it has upon *both,* the coloniser and the colonised.

(1) Memmi begins by rejecting the traditional assumption that the coloniser arrives in the colonies with a moral and cultural mission. There is only the economic basis for colonialism, argues Memmi. Even to the young adventurer, the economic advantages of his new situation (of being in the colony) soon reveal themselves. This revelation is also accompanied by the coloniser's recognition of his own privileges.

(2) The coloniser is aware of his "double illegitimacy." A foreigner, who arrives in another land by accident, he has (a) created a

place for himself and (b) taken away the place from the inhabitant. He legitimises this usurpation by substituting local laws with his own. He also states that the privileges of even the most favoured colonised still retains them in the position of *colonised.* Thus Memmi uncovers three developments in the processes of colonisation: profit, privilege and usurpation.

(3) The rigid adherence to routine and organisation by the coloniser is an attempt to impose the way of life of their own country from which, in Memmi's words, "they draw their administrative, political and cultural inspiration, and on which their eyes are constantly fixed."

(4) Memmi distinguishes between the *colonial*, the *coloniser* and the *colonialist.* A *colonial* is a European living in a colony, but without any special privileges, and with the same economic conditions as the colonised. The colonial is generally benevolent (Memmi also points out that such a category does not exist, because *all* Europeans in the colonies are privileged). The small *coloniser* defends the colonial system because he benefits from it. Though he is himself exploited by the bigger colonisers, the small coloniser defends the system because by protecting his very limited interests, he protects some larger ones. Every colonial immediately assumes the role of coloniser.

(5) Memmi argues that even if he tries the coloniser cannot escape the concrete realities of colonialism. He participates in and benefits from those privileges that he tries to denounce. He does not want to accept the role of coloniser. Then the other colonisers try to point out the advantages of his position to him. The coloniser cannot bring himself to go to the colonised in order to be loved by them, even if he morally supports them. He cannot bring himself to oppose his fellow countrymen openly. Racism also begins to assert its influence on this coloniser. He discovers the "primitiveness" of the native culture. Slowly he accepts his position and supports colonialism: he agrees to be a coloniser.

(6) There is always a disparity between the capabilities of the coloniser and his duties/benefits. The colonisers are generally of "small stature," it is the mediocre ones who stay in the colony for their whole life. And the process of recruitment—through

and within families of the mediocre—means that there is no new blood in the system. Memmi writes: "even if every colonialist is not mediocre, every coloniser must, in a certain measure, accept the mediocrity of colonial life and the men who thrive on it."

(7) Memmi suggests a "*Nero complex*" or "*The Usurper's Role*" for the features of the *coloniser*.

(a) The coloniser accepts his usurper role. He admits that what triumphs in his position are the very values that he once condemned. Now he needs to absolve himself of this usurpation and the conditions under which it took place. He begins to falsify history, rewrite laws, and extinguish memories.

(b) The more the usurper is downtrodden, the more the usurper triumphs, and thereafter confirms his guilt and self-condemnation. He seeks to defend himself—and the only way to do this is to wish for the disappearance of the usurped, because the usurped's very existence cause the coloniser to take the role of usurper. This is self-defeating: each time the coloniser hurts they colonised the more he coincides with the role of the tyrannical colonised that he tries to avoid.

(c) The colonialist, on the other hand, understands his unjust relationship with the colonised. He seeks to absolve himself of guilt by continually making a public show of his virtues and by degrading that of the natives. He will support police actions, massacres, and annihilation of the natives.

Thus colonialism "manufactures colonialist just as it manufactures the colonised.

(8) Every colonial nation carries the seeds of fascist temptation in its bosom. All administrative and political machinery is geared to a regime of oppression for the benefit of a few. The human relationships have arisen from the severest exploitation, founded on inequality and contempt, and guaranteed by police authoritarianism.

(9) There must be an overvaluation of the mother country by the colonialist, and a simultaneous "systematic devaluation of the

colonised." The distance between the master and the servant is never great enough in colonialism. The degradation of the colonised is explained as a natural order, the colony and the native are always inferior—by virtue of an inevitable and pre-established order.

(10) Colonial racism has three major ideologies:

(a) The gulf between the coloniser and the colonised: the colonialist stresses those things, which keep him separate.

(b) The exploitation of these differences for the benefit of the colonialist: In this, the colonised is always degraded, and thus the coloniser finds justification for rejecting his subjects.

(c) The use of these supposed differences as standards of absolute fact: the geographical or historical factor, which characterises the colonialist and contrasts him with the colonised, has been isolated. This gap must not be filled. What is essentially a sociological point becomes a biological, even metaphysical, point. It is attached to the colonised's basic nature. It becomes a definitive category: things cannot be changed.

Memmi argues that all racism and xenophobia consists of delusions about oneself, including absurd and unjust aggression towards others (this is in both the coloniser and the colonised)

(11) The colonised is associated with contradictory features, but the coloniser does not bother with this inverted logic. The colonised is projected as lazy, one with no sense of economy, jealous, fanatical, a weakling who requires protection. He is always considered in a negative light. He is depersonalised. The living conditions imposed upon the colonised do not grant them liberty. The colonised begins to identify with this image of himself. The colonised is, writes Memmi, forced to accept being colonised. Memmi also rejects the Mannoni notion of the dependency complex as a *cause* of colonisation. Like Fanon, Memmi also sees dependency as an *effect* of colonial rule.

(12) The colonised is no longer the subject of history, but only an object. He does not understand freedom any more. By being kept away from power, the colonised loses all capacity for con-

trol. Which is why, argues Memmi, there are so few men suitable for government among the colonised. As a result of colonisation, the colonised never experiences nationality or citizenship.

(13) There are only two options for the colonised: assimilation or petrifaction. Since assimilation is denied to him, he cannot plan his future, he must restrict himself to the present. He cannot recognise or remember his leaders: he even loses his memory. The material traces of his past are slowly erased. He must turn to the coloniser's institutions (cultural and political) for help. For instance, he is forced to celebrate the coloniser's holidays and festivals: his own are erased from the calendar. His biggest asset—his mother tongue now has no value. He must accept the language of the coloniser. His linguistic ambiguity is a cultural ambiguity. He forsakes his own language, but is saved from illiteracy, paradoxically and tragically, by adopting the *coloniser's* tongue.

(14) Other material developments such as highways and signs make the colonised feel like a foreigner in his own country.

(15) If the native writer were to write in his own language, he would be speaking before an audience of deaf men, because most of his people are uncultured and do not read any language. He must therefore write in the coloniser's language. But this is also a problem. He has to waste his imagination and energy in trying to achieve a proficiency that will never be fully realised. This is Memmi's explanation for the slow birth of colonial literature. Memmi writes that the colonised writer, having succeeded after much effort in being able to use the European languages can use them only to clamour for his own.

(16) Memmi argues that the only solution to the problem of the colonised is a complete end to colonisation—not a revolt but a revolution.

Aime Cesaire: Cesaire's *Discourse on Colonialism* (1972) was a passionate polemic on colonial domination, and one, which pleaded for "*negritude*" (a term coined by Cesaire). Cesaire's negritude was transnational (since he regarded the nation-state itself as a bourgeois phenomenon), and suggested a commonality between the African and Caribbean diaspora, while seeking a beyond-Europe civilisation and future.

(1) Cesaire mourns the destruction of native civilisations by colonialism. He argues that the "native societies were communal, never societies of the many for the few." He characterises these societies (non-European civilisations) as *ante-capitalist* (that is prior to, anterior to) and *anti-capitalist*. Arguing from a Marxist position, Cesaire suggests that the essential difference in European and non-European society could be seen as the difference between capitalism and non-capitalism.

(2) Cesaire argues that the terms "Negro" and "negritude: were adopted in defiance. Elaborating the term Cesaire charts the development of the negritude consciousness. Negritude is summarised in Cesaire's words thus: "we lived in an atmosphere of rejection, and we developed an inferiority complex . . . the black man was searching for his identity. And if we wanted to establish this identity, then we must have a concrete consciousness of what we are—that is the first fact of our lives: that we are black; that we were black and have a history . . . that there have been beautiful and important black civilisations." Cesaire in his writings (and especially in his poetry) seeks to derive an ethos common to all blacks, out of which an anti-colonial, anti-capitalist identity could be constructed. He thus indicates solidarity between the Caribbean and African "motherland."

(3) Cesaire sees Africa as the binary opposite of Europe. He sees Europe as decadent and "spiritually indefensible."

(4) For Cesaire, colonialism is not a philanthropic enterprise, or evangelisation mission, or driven by a desire to push back the frontiers of ignorance, disease and tyranny of native societies. It was not even a project undertaken for the glory of God. The decisive actor in the colonial programme were the adventurer, the pirate, the gold-digger, the wholesale grocer, shipowner and merchant (Hugh Ridley and Martin Green have demonstrated how adventure fiction of the 17th and 18th centuries were the motivational texts for the empire). Cesaire argues that no one colonises innocently. For Cesaire any civilisation that justifies colonisation is a sick civilisation.

(5) Colonialism's the same as "thingification," which is the reduction of the native into a mere object and instrument of production (labour). The coloniser is transformed into a "classroom monitor, an army sergeant, a slave driver, and the indigenous man into an instrument of production."

(6) Colonialism's essential equation was: Christianity = civilisation and paganism=savagery. Colonial activity is thus based upon contempt for the native.

(7) In a bitter indictment of colonialism, Cesaire writes in *Discourse on Colonialism*: colonisation works to "decivilise the coloniser, to brutalise him in the true sense of the word, to degrade him, to awaken him to buried instincts, to covetousness, violence, race hatred and moral relativism"

(8) Cesaire points out that people did not protest against Nazism when it was applied only to non-European peoples, it was only when they were its victims that they labelled it "barbaric." It is not the crime of humiliation of man as such, but the crime against the white man that causes protest.

(9) Between the coloniser and the colonised there is room only for forced labour, intimidation, pressure, police, taxation, contempt, mistrust, arrogance and the degraded masses.

Ngugi wa Thiong'o: Ngugi's *Decolonising the Mind* (1986) focussed primarily on the use of English as a weapon by the coloniser.

(1) Ngugi suggests that the study of Africa has always been restricted to the study of its tribes. Any trouble in the continent is attributed, immediately to the traditional conflict between its tribes. Even the literature was evaluated in terms of the "tribal" origins of the authors, or the "tribal" composition of the characters. Such a prejudice and informing principle helped the European to deflect the world's eyes from the real condition: that European imperialism was the root cause of Africa's troubles.

(2) In Africa the struggle is between two mutually opposed forces:

    (a) An imperialist tradition which is the tradition of the multinational and the native ruling classes, the native bourgoeis, the native intellectuals and the laureates of the neo-colonial establishment.

(b) The resistance tradition, which is the tradition of the peasantry, the proletariat and the patriotic students.

(3) The International Monetary Fund (IMF) holds mortgages of many African countries. The military threat from the West leaves no option to the natives but to accept theft (of resources by the West) or death.

(4) The "*cultural bomb*" is the biggest weapon of the West. This helps annihilate the peoples' belief in their names, unity, capacities and heritage. It makes them see their past as a wasteland of non-achievement. More importantly, it makes them want to identify themselves with other peoples' language and culture.

(5) The English language adopted by the African writers assumed that these European languages were the "natural" languages of literary and political mediation between African nations and other continents. Ngugi argues that we need not enrich other languages by translating African philosophy, folklore or imagery into other languages.

(6) Language, especially in schools, became the means of subjugation in the colonial period. Ngugi recounts his own problems in school, when he discovered that "the language of my education was no longer the language of my culture." The colonial child was made to see the world and where he stands in it as seen or reflected in the culture of the language of imposition.

(7) For the coloniser the most important area of domination was the mental domain of the colonised. This involved, argues Ngugi, two things:

(a) Destruction or undervaluing of a peoples' culture, art etc.

(b) The conscious elevation of the language of the coloniser.

Together these two resulted in the dissociation of the sensibility of the native from his natural and social environment. This is what Ngugi terms "*colonial alienation*."

(8) The colonial alienation is reinforced in the teaching of history and geography where Europe was always the centre of the universe. Eventually, over a period of time, this negative of image of Africa and the "centrality" of Europe became internalised even by the Africans.

Edward Said: Said's *Orientalism* is perhaps one of the most influential texts of the twentieth century (Spivak calls it a "source book" and Bhabha refers to it as "inaugurating the postcolonial field"). His pathbreaking work in this book and later ones such as *Culture and Imperialism*, his activist writings on the Palestine cause have made Said the leading intellectual of the postcolonial and marginalised people of the world.

(1) Said's argument borrows from Michel Foucault's dual notions of "discourse" and knowledge as inextricably linked to power. To recapitulate Foucault:
   (a) Discourse is the conceptual terrain of thought, a system of ideas and opinions that sanctions certain *forms* of knowing, and *expressions* of certain knowledges (see note on "discourse" at the conclusion of chapter one).
   (b) All "will to knowledge" is tied up with the will to power. There can be no expression/imposition of power without prior knowledge about the subject of power (for more details see the section on Foucault in the chapter on post-structuralism and deconstruction).

   Said argues that knowledge about the Orient (Asia, the East and non-European cultures) was not disinterested or knowledge for the sake of knowledge: it preceded *actual* colonial practices. In fact, colonial practices (political, economic) necessitated the production of such knowledge. Thus knowledge is bound up with power. Here Said adopts Gramsci's notion of the modes of hegemonic oppression—coercion and consent (see section on Gramsci in the chapter on Marxist criticism). The colonial power based on Orientalist knowledge does not rely on physical force as much as the *consent of the native*. Also, these texts and discourses present the imperialist programme as *natural* and *necessary*. The native *agrees* to be colonised when he accepts the colonial stereotypes of himself. The civil society apparatus of education, religion after adopting the stereotype, justifies and *consents* to being colonised subjects.

(2) One may now define Orientalism in Said's own terms The term originally referred to the work of Indologists like Sir William Jones and H.H. Wilson, who translated and compiled Indian lit-

erary works, laws and codes for use by colonial administrators. Said's use of the term sums up the colonial project when he defines Orientalism as "a manner of regularised (or Orientalised) writing, vision, and study dominated by imperatives, perspectives, and ideological biases ostensibly suited to the Orient. The Orient is taught, researched, administered, and pronounced in certain discrete ways." He adds "Orientalism is a style of thought based upon an ontological and epistemological distinction made between 'the Orient' and 'the Occident' . . . Orientalism as a Western style for dominating, restructuring and having authority over the Orient."

(3) The *discourse of Orientalism* is the production of ideas, knowledge and opinions about the Orient. This included certain modes of representation of the Orient through Othering (where the Orient was Europe's dark Other). Analysing this discourse, Said reads a range of texts—literary, philological, philosophical, administrative, ethnographic and others. Said demonstrates that these texts were the lens through which the Orient was viewed preliminary to being ruled. The texts were "worldly" in the sense they exhibit the pressures, preoccupations and prejudices of the world around them—therefore no text is free of its contexts of production. This meant that knowledge or literary imaginations could not be considered innocent, for they were complicit with the political agenda of colonialism. The Orient was interpreted in European fashion, to fulfil certain European ends. In Said's words "the Orient is something one judges (as in a court of law), something one studies (as in a curriculum), something one disciplines (as in a school or prison), or illustrates (as in a zoological museum)."

(4) Certain kinds of ideological assumptions informed these texts and produced stereotypes of the native: the ignorance of the natives, their effeminacy and indolence, their oversexed nature, their essential untrustworthiness, the superiority of the European and his knowledge, and others. These stereotypes of the weak and stupid native helped *justify* and even *necessitate* Western presence as the masculine, strong and rational protector. The Westerner must look after the poor native who could not look

after himself. Thus the stereotype helps introduce a Western presence in various guises and roles—of the protector (police, army), educator (teacher), administrator (bureaucracy and political presence), saviour (missionary). The *cultural* bias helped posit a *political* vision of otherness. As Said puts it, the Oriental man was first an Oriental and only secondly a man.

(5) There were various indices by which Orientalism was set up as a field of study.

  (a) 1765-1850 marked the period of discovery. The Orient was exotic, profound, and mysterious. The Orientalist, usually an expert in language (at this stage) travelled through the country, seeing the Orient through European eyes. The vision, which the Orientalist brought to the field of study, was European. They were rarely interested in anything except proving the value of *their* "truths."

  (b) Soon second-order knowledge was produced. This was the Oriental tale, the mythology of the mysterious Orient. All things in history, like History itself, were created for the Orient: it was set up as mysterious and barbarous long before anything was known about it. Later discoveries were to validate these early "findings." The completely new was seen as versions of a previously known thing. Thus Islam—a radically new way of life—was seen as a fraudulent version of Christianity. The Orient "vacillates" between the West's contempt for what is familiar and its shivers of delight or fear of novelty. The Orient is penalised for lying outside "our" world (the West). It is thus "Orientalised."

  (c) The Orientalist always chose the conquering West. The Orient existed and was treated not as something present, but for its series of valorised contacts it had had with a distant European past. The Orient itself was treated/perceived in some distant past, as unchanging and static, what Said identifies as a "*synchronic essentialism*" (the term is Talal Asad's). The Orient was static, an essential *vision* rather than a vibrant, changing *narrative*. This vision is under pressure from the narrative which introduces diachrony into the vision. The stability and unchanging nature of the Orient (vision) is threatened by the instability of narrative. This instability suggests that history, with its tendency towards growth, decline or dramatic movement is possible in the Orient. Narrative suggests that the vision is insufficient and does an injustice to the potential of reality for change. Narrative is the form taken by history to counter the permanence of vision. When the Orientalists were aware of some contemporary movements of/in Oriental thought or culture, these were perceived as silent shadows to be animated by the Orientalists, to be "brought into reality" by them.

(6) Modern Orientalism has four elements:
   (a) Expansion: of the Orient further east geographically loosened the Biblical framework. The reference points were no longer Christianity but India, China, Japan and Buddhism.
   (b) Historical confrontation: Capacity to deal historically with a non-European culture was to understand Europe in its objective relations with others.
   (c) Sympathy: Selective identification with regions and cultures not one's own wore down the unyielding categories/ definitions of self and identity. The notions of humanity were no longer restricted to the borders of Christian Europe.
   (d) Classification: of mankind multiplied.

(7) The Orientalist scholar had three intentions and categories of study:
   (a) Providing professional Orientalism with scientific knowledge. Here the Orientalist considers his stay in the Orient as a form of scientific observation.
   (b) He was less willing to sacrifice the individual consciousness to impersonal Orientalist definitions.
   (c) The writer saw the trip to the Orient as a fulfilment of some personal project.

(8) Said distinguishes between *latent* and *manifest* Orientalism. Latent Orientalism is the unconscious positivity. Here ideas and prejudices of Oriental backwardness, racial inequality and degeneracy exist. Manifest Orientalism is the various *stated* views about Oriental society, languages and culture, all of which relegate the native to a "dreadful secondariness," as Said terms it.

All the changes occurring in the knowledge of the Orient takes place in manifest Orientalism.

(9) There were two principal methods by which Orientalism delivered the "Orient" to the West in the early twentieth century:
   (a) Through apparatuses of learning—universities, professional societies, explorational and geographical organisations, publishing industry.
   (b) The relation between Orientalist and the Orient: the translation/interpretation of the Orient by the Orientalist, who remained "outside" the Orient.

(10) The Orientalist then provides his society with representations of the Orient. These representations:
   (a) bear his distinctive imprint
   (b) illustrate his conception of what the Orient can or ought to be
   (c) consciously contort someone else's view of the Orient
   (d) provide Orientalist discourse with what, at that moment, it seems most in need of
   (e) respond to certain cultural, professional, political and economic developments of the epoch.

(11) In *Culture and Imperialism*, Said undertakes a massive and brilliant rereading of canonical texts like *Heart of Darkness*, *Kim* and *A Passage to India* to demonstrate their implication in imperial discourse. His early comments on culture are useful in understanding the overall slant of his work here. Said argues that the power to narrate, or to block other narratives from forming and emerging is very important to culture and imperialism, and constitutes one of the main connections between them. Nations themselves are narrations.

(12) Culture soon comes to be associated with the nation or state, it becomes a source of identity. Culture becomes a theatre where various political and ideological causes engage one another. The "great cultural archive . . . is where the intellectual and aesthetic investments in overseas dominion are made."

(13) Said states that his purpose is to read individual texts as great products of the creative imagination *and then* as part of the relationship between culture and empire. Said suggests that there

are two perspectives possible: to see America, for instance, as an immigrant settler society superimposed on the considerable native one. To see American identity is to decide between a unitary identity and a complex but not reductively unified one. The former perspective is linear and subsuming, the latter is *contrapuntal* and *nomadic*. Said argues that the contrapuntal reading is sensitive to historical experience.

(14) Imperialism and colonialism are supported by (a) notions that certain territories require and beseech domination, (b) forms of knowledge affiliated with domination. These include notions of inferior subject races, dependency, expansion, and authority. Said argues that in all nationally defined cultures, there is an aspiration to sovereignty, and to dominance.

(15) When their hold on overseas territories began to fray, the European powers projected their power backward in time. This gave a history and legitimacy which only longevity could impart. Natives do similar constructions of what they supposed themselves to have been prior to colonialism (i.e. return to a precolonial "pure" golden age).

(16) People who protested against colonialism were heard only partially in the West and by the ruling authorities in their own societies (Ngugi, Faiz Ahmed Faiz). A "rhetoric of blame" is common to the Western and colonised people in postcolonial public discourse.

(17) Today's Western discourse is nostalgic and refers to the unappreciated magnanimity of the West by the natives. This assumes the primacy and centrality of the West.

(18) Said suggests that we need a contrapuntal perspective—think through and interpret together experiences that are discrepant, each with its own agenda, pace of development, internal formation and coherence, system of external relationships all coexisting and interacting with one another. Said is thus suggesting that we abandon a unified approach that goes by the master narrative, and adopt a technique where marginal and apparently contradictory narratives battle. This is contrapuntal reading informed and influenced by a "hermeneutics of suspicion": "a simultaneous awareness both of the metropolitan

history that is narrated and of those other histories against which the dominating discourse acts." What Said is suggesting, in short, is a disputational reading process, where the author's "given" must be seen in the light of texts/experiences which are effaced. (A parallel method may be seen in New Historicist readings, see chapter on the same above).

(19) Resistance has two phases: actual fighting against outside invasion and ideological resistance to save or restore the sense and fact of the community against the colonial system. Said argues that no matter how complete the dominance of imperialist ideology, there are parts of social experience that it does not cover. Said identifies three topics that manifest in decolonising cultural resistance:

(a) The insistence on the right to see the community's history whole, coherently and integrally. Thus national culture and memory is revived and emphasised. Local narratives, spiritual autobiographies, prison memoirs form a counterpoint to Western official discourses, histories or panoptic viewpoints.

(b) Resistance as an alternative way of conceiving human history. This seeks to disrupt European narratives, and replacing them with a more playful narrative style (Said uses *Midnight's Children* as example here). This may be the return of the once "*subjugated knowledges*" (Said adopts the term from Foucault). Thus the works of Marquez, Rushdie, Achebe and Soyinka interrogates the assumptions of imperialist discourse. The nomadic novel transgresses the limits imposed by imperial categories and also nativist/provincial nationalism.

(c) Pull away from separatist nationalism towards a more integrative view of human community and liberation. Said suggests that cultures are interdependent, and nationalism is an intellectual trend that favours more generous human realities of community among cultures. This community is the real human liberation heralded by the resistance to imperialism.

(20) Nativism reinforces the distinction (us/them) while revaluating the weaker partner. To accept nativism is "to accept the consequences of imperialism, the racial, religious and political divisions imposed by imperialism itself." Further, Said warns that abandonment of the historical world for the "metaphysics of essences like negritude, Irishness, Islam or Catholicism is to abandon history for essentialisms that have the power to turn human beings against each other." Postcolonial narratives progress from dependence and inferiority to nationalist revival, independent state formation and cultural autonomy in an "anxious partnership" with the West.

(21) Ideological and cultural wars against imperialism occur in the form of resistance in colonies. This later becomes the dissent in metropolises of Europe. The first phase produces nationalist independence struggles, the second leads to liberation struggles.

Gayatri Chakravorty Spivak: One of the most distinguished thinkers of the twentieth century, Spivak's work has been notable for its eclecticism, scope, brilliance, and not infrequently, its opaque prose. Harnessing feminism, deconstruction, postcolonialism, psychoanalysis and historiography Spivak is impossible to classify. The reason why she is discussed under the chapter on "postcolonial studies" is purely arbitrary. (Bart Moore-Gilbert writes of how he discovered Spivak listed under *five* disciplinary/theoretical heads—more than any other thinker!)! This is a bricoleur (which is how Spivak describes herself) who will not be classified. From her early translation of Derrida's *Of Grammatology* (1976), through essays ("Can the Subaltern Speak?," "How to Read a 'Culturally Different' Book" "Three Women's Texts and A Critique of Imperialism," "Feminism and Deconstruction," "Subaltern Studies: Deconstructing Historiography" among numerous others), books (*Outside in the Teaching Machine, In Other Worlds* and the recent *A Critique of Postcolonial Reason*) and interviews (mainly in *The Postcolonial Critic*, and *The Spivak Reader*) Spivak has written on democracy, development and gender, literary and cultural studies. Here we shall look at her contribution to postcolonial thought.

(1) Spivak rejects the ideas that there is precolonial past that we can recover. A nostalgia of lost origins, roots and nativist culture is a flawed project because there is no "pure" precolonial past that we can recover. All past has been worked over and irremediably changed by colonialism. One cannot separate the pre-colonial and colonial so easily. What one can do is to understand the "worlding" of the "third world." Spivak's "worlding" is a term that includes both a creation (similar to Said's "Orientalism") and a violation. "Worlding" is the process through which the local population was "persuaded" to accept the European version of reality for its own modes of understanding and structuring its social world.

(2) It is also, therefore, impossible to recover the "authentic" voice of the subaltern (the subaltern is a term used to signify the oppressed class. The term comes through Gramsci). Spivak's well-known (and controversial) argument is that the subaltern cannot speak for him/herself because the very *structure* of colonialism prevents the speaking. For the colonised woman, this is even more impossible because the double bind of colonialism and patriarchy represses her completely. She simply cannot represent herself. Using the case of sati (where no account of the woman-subject survives) and the suicide of Bhubaneswari Bhaduri (Calcutta, 1926), Spivak argues that the subaltern wrote her body because there was no other way of speaking. However, Spivak argues that the intellectual project must try to make visible the position of the marginalised. The subaltern must be "spoken for" (that is, represented), but not romanticised. There is also the warning that the term/category "subaltern" is not universally applicable, nor homogeneous (as has unfortunately happened). In her *A Critique of Postcolonial Reason*, Spivak reiterates: "Simply by being a postcolonial or the member of an ethnic minority we are not 'subaltern.' That word is reserved for the sheer heterogeneity of decolonised space." The subaltern may simply be a "native informant"—"a name for that mark of expulsion from the name of Man—mark crossing out the impossibility of the ethical relation."

(3) Spivak suggests that the appropriation of the marginalised as part of postcolonial studies and Western academies relegates them to perpetual marginality. The distinctions between centre and margin is retained, even more strengthened by the "third worldism" of postcolonial studies. What Spivak is suggesting is that the institutionalisation of marginality is a dangerous trend. Spivak writes: "I could easily construct a sort of 'pure east' . . . so that I could then define myself as the Easterner, as the marginal or as the specific, or as the para-institutional." The West's longing for the "pure Other of the West" figures in the institutional investments it makes in the form of postcolonialism (the theorist of diaspora, Rey Chow suggests, tongue in cheek, that the East is still a career—for the displaced Easterner, through a "self-subalternisation" which provides access to power in the metropolis/West!).

(4) Spivak also questions the role of Western feminist discourse in trying to recover (or speak for) the "gendered subaltern." In her reading of Julia Kristeva, Spivak points out that Kristeva is speaking for the Chinese women, in her own identity as a liberal Western feminist. As Spivak writes: "Her [Kristeva's] question, in the face of those silent women, is about her own identity rather than theirs." This is an "epistemic violence," an authoritative and ultimately colonial knowledge about the Other.

(5) Spivak, through her reading of *Jane Eyre*, argues that even in a liberal Western feminist text that apparently valorises the individualist and independent woman, the figure of the "native woman" (Bertha Mason, the white Creole from the Caribbean) is effaced. Spivak goes on to argue that the individualism of Jane Eyre is constructed out of the effacement of the gendered subaltern (Bertha Mason). Bertha's self-immolation is the displacement to the margins of her very existence. In fact, the West's praise of the individualist woman conceals the irony that this individualism was based on a series of exclusions and sacrifices: the native woman never figures in the discourse of triumphant feminist individualism: "As the female individualist, not quite/not male, articulates herself in shifting relation-

ship to what is at stake, the 'native female' as such (within discourse, as a signifier) is excluded from a share in this emerging norm." Spivak's attempt has been to reveal the figure of this gendered subject of colonialism. The native woman is doubly marginalised by virtue of her relative economic oppression and gender subordination. She includes the "homeworker" in her more recent studies of the gendered subaltern. In Mary Shelley's *Frankenstein*, the construction of the monster is the project of the subject-constitution of the colonial Other in denying the right of the monster to reproduce itself, and having failed to turn the monster into its creator's (Westerner's) mirror image, Frankenstein refuses it an identity. Spivak argues that Shelley's novel suggests that the Other have properties that cannot be "selfed" or contained.

(6) Spivak insists that postcolonial theory must recognise the "persistent . . . heterogeneity" of postcolonial cultures. Rather than a monolithic homogenising of Saidian version of the Orient and Orientalism, Spivak argues for a complexity of form full of differences and contradictions. Spivak suggests that the variations among experiences of oppression must be first admitted.

(7) Spivak is also conscious of the role of "socialised capital" in the contemporary world. Addressing the world from the privileged position of a third world academic in the Western academy, Spivak admits that "it is the structures of cultural imperialism that have enabled me." Spivak is thus aware of the ambiguous position she occupies: of a third world academic from a once-colonised nation incorporated into a system, which reproduced neo-colonialism. However, Spivak is cautious of the "appropriative" nature of this socialised capital and therefore is constantly critical of the alliance between Western capital/academy and the once-colonised. Spivak is thus interested in the "itineraries of silencing," through which political, cultural and literary narratives attain authority through marginalisation and exclusion.

(8) Spivak seeks to understand the methods through which third world cultural texts may be admitted into Western academy without blunting their (the third world text's) critical position.

To this end, Spivak argues for a truly "transnational study of culture," where single-author studies are substituted with non-Western texts, non-western languages, popular cultural forms and critical theory. Spivak questions the efficacy of modes of reading such as the New Critical one, where "reading literature 'well' is in itself a questionable good," since it prevents the reader from engaging with the material conditions of production of these texts/aesthetics.

(9) Spivak adopts a deconstructive reading process and a persistent self-critique. Her writing style which incorporates what she has termed a "bricolage," is a mixture that resists classification—an extremely self-conscious style that defies a label. Likewise, her deconstructive reading practice enables her to expose the "thematics of imperialism" in European texts, extend the relevance of texts such as those of Marx. Further, Spivak argues that the work of Foucault and Deleuze in analysing the micro-structures of power and oppression ignore the macrological and "objective" determinations and factors such as class, imperialism and global capitalism. The international division of labour cannot be ignored for Spivak. Spivak also argues that the economy of desire in Foucault and Deleuze reintroduces the notion of the undivided subject. Drawing on the work of Althusser on ideology and the decentred subject, Spivak suggests that the valorisation of the oppressed as subject (in Deleuze and Foucault) leads them to an "essentialist, utopian politics."

(10) Spivak's main contribution has been to harness deconstructive thought for postcolonial theorising. She seeks to reveal the manner in which colonial texts undermine their status and logic. Focussing on minor characters and subplots, Spivak is able to reveal the racial biases that constitute even apparently humanist texts. This process described by Spivak as "catachresis" places and reads canonical texts in alien contexts, by demonstrating how these texts reveal a contradictory meaning/subtext when wrenched out of their conventional narratives. She reveals the binary oppositions and exclusions that lie buried in these texts, and whose burial allows the text to parade itself as authoritative. Spivak, however, warns that mere reversal

of the dominant terms of the opposition would retain the "logic of the opponent," what is needed further is the displacement of the terms of the opposition itself. This is what Spivak terms a "supplementary distancing, a position and its counter-position." This involves a *negotiation* and *critique* to disturb the dominant from within.

(11) Spivak suggests that the subject must be treated as discursively constructed and decentred, a subject-effect which is part of discontinuous network of politics, ideology, economics, history, sexuality, language and others. The identity of the self is thus never self-present but *dispersed.* Spivak thus rejects all notions of the fixed subject. Thus she rejects the nativist stress on an "authentic" identity. It would be ridiculous, argues Spivak, to think that the native has some kind of transparent access to her/his condition. Local elites have no more direct and authentic access to the subaltern than the Western academic does (with this argument Spivak defends the use of so-called Western elite theory to understand/reclaim the subaltern). One cannot access the colonised subaltern's voice in isolation from the colonising formation and other sectors of local society. More importantly there is no pure or essential subaltern voice. In fact the subaltern's subject position is constructed out of the colonial discourse, and one cannot trace out the pure subaltern out of this network. The subaltern has been ascribed a subject-position by colonial officials as an "intending subject of resistance." However, Spivak defends the creation of the fiction of the true subaltern (in the subaltern studies project) as necessary to enable a critique of colonial historiography. As Spivak puts it, such a fiction is a "strategic use of positivist essentialism in a scrupulously visible political interest."

(12) Spivak points out that during imperialism the British assumed the authority and prerogative to speak for the oppressed native woman (especially in the colonial discourse on Sati). The construction of the oppressed native woman was necessary to justify the presence of the modernising Britisher. The native woman apparently "called out" for liberation. For Spivak this was the ascription of a true voice to the native woman. In real-

ity, the voice of the woman is "ventriloquised," spoken for. The nationalists also resurrected the voice of then native woman for their own ends but, as Spivak points out, the voice of the woman is effaced in the discourse of both nationalism and colonialism: she is only spoken for.

Homi K. Bhabha: In a series of essays in the 1980s and '90s Bhabha has suggested a rereading of the colonial experience and the issue of colonial identity. His *The Location of Culture* (1994) brought together some of his best known essays like "Signs Taken for Wonders," "The Other Question" and "Sly Civility."

(1) Bhabha argues that Edward Said's reading of the colonial encounter is unidirectional: it only treats colonial authority as proceeding from the coloniser to the colonised. This argument of Said also suggests that the identities of coloniser and colonised are fixed and stable. Bhabha asserts that colonial discourse is actually conflictual, ambivalent and riven with contradictions. The contradictory psychic relations between the coloniser and colonised—moving, for Bhabha, between fear and desire for the Other—prevents any stable unchanging identities for the coloniser and the colonised. The relationship between the two is one of negotiation and transaction and not a one-directional will to power, as Said implies.

(2) Bhabha argues, following poststructuralism and Lacanian psychoanalysis, that identities are possible only in *differential relations* and displacement. Identity for Bhabha is a liminal reality—constantly moving between positions, displacing others and being displaced in turn.

(3) The colonial regime creates a disciplinary gaze of power and control. It achieves power through the creation of set stereotypes such as those of the sly treacherous native, the noble savage or the lustful native. Bhabha argues that the stereotype is the indication not of the stable and supreme power of the coloniser, but rather of the fractured nature of the colonial power. Colonial discourse depends upon the representation of the unchanging nature of the native (as one of the above mentioned stereotypes). Thus what is already "known/established" has to be endlessly confirmed through repetitions. For Bhabha, this need for repeti-

tion points to a lack of certainty about the stereotypes, which indicates the essentially unstable and constructed nature of the stereotypes. For Bhabha this also suggests the lack in the colonial identity itself: that the coloniser can construct his identity only through the stereotype of the Other. That is, the identity of the colonial master is dependent upon the relationship with the oppositional native/Other. There would be no colonial power if he were not locked in a struggle with the resisting/oppositional native. The stereotypes thus help the formation of the coloniser's identity while simultaneously rendering it *unstable* and *dependent* (since the identity is always relational and never self-identical).

(4) The stereotype is a metonymy: substituting for the "real" object. It is also the point where the contradiction of colonial discourse is most visible. The stereotype and the "fetish/phobia" of colonial relations indicate

   (a) the affirmation and desire of the coloniser for wholeness and similarity with the native and
   (b) The simultaneous fear and anxiety at/of the lack and the different native.

   Simply put, colonial discourse is *ambivalent* in its attitudes because it *both* desires (fetishises) similarity/unity with the native and yet fears (phobic) the wholly Other nature of the native. This ambivalent nature is best seen in the contradictory representations of the colonised. The native is simultaneously beyond comprehension (the stereotype of the "inscrutable native") and yet completely knowable/controllable as the subject of colonial power (in the stereotype of the native as an innocent child, or as a vulnerable woman). Thus Bhabha argues that the colonial relation is full of contradictions and conflicts.

(5) Colonial discourse is never a monolithic authority. The discourse is dependent upon the repetition and perpetuation of colonial meaning. This is the authority of the *English book* (the "book" in Bhabha is initially the Bible and later comes to represent the whole text of Western culture). The English book is seen as original and originary. In the colonial context, it becomes necessary that this book be transmitted to the natives,

that it is repeated in a new context. Bhabha points out that the repetition is always a *difference* (here he borrows from Derrida)—that each time the book repeats in the colonial context (as translation), it moves further away from the original, simply because the repetition can never be *identical with the original*. Thus repetition of the book indicates a position of lack, of distance, of instability and of never being the same: "less than one and double" (as Bhabha puts it). This is the slippage of colonial discourse where narratives of authority are hybridised in the colonial context, and in the process lose some of the authority of the original. Thus colonial discourse that relies upon the repetition of its cultural texts discovers that with each repetition of the original is eroded and a newer form of the original emerges, one where the authority is *lost*.

(5) Bhabha suggests that "agonistic uncertainty" marks all colonial discourse. Using the figure of J.S. Mill as example, Bhabha argues that Mill's "On Liberty" was actually written as response to Macaulay's ideas on educating the natives. Mill, who agitated on behalf of democracy and individual liberty, also tried to justify despotism in India. This was the conflictual and fractured nature of colonialism itself: where Mill and Macaulay sought to integrate English culture but supported absolutism in India. As Bhabha asks: "Can despotism, however vigorous, inspire a colony of individuals when the dread letter of despotic law can only instil the spirit of servitude?"

(6) In his concept of *mimicry* Bhabha further analyses the fractured nature of the colonial condition. The colonial power requires that the natives adopt and internalise the forms and habits of the colonial master: the native should *mimic* the master. The entire colonial mission is to transform the native into "one like us," a copy of the coloniser. For Bhabha the mimicry is a defence, fraught with the resistance of the native. The native is in a position to return the gaze of the colonial master, since he is now camouflaged. A reversal has been achieved through the mimicry of the coloniser by the colonised. Mimicry is now active (transitive) resistance: it achieves something other than the purpose intended by the coloniser. On the one hand, the colonial power

tries to recast the native as one of themselves, and on the other tries to remember and reiterate the irreducible difference of the Other. Thus colonial discourse is fractured: "the desire for a reformed, recognisable Other, as a subject of a difference that is almost the same but not quite." The mimicry thus produces a subject who reflects a distorted image of the colonial master: what I see in the native is the same (me) and not-the-same (not fully me, a distorted me). In the attempt to produce the same-as-me, the colonial power induces a distorted self-identity, a reiteration of the difference. Otherness is brought back precisely at the moment when colonial authority seeks to remove it through mimicry. The authority of the colonial is thus changed in the very process of its replication. What is produced is the *hybrid* (the same *and* not-the-same native). This hybrid is "half-acquiescent, half-oppositional" and marks the site of the slipperiness of authority. The mimicry of the native combines *deference* and *disobedience* (what Bhabha terms "*sly civility*"), in the passage (translation) between the authority of colonial discourse into the native, there occurs a slippage, a misappropriation and the beginning of anti-colonial resistance. For Bhabha then, the resistance of the native is the *result* of the failure of the colonial power to effectively reproduce and extend itself.

(7) Resistance in the colonial situation is intransitive (passive) in the early Bhabha and transitive (active) in the later one.
   (a) When colonial discourse discovers that its authority and identity is partly dependent upon the colonised Other, there is the destabilising and undermining of colonial power. This is intransitive resistance.
   (b) The hybridised native who refuses to return the colonial gaze, and who refuses to acknowledge the coloniser's position and authority, is placed in a position of *in-betweenness*: between "adopted" Englishness and "original" Indiannness. This multiple subject positions mean that the colonial power cannot unify its discourse nor firmly *situate* the native subject. This is transitive resistance.

For Bhabha colonial presence is *ambivalent*, split between the two positions: of its appearance as authority and original (and therefore worthy of being mimicked); *and* its articulation as repetition and difference. This split is the failure of colonial discourse and the site of potential resistance by the colonised. In Bhabha's words "[resistance] is the effect of an ambivalence produced within the rules of recognition of dominating discourses as they articulate the signs of cultural difference." Hybridity and the *third space*, the result of the split and negotiation between coloniser and colonised, which is "neither the one nor the other" is thus the point where anti-colonial resistance is first articulated.

(8) Memory is the bridge between colonialism and cultural identity. Remembering is actually a *re-membering*, "a putting together of the dismembered past to make sense of the trauma of the present . . . of the history of race and racism." Memory is the submerged portion of existence. The repressed and silenced—results of colonial erasure of cultural memories—need to be resurrected from the unconscious. The colonial silencing may take the form of *repression* or *repudiation*. Repression is the censor that pushes painful memories deep into the unconscious. Repudiation transforms painful memories into delirium. The postcolonial subject suffers from both repression and repudiation. S/he is unwilling to recall the painful past and also repudiates these memories. The work of the postcolonial theorist has two components: to resurrect the memories, and to make the "delirious" or hostile memories more familiar and acceptable.

(9) Bhabha argues that the project of modernity is never complete because the postmodern simply replicates the negative aspects of modernity. For instance, the West's present (postmodern) continuation of ideological Othering and socio-political structures is an extension of the project of modernity from colonial times. Also, the role of the non-Western world in the construction of modernity has never been fully acknowledged: especially the role of slavery or colonial exploitation. Bhabha argues that the category of Man, which emerged in the post-Enlightenment age, was dependent upon the differential relation with the "pre-modern/primitive" non-Western man. Western rationality developed only through its distinction from the "barba-

rism" of the Other. Thus the French Revolution which is seen by Foucault as the critical moment of modernity ignores the role of smaller anti-colonial uprisings (such as those of Toussaint's). For Bhabha, the emergence of the modern universal "Man" is ethnocentric and dependent upon the non-Western "man."

(10) There is a belatedness, a *time-lag* which enables the formerly colonised to articulate the repressed. The postcolonial can point out the reprocessed elements in the West's construction of its own identity. The historical categories and identities (noble savage, for instance) can now be rethought by the postcolonial.

(11) Bhabha, however, is suspicious of both multi-culturalism and cultural relativism that postmodernism celebrates. For Bhabha multi-culturalism constructs cultures as implicitly equivalent and therefore interchangeable. Cultural relativism manages cultural difference in relation to a standard centre, which only serves to reinforce the authority of the cultural dominant. Both minimise the challenge of cultural difference. Bhabha argues that there can be no real equivalence between cultures (for example, the equivalence between oral and graphic literatures). Bhabha suggests that basic existential experiences of different groups are different and cannot be equated. Thus family, life and death, ageing is different for different cultural and social groups and cannot be considered equivalent to similar practices/experiences in other communities.

(12) Integration (of aliens and migrants) is essentially a problem of language and *translation*: how does one find exact transparent terms that apply equally in *both* languages? The notion of integration is built upon the supposition that the narratives and symbols of a particular culture can be translated into another, into a "unitary sign" of "human" culture.

(13) Bhabha suggests that the relation between the postcolonial/migrant and the dominant culture is not simply antagonistic. He adapts the Derridean notion of the hymen (both inside and outside) to suggest a model of difference: it is not synthesis, but it is not a negation either. This is the "third space," the "in-between." What is "outside" literally forms the "inside": in-

deed there is no inside without an outside. In the transactive, mutually dependent nature of the inside and outside where difference is emphasised, Bhabha locates the third space—which belongs neither to the inside nor to the outside, and is as a part of both. The third space "contests the terms and territories of both" (Robert Young's description).

Aijaz Ahmad: Ahmad's *In Theory* (1992) was one of the strongest critiques of Edward Said and postcolonial theory. Ahmad, writing from an avowed Marxist position, has called into question several of the assumptions that inform postcolonial theory—especially the latter's complicity with neo-imperialism, appropriation by Western academies and the notion of the subject.

(1) Ahmad begins by suggesting that the current "triumph" of literary theory is linked to the changes in the political and economic conditions of the world, to the rise of a category—the "Third World"—and Third Worldist political thought and nationalism, and to poststructuralism. Poststructuralism's and postmodernism's debunking of all efforts to speak of origins, collectivities and nationalism fails to distinguish between progressive and retrograde nationalism of the so-called "Third World." Literary Theory is the cement that constructs the counter-canon of Third World literature.

(2) When the theorists argue for nationalism as the only political imperative of the Third World, it rejects the oppositional traditions of our own cultures (which, for Ahmad, has frequently emerged from a Marxist political practice). Ahmad argues that to move from a Marxist critique based on class, colony and gender to one of simple nationalism is a "theoretical regresssion."

(3) Ahmad argues that "Third World" literature arrives as a category when they are appropriated, marketed, reviewed, and accepted as "counter-canonical" by the Western metropolitan academies. The global channels of communication and circulation coerce the book/texts into the category of Third World literature. The entire counter-canon is thus formed in the West. What is needed, according to Ahmad, is an inquiry into the principle of "selective incorporation" of texts into the Western

academy/canon. It is also aided by the fact that there is far greater assertion of the immigrant professional strata from non-Western countries (an argument that is paralleled by Arif Dirlik when he claims that postcolonialism begins with the arrival of the Third World academic in Western academies). The literary relations between the metropolitan countries and the former colonies is also instrumental here. The literary theorist in the US or Europe has access to at least one other European language, but rarely an Asian or African one. But the intellectual from the *imperialised formation* will need at least one European language. Therefore the few writers who write in English are praised and valorised "beyond measure." The metropolitan country sees the text in English as representing, speaking for the whole colony/Third World. In the division of the world into the First (capitalist), Second (socialist) and the Third World, each is made fundamentally coherent and external to one another. Differences within particular national structures are then minimised, and one is forced to speak only in terms of the First or Third Worlds. Class and gender formations and conflicts are thus conveniently ignored.

(4) Rejecting Bhabha's notions of the interventionary nature of poststructuralism, Ahmad argues that Bhabha writes from within the material conditions of postmodernity. Ahmad argues that the luxury of debunking myths of progress and modernity is available only to the intellectuals who have availed its plenitude: the vast majority in the "Third World" have no access to the actual benefits of modernity (health, education and so on). Ahmad also rejects Bhabha's idea that magic realism is the "literary language of the emergent postcolonial world." This, for Ahmad, is the "inflationary rhetoric" of contemporary theory which prescribes a norm for all such writing (Tim Brennan, in an argument that parallels Ahmad's, also argues that the novel in the once-colonised countries is "the form through which a thin, foreign-educated stratum has communicated to metropolitan reading publics"). Such assumptions proceed from the metropolis, and from Western personnel. Non-Western individuals have also been appropriated into the

Western programmes in an "institutionalised symbiosis between the Western scholar and the local informant."

(5) Attacking the postcolonial theorist, Ahmad suggests that immigration has its own politics. The combination of origins, professional ambitions and the absence of socialist agenda cause the immigrant intellectual to seek a Third Worldism-as-oppositional politics. Exile is over-romanticised and, for Ahmad, does not quite carry the same meaning to describe the upper-class Indian who *chooses* to live in the metropolitan country.

(6) Jameson's idea that all the third world texts are "*national allegories*" also comes in for criticism in Ahmad. Ahmad notes that Jameson's definitions of the First and Second worlds are based on the criteria of *modes of production*, while the Third World is described as that which has once *experienced imperialism*. Thus the Third World is defined entirely in terms of an externally inserted phenomena. This, for Ahmad merely repeats the age old idea that history is created *by* the First world, and happens *to* the Third World. Also nationalism is not a simple unitary thing there are variation in the type of nationalism, which Jameson does not seem to recognise. Moreover, if the Third World has only the experience of the oppression and imperialism (and not the conflicts of class or gender), then (asks Ahmad) what else does the Third World have to narrate? Also, by freezing the Third World into the ideal typology of master-slave, Jameson has set up the criteria for judging the work of the Third World writer. We need to, therefore narrate ourselves in conformity with this ideal type. That is, any text which is not a national allegory cannot be considered as an authentic Third World text. This implication of Jameson's argument comes in for severe attack from Ahmad.

(7) For Ahmad, Jameson also reiterates the "primordial" difference between the First and Third Worlds, rooted in things far older than capitalism itself when he speaks of the civilisational categories. Ahmad argues that one must recognise transformative powers of capitalism in the colonialism. One needs to look at the forced transfers of values *from* the colonies to the imperial

powers and the intensification of capital *within* those formations (colonies) in imperialism. As this process proceeds the private and the public domains are separated, the intellectual is slowly alienated from the actualities of concrete economic experiences. The self is experienced as isolated and alienated, they (the authors) then produce texts of the capitalist era, which is the same type as any Western text of the First World.

(8) Moving onto Said, Ahmad has a number of charges against *Orientalism*. Ahmad argues that Said is steeped in the High Humanist tradition, when he (Said) presupposes (a) a unified European identity which is at the origin of history (b) this history—visible in a set of beliefs, values and attitudes—remains essentially the same right upto the twentieth century (c) this history and beliefs are immanent in the great *books* of the Western canon.

(9) Ahmad also accuses Said of ignoring the manner in which the Western texts about the Orient were received and circulated, modified, challenged or assimilated among the intelligentsia of the colonies. In *Orientalism*, Ahmad notes there is hardly any non-Western source—precisely the problem Said raised about the Orientalist texts! Said also ignores the numerous anti-colonial texts that have been in circulation in colonies since the nineteenth century.

(10) Further, Ahmad objects to Said's assumption that difference and identity in the colonial contexts were the effects of *discourse* rather than political economy. The Saidian assumption that the entire Western civilisation was diseased and paranoid about the Other and itself is too fantastic for Ahmad to accept.

(11) Said also posits stable subject-objects identities and relations. He is thus himself an "Orientalist-in-reverse" (Ahmad uses the term from Sadek el-Azm). Ahmad argues that the xenophobic crisis of identity have been prevalent in all civilisations, including non-European ones. "What gave the European forms of these prejudices their special force in history . . . was not some gathering of unique force in domains of discourses [but] the power of colonial capital." (Ahmad's argument that Said homogenises all colonial oppression in his suggestion of the

stable identities has been a point raised by numerous thinkers. Meenakshi Mukherjee notes in *Interrogating Post-colonialism* that we should be wary of "the possible risks inherent in the formulation of post-coloniality as the common condition of contemporary civilisation cutting across continents, or of making the specific configuration of circumstances in particular regions subservient to a global paradigm").

(12) Said also attaches great importance to being able to address the metropolitan centre, what Said calls the "voyage in." There is thus an excess emphasis on techniques and forms of such an address. Only those discourses that "answer back" to the centre are acceptable. Those that do not are rejected as "cultural nationalist." Ahmad attacks the so-called representatives of the Third World, where the elite academic intelligentsia claims for itself "the role of the world's revolutionary vanguard." One must, notes Ahmad, be aware of the fact that the "combination of the comprador class origin, Western location, exiled self" produces the so-called revolutionary postcolonial position. Ahmad points out that postcolonial intellectuals do their theorising in the *West* (Harish Trivedi addresses a similar issue in his response to Spivak's question, "Can the Subaltern Speak?" Trivedi argues that the subaltern has always spoken, although in a native tongue. The issue is not whether the subaltern can speak, rather it is whether the subaltern can speak the language of the *metropolitan centre*, that is English and the language of high theory. As Trivedi puts it, "can the subaltern spivak?")

(13) Ahmad, in his essay "The Politics of Literary Postcoloniality," argues that Spivak's notion of postcoloniality as "the heritage of imperialism" is simply untenable. Spivak, argues Ahmad, relies upon *political* concepts of nationhood, democracy and socialism for her definition. For Ahmad, the "historically adequate referent" for the legacy of imperialism (which, Spivak claims, is not available from the postcolonial space) is available in the national movement itself. Ahmad claims that Spivak is relying upon the European meanings of these concepts and words. This closely parallels the present idea that there is no secular India because secularism is a Western product. Democ-

racy, socialism and constitutionality are not simply the heritage of imperialism. Ahmad argues that we need to speak not of colonialism or postcolonialism but of capitalist modernity.

(14) Rejecting Bhabha's notion of hybridity, Ahmad comments that the hybrid intellectual in Bhabha is "remarkably free of gender, class, identifiable political location." A politics of contingency (based on the ideas of the hybrid and displacement) that Bhabha recommends denies the specific prior structural nature of categories like caste or class. Members of particular castes and classes are bearers of *earlier specific histories* of power and dispossession. The present politics of conflict are inseparable from these histories. Further, the assertion that human action must be non-rational and displaced precludes the very base of human action. Ahmad argues: what the migrants seek is "not displacement but, precisely, a place from where they may begin anew, with some sense of a stable future. Postcoloniality is also, like most things, a matter of class."

English Studies, Religious Reform and India: A Note

The role of English literature, and English studies in the extension and reinforcement of the colonial enterprise was hinted at in the work of Edward Said. Said suggested that the "encoding" of colonialism took place in the texts it produced about the Orient. These texts, consumed by the natives, *naturalised* the order of imperialism as necessary, and benevolent. The seminal work of Harish Trivedi in *Colonial Transactions,* Gauri Viswanathan in *Masks of Conquest* analyses the specific role of English studies and English literature in the consolidation of English rule in India. The English language was treated as politically neutral. Viswanathan argues that the introduction of English studies in India was necessitated by the need for native administrators. Macaulay, in his infamous 1835 Minute on Education, dismissed Indian and native knowledges as useless and recommended the introduction of Western education, mainly to produce a class "Indian in blood and colour . . . [but] English in taste, in opinions, in morals, and in intellect." What the system produced was not a ruling class but a group of clerks (as Susie Tharu has pointed out). English literary studies, argues Viswanathan, and was instrumental in propagating Western ideals among the natives. Aesthetics, political ideas and the "humanistic tradition" were spread into the natives through these means, which were merely the cover for economic exploitation. Viswanathan writes: "the English literary text, functioning as a surrogate Englishman in his highest and most perfect state, becomes a mask for economic exploitation." Native texts such as Kalidasa's *Shankuntala*, which were consumed avidly in Europe, were considered unfit for the natives because these texts apparently inculcated immorality in these weak minds. This meant that "raising Indians to the intellectual level of their Western counterparts" had to "forestall the danger of having unfortified minds falsely seduced by the 'impurities' of the traditional literature of the East." Education was, in Susie Tharu's words, "a means of shaping Indian subjects, who, equipped with disciplined minds and bodies, would not only be in a better position to understand Imperial laws, but also have the necessary ethical discrimination and mental cultivation to desire and appreciate the rational, humane and impartial government that the new rulers were trying to set up." In the postcolonial context, a similar strain continues where the access to English by certain segments of society ensures the retention of class/caste privileges. As Susie Tharu points out, this retention of the status quo by the new elite was predicated upon the assumption of the idea of a universal man, and the "bourgeois-mercantile (but also imperial and patriarchal) agenda is endowed with finality and designated as embodying the aspirations of all humanity." The English language was treated as politically neutral and the colonial history of the language, its role in the oppressive structures of the Raj was ignored in post-Independence India, for instance.

English studies also projected the colonial system as natural and necessary, that the system was a humanistic enterprise rather than a politically exploitative/oppressive one. The natives, brought up on the diet of these texts began to accept the colonial presence as natural and necessary. The choice of texts transcended the realities of time and place—and projected as universal. The colonisers in India conveniently ignored the institutional matrix within which these texts were canonised as universal. Texts were supposedly "unmediated by the political and historical realities [of colonial power]." This becomes the Gramscian *oppression by consent*, when the natives, convince about the good of colonialism, actually demanded English studies and Western rule. The role of the native supporters of English education (Raja Ram Mohun Roy, for instance) is thus crucial to our understanding of the use of English education. This also meant that English studies aimed to curb any native tendency towards insubordination and rebellion—since they believed colonialism and the inferiority of their race as "natural" they would not rebel. What Viswanathan suggests is a close link between the materials and political practice of colonialism and the textual aspect of the same. Slowly this also meant a distancing from their own culture and language (as Ngugi Wa Thiong'o has argued).

English studies also went hand in hand with the "civilising mission" of the coloniser. The colonial powers first *constructed* a communal India, and then set about *restoring* harmony, as Gyanendra Pandey argues in *The Construction of Communalism in Colonial North India*. Pandey argues that communalism is a form of colonialist knowledge, it stands for the "puerile" and the "primitive." Pandey demonstrates how the religious violence of the colonial time was seen as just another "convulsion" in a long *history* of similar violence in an intolerant Indian society. To curb this intolerance what was needed was the strong arm of the European presence—namely the legal/juridical and military power. Communalism seen as fanaticism and irrationality helped establish the inherent perversity of the native. The violence seen as a part of a continuum (a pre-colonial past) becomes the justification for colonial rule. The violence of the fanatic natives is contrasted with the legitimate and rational violence of the colonial state. The colonial state thus emerges as the "hero" in this "communal riot narrative."

Religious conversion, as Viswanathan's essays "Coping with (Civil) Death" (in Gyan Prakash's *After Colonialism*) and *Outside the Fold* demonstrate, was also a means of exploitation that left the native with an "impasse of identity." Viswanathan points out that the native converts to Christianity were treated as neither Christians nor heathens. Thus, converts to Christianity "could still remain Hindus for purposes of law." This was "civil death" for the natives. The essential result of this was tragic for the converts: "[they were] treated as dead by their former religious community [and] the lease of life they were given by civil courts was founded on an equally unreal fiction, a perverse denial of their adopted religious identity." Viswanathan argues that religious conversion rather than acting as a "catalyst of social and cultural change" actually functioned to preserve the status quo. It privileged a legislative religious identity over private or subjective religious experience."

Women and Colonialism: One of the most interesting areas of research in colonial studies is the gendering effects of colonial rule and the link between sexuality, race and empire. A large amount of material is now available, notably in the writings of Anne McClintock, Jenny Sharpe, Mary L. Pratt and others. Rajeshwari Sundar Rajan and Lata Mani have analysed the colonial discourse on Sati in British India. Sati, argue Mani and others, provided a context where the European social mission could best be articulated. The ritual apparently symbolised the barbarity of native religion and the vulnerability of the native woman. The writings of English reformers like William Jones, William Bentinck and the Clapham Sect thus contain numerous references to the fundamental barbarity of Hinduism, which can be erased only through English intervention.

The image of the "virgin land" awaiting discovery and conquest is the sexualisation of colonial rule. The land is inevitably seen as a female body that invokes desire. The vulnerability of the native woman who needs to be protected from her fellow men by the European rulers is another recurrent image (as Spivak puts it, "White men are saving brown women from brown men"). The native women are immoral, sexually promiscuous and are *both* dangerous seductresses and vulnerable/innocent creatures. The European is thus "suspended between a fantasy of conquest and a dread of engulfment" (Anne McClintock). The woman is the "boundary marker" where colonialism functions. Anne McClintock writes that women mark the boundaries of the New World. This reflects the anxiety (of the male) of the loss of his boundary (his native land) and the desire/fantasy of potentially newer ones (the colony). Forbidden desires could be projected onto the native female because they are less than women are and promiscuous in any case. These are the "porno-tropics" of colonial discourse (the term is McClintock's). The European thus seeks to pierce the obfuscatory veil of the native woman (because the veil prevents the European male from *seeing* her clearly, as Meyda Yegenoglu's work has pointed out), to enter the prohibited space of the woman's quarters (Anthony King has argued that the laws on building construction in colonial Lucknow, which prohibited high walls around houses in the name of "hygiene" was primarily due to this European need to see into the prohibited quarters). The woman was also the guardian of morality and hence the European woman was discouraged from mingling too closely with the native males. The control of woman's sexuality and breeding a race of empire builders was paramount in the colonial agenda (and, as Partha Chatterjee points out, this role of the native woman as guardian of tradition was also the emphasis in the nationalist agenda during the anti-colonial movement). The threat of rape of the white woman by the oversexed native male was a direct result of the colonial emphasis on the woman as the boundary figure. The purity of the English woman has to maintained, and thus the fear of rape (for a discussion of the colonial discourse of rape, see the seminal work of Jenny Sharpe). Also, the native comes to see the white woman as a possible possession. The possession of the white woman could effectively (for the native) neutralise the strength of the white master. The woman is thus effectively invisible *except* as the man's dark side, as a possible bargaining counter in the transaction between the native and the coloniser male. This is the *Miranda complex*, as Laura Donaldson terms it, of colonialism's sexualising aspect. In the colony the health of the colonial male must be maintained at all cost. Hence regulations of the movement of prostitutes in barracks, the compulsory segregation and medical examination of these women was undertaken, as the work of Kenneth Ballhatchet demonstrates. The role of the European *woman* reformer has also come in for scrutiny in the issue of gender, sexuality and race (notably in the work of Vron Ware).

Subaltern Studies: The ongoing work of the Subaltern Studies group (Ranajit Guha, David Arnold, Partha Chatterjee and others) is an attempt to write a historiography that is different from the colonial one. The theories of nationalism, identity and ethnicity come in for special scrutiny here. Gyan Prakash explicitly links the subaltern studies project with postcolonial studies in its combination of post-structuralism, Marxism and archival research. Tejaswini Niranjana writes: "post-structuralism's questioning of universalism and essentialism as well as its critique of humanism not only aligns it with anti-colonial critique, but is also indebted to such a critique in ways that as yet remain largely unmapped." The focus is on "the general attribute of subordination in South Asian society whether this is expressed in terms of class, caste, age, gender and office . . . along with the attitudes, ideologies and belief systems." It looks at "history from below," that is the history of those common people (tribals, lower classes/castes and women) that have been silenced in accepted histories of the nationalist movement. The oppressed people would finally find a voice here. As Guha puts it, the accepted history has always been of the elite, the "dominant groups, foreign as well as indigenous . . . the foreign industrialists, merchants, planters . . . and the native recruits to the uppermost levels of the bureaucracy." Some sections have evidently been left out of such histories—these are the subalterns, the oppressed class. The entire project is premised upon the assumption that nationalism and anti-colonial movements cannot be understood without analysing the role of the women and the tribals in it. Thus the focus is on small peasant uprisings and individual acts of rebellion that were *not* part of the larger nationalist movement (these were even considered criminal acts). Gyan Prakash's summing up in *After Colonialism* is adequate to understand the assumptions of the project: "The subalterns' social location defied the identities of nation and class, and their insurgent consciousness, religiosity, mythic visions, and notions of political community were at odds with the model of causality and rational action advanced by the nationalist elites." Local resistance to colonialism and the use of oral/local traditions rather than a pan-Indian agenda come in for analysis here. Other factors like the gender, class, region are also included in the analysis, which is seen as a counter to the homogenising discourse of the nation-state which elides/erases these local variations in favour of a particular elite/religion/caste/class. The subaltern studies project thus provides rigorous reconstruction through empirical analysis and archival research to put together an alternative history.

IV Relationship with Other Disciplines

Postcolonialism has now moved into territories such as psychology (notably in the work of Ashis Nandy) in works that deal with the actual psychological modes of colonial context. Feminism and the issue of representation in the work of Trinh ti Minh-Ha, Spivak, Jenny Sharpe and Anne McClintock have looked at the gendering effects of colonialism. Geography, feminism, masculinist scientific epistemology (Laura Donaldson, Sandra Harding), the role/status of English language and literature in the colonial and postcolonial context (Ngugi, Probal Dasgupta, Svati Joshi, Susie Tharu, Rajeshwari Sundar Rajan, Harish Trivedi), the discourse of medical science in colonialism (David Arnold), nationalism and identity (Partha Chatterjee, Benedict Anderson), religion and communalism (Gyan Prakash, Gyanendra Pandey), cartography and empire (Mathew Edney) architecture and town planning in the colonial context (Thomas Metcalf, Anthony King), art (Partha Mitter), scientific developments (Deepak Kumar, Zaheer Babar, Michael Adas), translation and colonialism (Tejaswini Niranjana), ecology and colonial land use (Madhav Gadgil, Vandana Shiva, Ramachandra Guha, Ariel Salleh, Alfred Crosby), decolonisation, nativism and nationalism (Ngugi, Balachandra Nemade, Benita Parry, Makarand Paranjape), displacement and diasporic identity (Rey Chow, Arun Mukherjee), modernity and colonialism (Ashis Nandy, Stuart Hall). Textuality and representation in the colonial writing has of course been the subject of extensive analysis in the work of Tim Brennan, Tom Nairn, Kate Teltscher, Elleke Boehmer, Helen Tiffin, Alan Lawson and several other thinkers. There is also the attempt to interrogate and explore the possible interfacing of postcolonialism and postmodernism. Thinkers like Ato Quayson suggest that postmodernism's emphasis on the local and the different may be usefully tied up with postcolonialism's dual emphasis on the common-yet-different denominator of colonial oppression. Quayson's summary of this interfacing position is worth citing. Quayson writes: "The first thing to note is the need to factor images, tropes and texts simultaneously into specific socio-cultural domains while at the same time attempting to alienate them from themselves by reading them against other images, tropes and texts that do not seem to share historical similarities."

Further Reading

Loomba, Ania. *Colonialism/Postcolonialism.* London: Routledge, 1998.

Gandhi, Leela. *Postcolonial Theory: A Critical Introduction.* Delhi: Oxford University Press, 1999.

Quatson, Ato. *Postcolonialism: Theory, Practice or Process*? Cambridge: Cambridge University Press, 2000.

Ashcroft, Bill et al, ed. *The Postcolonial Studies Reader.* London: Routledge, 1995.

Trivedi, Harish. *Colonial Transactions: English Literature and India.* Calcutta: Papyrus, 1993.

Chapter Eight

Postmodernism

The term "postmodernism" was popularised in literary criticism during the 1960s and 70s by critics like Ihab Hassan, Irving Howe, Leslie Fiedler and others. The term has now acquired a catchall scope, being used to describe politics, International Relations, art and architecture, philosophy, popular culture, cyberculture etc. Postmodernism is essentially a philosophic and theoretical position that privileges the local over the universal, differences rather than similarities, resistance rather than conformity, the temporal and a state of flux rather than permanence and stability, and hybridity rather than purity. It supports the "play" of meanings, the contingent nature of all decisions (political, ethical), the narrativist and discursive nature of "history" and the relational, "collage" nature of lives/truths/stories.

I Background and Origins

The first usage of the term "postmodernism" is attributed to Charles Jencks in 1947. The term was used to describe a new style of architecture that emerged in the early part of the twentieth century (see section on postmodernism and architecture below). In the 1950s-1970s, the term was used in literary criticism (usually in conjunction with terms like *metafiction*) to describe the complex work of authors like Donald Barthelme, John Barth, Samuel Beckett, Thomas Pynchon, Kurt Vonnegut and even James Joyce (especially his *Finnegans Wake*). Eventually the term began to be used to describe the state of contemporary culture with its apparently incongruous and irreverent mix of classicism and popular art (pop-culture) forms, the disregard for generic conventions, the intensely self-conscious and self-reflexive mode in films and fiction, the blurring of reality and illusion, and the rise of digital technology, the global communication networks, the proliferation of data and cyberspace and its influence on art forms (including cybertexts and cyber art) and the increasingly problematic distinction of private and public space (home and office and now homeoffice, the individual and the collective in the age of networking, and the media-run lives). The term is used to identify new trends in architecture (the work of Corbusier, Robert Venturi, Peter Eisenman, and James Stirling), photography and representation (Barbara Kruger, Robert Rauschenberg, Victor Burgin, Martha Rosler), painting (Robert Kushner, Brad Davis, Georg Baselitz, Susan Rothenberg, Ashley Bickerton, Julian Opie, Tony Cragg, Michael Gorman and Richard Estes), furniture and design (Hans Hollein).

The major philosophers and theoreticians of the postmodern (in terms of literary and cultural studies) who will be discussed here are Jean-Francois Lyotard, Jean Baudrillard, Craig Owens and Stuart Hall. Short notes on postmodernism in architecture, postmodern literature, postmodernism in visual arts, design, sculpture, postmodern politics and popular culture are also included.

II Assumptions and General Methods

As in most contemporary theory, there are no identifiable and cogent "groups" or "schools" in postmodern theory. One can, however, organise the central assumptions of a postmodern literary and cultural theory.

(1) *Postmodernity* is the social, economic and political state, *postmodernism* is the intellectual, philosophical and theoretical enterprise that seeks to understand and explain the state of postmodernity.

(2) If the modernists *mourned* the fragmentation of experience, history, subjectivity and narratives in their nostalgia for a unified state of affairs, the postmodern *celebrates* fragmentation and anarchy. Fragmentation is an ecstatic state for the postmodernist.

(3) Postmodernism adopts a tone of irreverence towards established icons, installs unexpected figures as cultural icons (Andy Warhol and Marilyn Monroe, the Beatles and Elvis Presley, the star-status of rock musicians) and interrogates traditions and canons.

(4) It rejects the opposition between "high" or elite culture and "low" or mass culture. It questions the criteria by which certain forms/texts/assumptions are canonised, projected and imposed as "good taste," "classics," permanent ("for all times to come") and universal, and which implicitly rejects the mass forms of culture as degenerate, and a passing "fad."

(5) It interrogates any notion, philosophy or ideal of a general, universal and overarching nature. It rejects the claim of any universal or totalising theory, a common "end' of all life, or a common ideal and aim (such as the Marxist idea of the ultimate emancipation of all mankind, the Enlightenment idea of the role of science in human lives all over the world, the Freudian repressive psychosis of all civilisation). In Lyotard's words, this is the resistance towards all such "*grand narratives*." It instead celebrates plurality, heterogeneity, and the small, local, innovative, marginalised and unfinished narratives that respect differences and specifities of cultures, individuals and regions. It is thus "*anti-foundationalist*," refusing any stable or unified foundation to subjectivity, lives, history and reality. It prefers the *liminal* (borderfigures, thresholds, mobile and constantly re-forming) positions rather than stable or fixed locations.

(6) Meaning is seen as differential (see poststructuralism and deconstruction above), contingent and purely arbitrary. Signification and narration are seen as *ends in themselves*, rather than as sources of any Truth. That is, the process of representation seeks not to offer any insights into reality (Truth), but to call attention to itself as *nothing more than a game of representation.* It concedes, like the poststructuralists, that there is no reality that lies beyond language. It seeks, in Lyotard's formulation, to "present the unpresentable."

(7) In literature it collapses the distinctions between genres and conventions. The thriller format becomes part of the "serious" novel. Comic elements and absurdity mark the author's attitude to tragic and sad events like death, suffering, the Holocaust (Joseph Heller's *Catch 22*, the fiction of Kurt Vonnegut, Jr). There are deliberate references to earlier texts (intertextuality)

in the form of parody, explicit borrowings, indirect references, quotes. Myths, fairy tales, legends and contemporary realities merge (in the fiction of Donald Barthelme, Gunter Grass, Salman Rushdie and Gabriel Marquez). Historical figures jostle with contemporary man (for instance, the use of Goethe and Hemingway as characters in Milan Kundera). It becomes impossible to distinguish between reality and illusion, for both the characters and the reader (the work of John Barth, Pynchon's *The Crying of Lot 49*, for instance). The distinction between "real" history and "mere" fiction is called into question (Graham Swift's *Waterland*). The narrator continually undermines his own apparently "reliable" narrative, thus drawing our attention to the essentially contingent, *representational* and *linguistic* nature of reality (the fiction of Italo Calvino, Donald Barthelme). The use of unconventional forms of writing (loose sheets of the novel that may be rearranged in any manner by the reader, as in B.S. Johnson's "shuffle novels"), cybertexts with scope for the reader/viewer to alter the storyline in an interactive "production" of the novel are all examples of postmodern techniques in fiction. Irony and scepticism, self-conscious narration, the interrogation of their own assumptions and narrative techniques, language games, the self-confessed inadequacy of the author are general traits of the postmodern novel.

(8) Rationality and rational explanations are also treated with suspicion. Postmodernism is constantly aware that "truth" and reality are constructs of discourse. Postmodernism suggests that rationality is the sanctioned approach of a particular episteme, and that power relations structure all social truths, approaches and even conceptions of reality (see section on Foucault in the chapter on poststructuralism for his notion of discourse, episteme and power).

(9) The everyday, the body and its "permanent flux" of desire, and the ordinary become subjects for "serious" art, philosophy and criticism. The *presentism* of postmodernism undercuts the thrust on history and the future in modernism. All knowledge, truths, experience and pleasure are only of *immediate* value

and relevance. No universality or permanence is advocated by postmodernism.

(10) The postmodern sensibility has been summed up by Scott Lash and John Urry thus (in their 1987 essay, "Postmodern Sensibility" reprinted in *The Polity Reader in Cultural Theory*, 1994). Postmodernism rejects the aesthetic "aura" (the emphasis on aesthetic value in the modernist phase) though:

(i) It proclaims not its uniqueness but its location in a proliferating context of mechanical and electronic reproduction.

(ii) It denies the high modernist separation of the aesthetic from the social and the everyday.

(iii) It disputes the high modernist valuation of such unity through pastiche, parody and collage.

(iv) Where audiences in a state of "contemplation" (Walter Benjamin) received high modernist cultural forms, postmodern cultural forms are received in a state of distraction.

(v) Where high modernist art is appreciated for coherent use and the formal properties of the aesthetic, material postmodern culture affects the audiences through its immediate impact, the "economy of pleasure" [the presentism of postmodernism, as we have already noted].

(vi) Postmodernism does not distinguish between high and low culture.

III Key Concepts and Thinkers

Jean-Francois Lyotard: With his *The Postmodern Condition* (English translation, 1984), *The Differend* (1988), *Just Gaming* (1985) Lyotard has emerged as the most important philosopher of postmodernism. Lyotard's work has focussed on a range of issues such as postmodernism and language, ethics, the issues of representation and notions of truth.

(1) Lyotard's definition of the postmodern must begin any discussion of his work. Lyotard defines the postmodern (in *The Postmodern Condition*) as "*the incredulity towards metanarratives.*" He adds, "the narrative is losing its functions, its great hero, its great dangers, its great voyages, its great goal." Instead of such macro- or meta- narratives (the "*grandes his-*

toires," as Lyotard terms it) Lyotard suggests the *petites* or *micronarratives*.

(2) The "incredulity towards metanarratives" is the disillusionment with totalising and foundationalist explanations of reality. This includes the narrative of science, philosophy and religion. For instance, the Marxist ideal of an emancipatory agenda and aim for communism, the Christian narrative of redemption, the psychoanalytic one of the repressive nature of all human civilisation are totalising narratives because they ignore differences, variations at local, individual and regional levels in favour of an overarching universal programme or explanation.

(3) These knowledges and explanations are therefore tyrannical, false and oppressive because they ignore differences in order to impose a false unity on knowledge and reality. Such grand narratives prevent the full development of individuals and cultures. These knowledges also conceal beneath their apparent objectivity an "exercise of terror." Lyotard suggests that scientists and scientific discourses are not employed to disseminate "Truth" but to "augment power." That is, scientific discourses that seek to *legitimate* certain knowledges actually suppress oppositional knowledges in order to retain their stranglehold of power (not the parallels with Foucault here).

(4) Lyotard argues further that "proof" belongs to the wealthy. That is, there is an irreducible relation between "wealth efficiency and truth," where the "games of scientific language become the games of the rich, in which whoever is the wealthiest has the best chance of being right." Lyotard is here pointing to the abuse of power by institutions (such as the scientific establishments, religion, the education system and the state) in their drive to legitimise their authority and versions of truth as universal.

(5) There is a "mercantilisation of knowledge" where the *saleability* of the truth is all that matters. The question "what use is it" replaces, according to Lyotard, the query "Is it true?" Lyotard writes that "knowledge is and will be produced in order to be sold." In fact (argues Lyotard), knowledge is the major stake in the world's quest for power. He suggests that one day the

world will fight for control of information just as it now fights for the control of territory. Those who control the metanarrative will control knowledge.

(6) Postmodernism is interested in the "undecidables, the limits of precise control, conflicts characterised by incomplete information, "fracta" [fractions], catastrophes and pragmatic paradoxes" (Lyotard). Postmodernism acknowledges that all knowledge is fragmentary, partial and incomplete. One can only utilise local knowledge to know a *part* of the truth. Thus the individual's experience, knowledge and voice is to be retrieved as a resistance and *delegitimation* towards grand narratives that simply pass off *one version* of knowledge and reality as universal. This is the *anti-foundationalist* aspect of postmodern thought. As Lyotard writes in a famously prophetic-and prescriptive-tone, "Let us wage a war on totality; let us be witnesses to the unpresentable; let us activate the differences and save the honour of the name."

(7) "*Language games*" for Lyotard are essential for the full development of the individual. He calls for the complete dissemination of knowledge and an opening up of the data banks to this end. The "reserve of knowledge" is for Lyotard, the reserve of language's reserve of all possible utterances" (the parallel with Richard Rorty's arguments that the import of new "languages" or metaphors caries the potential for new politics and ethics is striking here). Lyotard thus argues that individuals rather than systems should control knowledge. Lyotard believes that individual resistance—what he terms "*agonistics*"—to the system will help keep the narrative from becoming oppressive. The multiplicity of small narratives is thus agonistic. Lyotard explicitly emphasises the political implication of this role of the individual and mini-narratives when he writes: "the idea that I think we need today in order to make decisions in political matters cannot be the idea of the totality, or of the unity, of the body. It can only be the idea of a multiplicity or of diversity."

(8) There is a political implication to Lyotard's arguments against foundationalism. The exploration of the legitimation of truth through a suppression of alternatives and differences by insti-

tutions is Lyotard's contribution to the political aspect of postmodernism. In place of the oppressive drive towards legitimation—through the creation of universal criteria of morality and goodness—Lyotard suggests a "*paganism*," where "one judges without criteria."

(9) Lyotard suggests short-term contracts instead of permanent ones. The emphasis is on process rather than fixity, on contingency and adaptability rather than stability. Lyotard writes: "the temporary contract is in practice supplanting permanent institutions in professional, emotional, sexual, cultural, family and international; domains, as well as in political areas (once more, a parallel needs to be drawn with the "[postmodern] politics of contingency" as advocated by Ulrich Beck and Zygmunt Bauman).

(10) Lyotard focuses on *narrativity* as anti-foundationalist. The narrative drive is at the heart of all human affairs. Scientists speak of their discoveries and play by the "rules of the narrative game." Lyotard argues that narrative games are all around us, that "we have always already been told something . . . we have always already been spoken." Narrative knowledge approaches other discourse as a variant in the family of narrative discourses.

(11) Postmodernism invokes the *sublime*, which is the "unpresentable in presentation itself." It does not favour "good forms" for the sake of unity or "good taste." Instead, it draws attention to the unattainable in any presentation. Hence postmodernism constantly reinvents itself and its forms of presentation. In this search lies the ecstasy of the postmodern.

(12) In an important move for literary studies, Lyotard argues that the "*actuality*" or "density" of real things cannot be opposed to the "*artificiality*" of *texts* and representations (the traditional opposition of the reality and solidity of things and the merely reflective/representational nature of texts about these things). Things escape textuality not because they (things) have any real identity, but because the difference between the two (things and texts) cannot be *reduced* to a simple set of *oppositional concepts* (the sensory reality of things *versus* the textual

imaginary/fiction). What Lyotard is suggesting (in the Derridean line of thought) is the very deconstruction of the binary opposition "figural/real."

(13) The "differend" is Lyotard's term for the *incommensurability* of ideas and basis for argument and judgement. When there is no rule of judgement applicable to both arguments, when the application of a single rule of judgement to both would wrong at least one of them, we have the differend, the silencing of the player in the language game. There is no ultimate genre of discourse to appeal to in the case of a conflict between genres. Thus the universe of discourse is highly fragmentary. This means simply that *one* universal, absolute standard of judgement is not applicable to all genres/cases/individuals. One must account for the *basic* incommensurability of the genres. Our duty, insists Lyotard, is to "bear witness to the differend." This also means that there is no truly objective infallible, impartial "third party" to whom one may appeal to resolve the conflict. A third party (like god) who is able to perceive what is hidden in the narratives of the litigants/genres, and who is outside the genres under dispute does not exist any such authority or standard is itself "locked into," is a *part* of the dispute. The criterion for such a judgement is itself part of the genre or narrative. Lyotard is again contesting the idea of a "transcendental signified," referent or authority that remains *outside* the games of narrative and is therefore able to indicate possible final resolutions/truths in the dispute. The differend is the term for this basic incommensurability of disputes and narratives, which prevents seizure of the narrative by any totalising authority.

(14) Lyotard, continuing his argument on individual resistance, puts forward the idea of "*sveltness*." Sveltness, as Stuart Sim defines it, is a guerrilla-like attitude, a flexible and creative response by the individual to late capitalism's pressures. Lyotard describes it as "suppleness, speed, strength, the ability to metamorphose." It is a condition of the mind, the readiness to confront and displace metanarratives, a permanently vigilance against universalities (reminiscent of Foucault's permanent resistance). It is based on individual need rather than administra-

tive convenience, and is the resistance against legitimation through a tactic of unpredictability, contingency and immediacy. Such a state of unpredictability is destabilising in its effect and is the only answer to grand narratives. Agonistics is the founding principle of such a sveltness. The boundaries of institutions are displaced, a poetics is introduced into the "formal" discourse of power (the example Lyotard uses is of whether the university would allow language games—poetics, and whether one may tell stories at the cabinet meeting). The agonistic svelte individual thus becomes the living antithesis of authoritarianism and totalitarianism.

Jean Baudrillard: Baudrillard's poetic and distinctly "unacademically" styled prose in works like *Simulations* (1983), *America* (1988), *Seduction* (1990) and *Cool Memories* (1990), *The Illusion of the End* (1994) has presented twentieth century with some of the most radical theories. Baudrillard's work has invariably taken into account the proliferation of digital technology, the emphasis on the image, the development of "virtual" models of reality and the commodity-consumerist culture of contemporary life.

(1) Baudrillard's central argument is that in the age of perfect reproduction and endless repetition of images, the distinction between the real and the illusory, between original and "copy," between superficiality and depth has broken down. What we now have is a culture of "*hyperreality*."

(2) Baudrillard suggests that the *sign* is not an index of some underlying reality. A sign merely refers to other signs. The entire system, constituted by such signs that are ultimately empty (because they only refer to other similar signs rather than "truth") is thus a *simulacrum* of the real. The process is what Baudrillard terms *simulation*. Simulation is when the image/model becomes more real than real. In Baudrillard's words, in simulation there is a "generation by models of a real without origin or reality: a hyperreal." And when the distinction between the real object and the image/representation of the object breaks down, we have the simulacra of the real. This means that notions of aesthetics and the criteria for aesthetic judgement will have to be radically redefined to account for the ab-

sence of originals. This is the *post-aesthetic* phase, as Stuart Sim has termed it in his comments on Baudrillard.

(3) Baudrillard's notion of the code is crucial here. Baudrillard argues that contemporary life is governed by the code: the DNA code in biology, the digital code of sound reproduction, the binary code of computer technology. The code ensures that the object reproduced is not *simply a copy*. Since the code enables an exact replication, the distinction between the original and the copy breaks down. Virtual reality, global communications, the infinite reproductions of data banks, holograms are examples of the redundancy of the distinction between real and imagined, between "true" and copy.

(4) In an age when the natural object is no longer credible, the code has raised simulation to an unprecedented importance. Simulation and models are pure reproductions. When the code enables reality to be bypassed, a curious *reversibility* emerges where all finalities disappear. The origin of things is *not* an original thing but a *code* or formula (as noted above). The last "original" may now be exactly reproduced through the master code to the original-reversibility. That is, the "last original" actually does not exist: it may be infinitely reproduced. This is the *hyperreal*. In the hyperreal, then, the image is the reality. Our experiences (of reality) are simulated through technology. Examples of this simulated reality abound: home shopping via the television, electronic shopping, holographic images etc. Baudrillard describes the situation thus: we will never again in the future be able to separate reality from its statistical, simulative projection in the media, a state of suspense and of definitive uncertainty about reality. This uncertainty results not from a lack of information, but from information itself, and even from an *excess* of information.

(5) The pervasiveness of the code therefore opens up hyperreality. There are four different logics of the code:

   (a) The logic of practical operation: This corresponds to the use-value (or practical benefits derived from using the particular object) of the object. The object is here an instrument, and the logic of utility governs the code.

(b) The logic of equivalence: This corresponds to exchange value (or the fact that one object may be given as equivalent to/for another object since both carry the same value) of the object. Here it is the logic of the market in operation.

(c) The logic of ambivalence: This corresponds to symbolic exchange. Here the principle of the gift operates (Baudrillard adopts the Maussian notion of the gift). The object is a symbol for something (a wedding ring, for instance)

(d) The logic of difference: This is the sign-value of the object. Here the logic of status and prestige operates, where the object is a sign for something (class, professional position).

(6) Baudrillard argues that in a consumer society objects are not simply consumed. They are produced to signify a *status* rather than satisfy a need. Hence Baudrillard's argument that in a consumer society objects become signs. In fact, he argues that what we consume are not objects but signs: the signs of advertisements, of television. The objects have value for us *as signs*. Therefore we consume *images*, and the exchange value is transformed into *sign-value*.

(7) Baudrillard's analysis of the types of signs suggests four stages in the "development" of the sign.

(a) Initially the sign was "full." That is, a sign was a surface indication of the reality below. It therefore represents a basic reality.

(b) In the second stage, the sign misrepresents or distorts the reality behind it.

(c) In the third stage, the sign conceals the fact that there is any reality under it at all. What we have is the sign that simply points to another sign. The sign thus ceases to have any authority as representation.

(d) In the fourth stage, the sign bears no relation to reality at all. Everything is merely a *model*, a simulation of the real. Reality itself no longer exists *outside these representations*. This is the *hyperreal*.

(8) Baudrillard noted the following stages in the sign's movement towards simulation. These correspond to three kinds of simulation.

(a) *Counterfeit*: In the age of the Renaissance. Here the distinction between the real/natural and the counterfeit is made apparent.

(b) *Production*: In the Industrial Age. Here the difference between labour and object is made evident.

(c) *Simulation*: The contemporary. Governed by the code. The reproduction becomes more important than the production.

(9) In the discourse of consumption, Baudrillard detects a counter or anti-discourse. The exalted discourse of overabundance is duplicated by the critique of consumer society. Thus, advertising intentionally parodies advertising, suggesting the existence of an anti-discourse. In Baudrillard's terms, the society of consumption is also the society of the *denunciation* of this consumption.

(10) The world—its objects and events—can never be fully captured. The object of enquiry forever remains out of our reach. This is the "revenge of the object," it seduces us into believing that we shall possess it next time, that the next time its Otherness will be ours. But it remains forever elusive. That is, there is always a beyond. No closure is complete, no presence is "full." Politically and socially, this theory of Baudrillard has certain important implications. If no closure or certainty is possible, then no social-formation is stable. The factors that are believed to stabilise things (culture, religious truths, the state, law) are seen as themselves temporary and simulations. We need, suggests Baudrillard, to accept that the world is unintelligible. Further, we should also resist all attempts to make it intelligible.

(11) For Baudrillard, then, the postmodern is characterised by the hyperreal, by the collapse of distinction between the private and the public (home, office, and now homeoffice, as pointed out earlier; the experience of home shopping, simulated participation in events etc). This is the *implosion* of meaning in the media: "only signs without referents, empty, senseless, absurd and elliptical signs absorb us."

(12) There is an anti-judgmental strain in Baudrillard's thought. We have already noted that criteria for aesthetic judgement must be

redefined now that the notion of the original has itself become redundant. Extending the argument into social and cultural; areas, law and order themselves become problematic, since standards are hard to decide in the face of simulated reality. In fact, law and order may themselves be simulations. There can be no ground for political authority (Baudrillard reached the height of his controversy when, extending his notion of simulation, he claimed that the 1991 Gulf War did not really happen!).

(13) Baudrillard put forward his notion of *seduction* to suggest a means of undermining authority, systems and meaning. Seduction for Baudrillard is a specifically feminine trait. Power and authority must not be challenged but seduced so that it loses its pretensions of/to truth. The masculine prides itself (argues Baudrillard) upon its "unfailing powers of discrimination and absolute criteria for pronouncing the truth." The feminine on the other hand is "insoluble." Seduction is a permanent antithesis and prevents power from being properly established. Baudrillard's definition of seduction goes thus: "seduction need not be demonstrated, nor justified—it is there all at once, in the reversal of all the alleged depth of the real, of all psychology, anatomy, truth, or power. It knows (this is its secret) that there is no anatomy, no psychology, that all signs are reversible." Seduction is thus a game that relies on contingency, unpredictability and flexibility. The system becomes powerless against such a seductive policy of the individual. (Baudrillard's notion of the essentially *uncertain* nature of femininity and of seduction as a feminine strategy that is opposed to the masculine authority has important consequences for feminism).

(14) Baudrillard argues that in the postmodern there is no actual ground to rely on. We need to therefore push towards theoretical violence, the very extremes of theoretical speculation. We need to speculate (writes Baudrillard in a scintillatingly poetic prose) "to the death, whose only method is the radicalisation of all hypothesis . . . the only strategy is catastrophic . . . at the peak of value ambivalence intensifies; and at the height of their coherence, the redoubled signs of the code are haunted by the

abyss of reversal. The play of simulation must be taken further than the system permits."

(15) In his book, *America*, Baudrillard argues that America is the complete hyperreal society. Writing in a reflective intensely subjective mood, Baudrillard comments on the issue of desire and the simulated realities of American life. Baudrillard suggests that America's insistence on the present is a "trip without any objective." America is a vast dislocating spectacle: "every special effect can be found here." American society has erased all reference and meaning, reason for its existence and has gone beyond human rationality. There is no relationship between people. They are linked together simply because they crowd together. Sheer existence is an end in itself (a *presentism* without meaning or telos). There is the "liquidation of all culture" and the "consecration of indifference." Self-absorption is the American way of life (Baudrillard gives as example for this self-absorption, breakdancing, and the jogger absorbed in the jogging and the music from the walkman). America seeks the "sign from beyond," from beyond history. Baudrillard thus suggests that the idea of history having an end is illusory. History, however, has ended because it is "no longer able to transcend itself . . . to dream of its own end; it is buried beneath its own immediate effect . . . imploding into current events" (as Baudrillard puts it in *The Illusion of the End*). The prestige of events, the sense of purpose, the meaning and significance has disappeared.

(16) *Indifference* is a major concept in Baudrillard. We need to be not nihilistic or nostalgic about the world, but indifferent. This opposes any value or solution. The indifference must be the "rule of the game." In such an indifference, in the state of complete reversibility (see above) Baudrillard locates the possibility of democracy and emancipation. Baudrillard writes that the law is actually a principle of "profound inequality." But indifference being arbitrary renders everyone equal because in the state of reversibility everyone has the same *potential* (there being no originary potential, such as the potential enshrined

originally in the Constitution. Reversibility and simulation suggests that the copy or reproduction *is* the original).

(17) All solutions are *imaginary* solutions, an acting out. This is pataphysics. It is both inside and outside metaphysics. Pataphysics is an epiphenomenon that occurs during the process of a phenomenon. Thus it is both extra, superfluous and part of the phenomena. It extends beyond the phenomenon. And, as we have seen in Baudrillard, the extreme position is the only one available to us. Once a system reaches perfection, for Baudrillard one single push will ensure its collapse.

(18) In terms of social action and politics Baudrillard argues that the individual is no longer confronted with her/his own will. In his famous essay "The Masses: The Implosion of the Social in the Media," Baudrillard writes: "each individual is forced into the undivided coherency of statistics, a positive absorption into the transparency of computers which is something worse than alienation." Baudrillard suggests that there is no Other anymore, and the scene of the Other has disappeared. Further the groups/society are/is self-absorbed and "auto-intoxicated." It must know what it wants, know what it thinks, and see itself continually on the videoscreen of statistics. Postmodern society thrives on images of itself (opinion polls, for example). Therefore, obsessed with itself the society or the group can no longer enact itself: it is confused with its own image. Baudrillard writes: "it loses its scene and becomes ob-scene."

Stuart Hall: Hall's extensive work on postmodernity and question of identity, culture and social action has been important interventions in the debates. Hall argues that there were five major advances in the history of ideas that de-centred the Cartesian subject and heralded the advent of the fragmented, unfinished, open, and contradictory identity of the postmodern subject. Hall identifies these historic moments: Marxism, Freud and psychoanalysis, Foucault, Feminism (as both theory and social movement). Hall argues that the New Social Movements—student upheavals, anti-war and counterculture movements, civil rights struggles, "Third World" revolutionary movements, peace movements—are based on an identity politics. On feminism and such social movements, Hall suggests that they introduced a whole new form of identity.

(i) Opposed both the corporate liberal politics of the West and the Stalinist politics of the Soviet Union.
(ii) Affirmed the subjective and objective dimension of politics.
(iii) Were suspicious of all bureaucratic forms of organisation and favoured spontaneity and acts of political will.
(iv) Had a powerful *cultural* emphasis and form.
(v) Reflected the weakening or break-up of class politics, and the mass political organisations associated with it and their fragmentation into various and separate social movements.
(vi) Each movement appealed to the social identity of its supporters. Thus feminism appealed to women, sexual politics to gays/ lesbians, racial struggles to blacks, anti-war to peaceniks etc. This introduces *identity politics* into the social movement

Postmodern Literature: Postmodernism has seen its most emphatic expression in fiction. Barth, Pynchon, Beckett, Graham Swift, Barthelme, Malcolm Bradbury and several others have developed narrative techniques that can readily be linked to the postmodern condition. The work of Niall Lucy, Brian McHale, Andrew Gibson, Linda Hutcheon, Ihab Hassan and others have contributed to the understanding of this genre of postmodern literature and postmodern narrative. The features of postmodern fiction may be summarised as follows.

(i) It extends certain features of modernist fiction, such as the use of the past, myths and history. A novel like Graham Swift's *Waterland* combines the traditions of historical narrative, fiction, nature writing in a truly postmodern style of mixed genres. Traditional concepts of time and space are interrogated. These novelists frequently use the relational nature of time (time as an order of movements and of their units), and the incommensurable, measureless nature of time. Ideas from contemporary physics, electronic technology and chemistry (chaos theory, virtual reality, entropy, space-time continuum, to mention a few. See appendix "Technocriticism") are adapted by novelists like Pynchon, Alain Robbe-Grillet, Jorge Louis Borges and Swift.

(ii) It is intensely self-reflexive, and constantly draws attention to the very *act* of writing, as the narrative styles of Italo Calvino or Donald Barthelme indicate. The term metafiction or "*histo-riographic metafiction*" (the latter term is from Linda Hutcheon's seminal *A Poetics of Postmodernism*) is thus frequently applied to describe the self-reflexive style.

(iii) These novels celebrate and favour fragmentation of narrative, linguistic experiments, the use of different registers (the serious tone combines or alternates with advertisement jingles, newspaper reports, popular songs etc.), interplay of genres and so on. Thus the postmodern novel is a hybridised form.

(iv) Conventional notions of reality are questioned. The narrative calls attention to its *representational* rather than presentational status. That is, the narrative rejects its role/status as a presenter of universal truth. It constantly emphasises that it is only a version of the truth, that all truth is narrative, and that there is very little distinction between reality and the narrative representation of reality. Mimetic realism, therefore, is not a favoured narrative style here. Instead we have an anti-mimetic mode. The reader is left unsure about the truth of what s/he has read. In a reversal of the Lawrence dictum, postmodern fiction suggests that one can trust neither the teller nor the tale!

(v) Irony is a favourite mode for postmodern novelists. There is also the irreverent tone, the apocalyptic vision, and black humour that plays an important role in postmodern fiction. Heller's *Catch 22*, Vonnegut's *Slaughterhouse Five* are examples of the black humour that satirises the "pity of war" and the Holocaust.

(vi) The postmodern novel is generally characterised by the presence of many narrative voices (polyphony). None of these are "reliable." Indeterminacy is a key feature of all postmodern texts. Child narrators, letters, notes, songs and cryptographic (literally, secret writing) subtexts undermine each other's narrative. The novel suggests that each of the voices functions and speaks for certain subjective positions and hence can deliver only particular or mini versions of the story, there is rarely a unifying grand narrative. Many meanings (from the many stories) fight for dominance (polyvalence). The postmodern novel celebrates this state of hermeneutic anarchy, where no meaning can be privileged over another. Andrew Gibson's notion of "*narrative laterality*" and Deleuze-Guattari's "*rhizome*" are attempts to formulate a poetics of such a multiplicity.

(vii) The absence of a "conclusion," and leaving the narrative open-ended without offering any solution/resolution is a characteristic feature. For instance, in Pynchon's *V* the novel gives no definite clue as to the exact nature of V. In *The Crying of Lot 49* we do not know (just as Oedipa Mass does not know) whether there really was/is a parallel secret postal service.

(viii)The postmodern narrative interrogates the notion of being, of subjectivity, rationality and logic. It celebrates irrationality, indeterminacy, temporality (impermanence). It delivers images rather than truths (as noted above).

Postmodern Architecture: Postmodern architecture was a revolt against the "International Style" popularised by architects such as Le Corbusier, Maison Citrohan (characterised by an insistence on low cost, clarity of structure rationalised and standardised architecture, preoccupation with functionalist use of space, and strictly non-decorative where "ornament was crime"). Robert Venturi, Robert Stern and Charles Moore initiated postmodern architecture. Charles Jencks provided the theoretical discussion and elaboration of postmodernism in architecture, though Joseph Hudnut first applied the term post-modern to architecture in 1949. Jencks suggested that postmodern architecture was informed by a "double coding": (a) it addresses the architecturally minded with its experimentation and (b) the public at large, the inhabitants who are more concerned about comfort and function. Jencks was thus suggesting a conscious architectural irony. Postmodern architecture has the following characteristics:

(i) Architecture is now conceived as a literal language, it encodes parts of the body, the outlines of animal forms and other physical features into the building.

(ii) A deconstructive architectural style is visible in the 1980s and 90s in the work of Peter Eisenman, Frank Gehry, Coop Himmelblau. Here exaggerated perspective, ambiguous spacing, idiosyncratic meeting (corners) of walls, unclear boundaries play an important role. It adopts aesthetics of fragmentation. Structure and ornamentation collide in these buildings in the excessive use of promenades, the uncertain distinction between interior and exterior (notably in the work of Bernard Tschumi. It is interesting note that chief practitioners of deconstructive architecture Tschumi and Eisenman have both collaborated with Jacques Derrida. For an interesting account of deconstruction in architecture, see Andreas Papadakis, ed., *Deconstruction in Architecture*, 1988).

(iii) There is a celebration of the spectacle. There is heightened theatricality, and strives for a disorienting effect. There is playfulness, functionalism and the fantastic mixing in the same "space."

(iv) It uses a large variety of styles and traditions. Classicism and popular forms jostle here.

(v) Numerous "collections" are displayed, but not as historically significant objects. The subjects are selected merely for their aesthetic interest.

(vi) Normal categories of time and space are called into question. Irrationality is the key here, where the logic of everyday life, functionalism and mere ornamentation are squeezed together into a schizophrenic mixture.

(vii) It parodies earlier forms and styles. For example, the need to communicate meaning through form is exaggerated. Buried faces, bodies are insinuated into designs here.

(viii) The everyday and the common become part of the environment. It mixes, as Venturi described it, the sacred and the profane.

Postmodernism in the Visual Arts, Sculpture and Design: The best surveys to date on the postmodern trend in the visual art, sculpture and designs are David Britt's *Modern Art: Impressionism to Post-Modernism* (1989) and Arthur Danto's *After the End of Art* (1997). With the 1960s, new forms of visual art emerged. These included *pattern painting* (Brad Davis and Cynthia Carlson), *Neo-Expressionism* (Susan Rothenberg, Georg Baselitz and Julian Schnabel), *Neo-Geo* (Ashley Bickerton, Jeff Koons), *New British*

Sculpture (Julian Opie, Tony Cragg), *Super-Realism* (Richard Estes, Michael Gorman). The most influential theorist of postmodernism in the visual arts is Craig Owens whose essays in the journal *October* formulated a detailed study of the postmodern turn. Owens suggests that the postmodern visual art forms returned to the allegorical mode. Owens identifies the following features of postmodern visual art:

(i) Appropriation: The multiple reproduction of images where the uniqueness of the artefact is undermined. Thus reproduction of the images challenges the notion of the unique or speciality of the work of art. Artists, writes Owens in a crucial observation, generate images through the reproduction of other images.

(ii) Site-specificity: where the environment of the work of art is elaborately defined and created. This emphasises the *local* and *present* context of the artefact rather than any timeless or universal status of the same.

(iii) Impermanence: The use of perishable materials (for instance, earth and mud, vegetables) and themes of a purely temporary nature. Once again, this undermines the artefact's claim to permanent fame or universality.

(iv) Agglomeration: The use of repetitive logic, the sequential nature of images. This means that fragments are accumulated. The daily, the mundane and the ordinary are invested with great symbolic significance.

(v) Discursivity: The link and the interdependency of the visual and the verbal. Frequently termed conceptual art (notably in the work of Lawrence Weiner), this mode treats the visual artefact as a script to be deciphered and the text as a visual design. The two are meant to complement each other in a reciprocal relationship.

(vi) Hybridisation: The use of many diverse and apparently incompatible materials, genres, styles and modes. Thus broken crockery, newspaper bits, vegetables and paint figure in the same artefact. This is also related to the term "*kitsch*" which refers to the use of apparently useless objects and rubbish as/to make artefacts. For instance the use of garbage, old newspapers, plastic wrappings, even toiletries as art forms constitute kitsch. This is the extreme from of the *anti-aesthetics* of postmodernism.

The characteristics of postmodern visual art, sculpture, plastic art and designs may be summarised as follows:

(i) Incompatible styles are a favourite device. Classical "clean" images boundaries and the fragmented modern aesthetic style are used simultaneously. It does not respect traditional forms, and prefers a playful attitude towards the process of creativity itself. Art is not the sacred space or the supreme creation anymore.

(ii) The use of the vernacular and slang in art. This rejects the distinction between high/elite and low/popular art when the artists adopt the style, language of the masses.

(iii) The celebration of colours, the excessive use of ornamentation, and the exuberance of both geometric and non-geometric shapes.

(iv) A streak of narcissism and highly subjective strain is present. This combines with the ironic and the objective in the *same* artefact.

(v) An increased use of the technological media (videos, digital images) and electronics.

(vi) The body returns as a central artefact (body art, tattoos, piercing are examples).

(vii) "Open" artefacts where the object is made deliberately accessible to the elements (wind, ageing, people passing by) to suggest the continual re-formation of the art object.

(viii) Use of anti-functional devices—garish colours, sharp angles, projections, and rough texture.

(ix) The emphasis on privacy and individual use of goods rather than products for the masses (especially in furniture and cutlery/crockery). Perhaps the stress and demand for the "exclusive" is part of the postmodern redefinition of necessity and fashion.

(x) The interactive artefact, where the spectator is not kept away from the art object. The art object is not a sacrosanct object anymore, but opens to touch and views.

(xi) The prevalence of "*Schlock.*" Schlock is the term used to describe the trivia that function as memorabilia in our lives. The schlock item has rarely any functional use. The toy dog hanging in the car, the stickers in the car window, the toy models, the wood/plastic/metal artefacts that constitute much gift exchange today all classify as schlock.

Postmodernism and Popular Culture: The arrival of rock music, MTV, films such as Ridley Scott's *Blade Runner* (based on the 1968 novel *Do Androids Dream of Electric Sheep?* by Philip Dick) has created a whole postmodern popular culture (for a discussion of cyborgs, cybernetics, virtual reality and the arts, see the appendix on "*Technocriticism*"). In fact Andreas Huyssen agues that pop music is "the context in which a notion of the postmodern first took shape." Simon Frith argues that popular music is crucial to our understanding of contemporary culture because here the effect on emotions is tremendous. Peer pressure, groupism and anti-hegemonic moves may be located and traced to pop music. Dick Hebdige terms these new forms of cultures, produced by marginalised groups, "*subcultures.*" These subcultures evaded the hegemony imposed by the "high" cultural forms. It marks a strategic reversal: from "being under scrutiny into the pleasure of being watched." Thus the emergence of popular and subcultures altered power structures and social formations, leaving the society and art forms in a state of permanent evolution and change where no form/style occupies any privileged position. (The emergence of punk rock is a case in point. Subcultures also get co-opted into mainstream culture. Punk remained essentially a *white* subculture. The New York based "Riot Grrrls" was a group that sought to combine punk rock with feminism. And yet, a streak of elitism permeated even this subculture within subculture, when the race issue was never resolved even in this new attempt to radicalise in egalitarian fashion the challenge to "high culture" [I am indebted to Sara Valentine, programme curator and perfomer, for her insights into punk rock and Riot Grrrls.]). Popular culture and popular music may be characterised as follows.

(i) The recycling of traditional styles, songs, forms. Folk tunes, other cultural forms—classicism, jazz and such varied styles/

forms combine (fusion music, where eastern and Western styles mix). Rap, rock'n'roll, beat, progressive rock are styles that have developed and held sway in this category of popular music.

(ii) The use of certain specific modes (this is common to popular music and postmodern literary techniques. See section on postmodern literature) in the recycling: *pastiche* and *parody*. Pastiche is a technique where genres are mixed and boundaries between the various arts are dissolved. Parody, on the other hand, is a work in the same genre, following the conventions of the genre but only to subvert it. The principal difference is thus the wide-ranging, intergeneric nature of pastiche and the subversion within the genre in parody.

(iii) A condition of "*autoreferentiality*" where the cultural form refers to the manner of its own composition (self-reflexive), and suggests that its significance is local, present and immediate. Thus plagiarism, authenticity and copying lose their derogatory connotation. In pop music borrowings, echoes and cut-and-paste modes are accepted forms. Indeed the artist deliberately calls attention to her/his sources and acknowledges the borrowings.

(iv) There is the large-scale use of technology. The work of art features itself as a part of this simulated reality ("live music," for instance).

(v) The emphasis is on style, spectacle and presentation rather than substance. Thus we have the image making of the stars and their transformation into cult figures, (Madonna and Michael Jackson to name two cult figures of pop), the extensive publicity, use of colourful and vibrant visuals through the widespread use of technological devices (large screens in stadia, for example), the marketing of memorabilia and artefacts (medallions, T-shirts and jewellery that carry portraits/pictures of the stars), the live mass performances, the appeal to the "natural" and the uninhibited in individuals, the suggestion that "image is everything" (as the always-in-the-news tennis star Andre Agassi announced), and the emphasis on the rebellious and anti-traditional nature of this art.

(vi) Camp: This emerged primarily as the culture of the minorities, ethnic or select groups. It refers mostly to homosexuals and sexually marginalised groups. Camp culture also refers to groups like those of the dandies, the declassed intellectuals, transvestites. Crossdressing, dandyism, male dancing, streaking are examples. Camp seeks to value and even valorise objects that have been traditionally despised. A taste, style, manner or habit that is conventionally rejected as "bad taste" by high culture is cultivated as a cult and private "language" by select groups. Camp is thus a prime example of the counterculture facet of postmodernism.

Postmodernism and Politics: The work of thinkers like Zygmunt Bauman, Ulrich Beck, Jurgen Habermas and Richard Rorty has enormous implications for politics in the postmodern world. Agnes Heller and Ferenc Feher's *The Postmodern Political Condition* (1988) is a useful description of the condition of politics in the post-Lyotardian world. There is the prevalence of the functional over the structural and the gradual weakening of a politics based solely on class interests. Postmodern politics has movements that are single-issue actions and oriented towards the elimination of a single function of modernity. That is, these movements are more narrowly focussed, and are completely functionalist. There are attempts at reordering the given network of functions in a particular society. These are again purely functionalist and cannot be seen or explained simply in terms of class conflict (the examples are of the Thatcherite "popular capitalism" and the radical left's 1968 "rebellion" in Paris). Postmodernity's "presentism" excludes attempts at transcendence. It rejects any kind of Utopianism that is aimed at the future. It reduces history to mere temporality. There is also the "recycling of theories" (or political solutions) in postmodern politics. It seeks to repossess and rework all histories. Postmodern politics also accepts the plurality of cultures and discourses. Various ethnic, religious, linguistic, local identities jostle for expressive and political space here, since postmodernism has announced the end of a unifying grand narrative. This may move between absolute cultural relativism and the inauthentic valorisation of the Other. There is a streak of "holistic anti-universalism" and anti-humanism. By denying that humanity has a common origin/history, postmodern politics suggests that "humankind" cannot be a category for concerted political action. The collapse of the grand narrative of secularisation has inaugurated the proliferation of widely pluralistic religious revival of versions of "established" religion and religious fundamentalism. There is also the reconceptualisation of the state as merely an extension of certain class interests. Postmodern politics are also irrational and unpredictable. With a constant interrogation of the nation-state, the irrational element of postmodern politics comes to be emphasised. For instance, with the debate moving away from the "national interest" (which, during modernity, elided ethnic, linguistic differences in the stress on the unified nation-state), the ethnicity component has been revived and become the source of conflict. The role of social movements such as environmentalism has become prominent in postmodern politics. Politics is thus no longer the province of classes or political parties. Thus Anthony Giddens in *Beyond Left and Right* suggests that the future politics—which he terms a "politics of life chances"—will be in the domain of the New Social Movements. Ulrich Beck argues in *The Reinvention of Politics* that socio-political movements like the Greens abolish the distinction between private (domestic and a political) and public (political) because every individual is forced to co-operate as a minor activist in order to save the earth. The total moral relativism of postmodernism also produces a new problem. Questions of judgement become difficult and criteria for such judgements become impossible to formulate. Thus even genocide, "ethnic cleansing" xenophobic nativism can all be accommodated within a postmodern politics simply because the moral relativism prevents classifying them as "evil." Zygmunt Bauman suggests that, in the postmodern condition, it is easy to acquire an identity, but difficult to retain it. Identity may be revoked at short notice, and is therefore completely contingent. Bauman vividly characterises postmodern life as "one lived in a city in which traffic is daily re-routed and street names are liable to be changed without short notice." One needs to be a vagrant or tourist in the postmodern condition. One is then physically close to the locals, but spiritually distant. This is the politics and ethics of contingency in postmodernity. Scott Lash and John Urry argue that Baudrillard's insistence on the implosion of the social into flat hyperreality denied the possibility of active resistance (Baudrillard had argued that forced silence for the masses in the media is "an original response in the form of a challenge"). Resistance, argue Lash and Urry, is dependent upon the coherence of certain identities, especially collective identities. If there are only images and simulation of identities, then there is no possibility of any collective action against the oppressive structures of power, argue Lash and Urry in an important turn in the debates within postmodern politics. Thinkers like Barbara Marshall and Susan Hekman interrogate the epistemological basis of modernism. Arguing from a feminist position, they retain a postmodern scepticism regarding a coherent subject. They also reject science as objective truth and the "universalising impulses of modernism" (Marshall).

Detraditionalisation: The notion of detraditionalisation is postmodern in its stress on the realignment of power structures. Paul Heelas (in *Detraditionalisation*, 1996) defines it as a "shift of authority from without to within. It entails the decline of belief in pre-given/natural order of things. Individual subjects are themselves called upon to exercise authority in the face of disorder and contingency." There are two principal approaches to detraditionalisation.

(i) The Radical Thesis, advocated by thinkers like John B. Thompson, suggests a past to present/future opposition. Detraditionalisation here involves *replacement* of the closed, ritualised, preordained, differentiated culture with open, contingent, risky, uncertain one. Traditional culture is seen as dominated by fate and excluding choices.

(ii) The Coexistence Thesis, advocated by thinkers like Timothy Luke, suggests that we cannot treat tradition as completely silencing autonomous voices. They recommend not an eradication of tradition but competing and interpenetrating. They argue that tradition-preservation always faces conflicting demands. There is always the co-existence of such opposing positions, and therefore the chances of rejuvenation.

IV Relationship with Other Disciplines

This has been already anticipated in the sections detailed above. Postmodernism has influenced disciplines like geography (Edward

Soja), International Relations (James Der Derian), sociology (Zygmunt Bauman, Anthony Giddens), law (Mary Joe Frug), ethnography (James Clifford, Stephen Tyler), and politics, ethics and identity (John Urry, Scott Lash). Postmodernism's emphasis on the local, marginal and the anti-foundational/anti-hegemonic has also helped the development of resistance theories and philosophies like gay/lesbian theory (see chapter on gay/lesbian theory below) and certain branches of feminism (notably in the area of epistemology and gender in the work of Susan Hekman). Sexual politics, cultural identity and postmodernism have found its best spokesman in Steven Seidman. Donna Harraway's work on cybernetics, gender and contemporary culture, and Katherine Hayles's writings on modern electronic technology, the new sciences (chaos theory) and literature reveal the influence of postmodern literary and cultural theories.

Further Reading

Docherty, Thomas, ed. *Postmodernism: A Reader*. Brighton: Harvester Wheatsheaf, 1993.

Hutcheon, Linda. *A Poetics of Postmodernism: History, Theory, Fiction*. London: Routledge, 1995.

Lucy, Niall. *Postmodern Literary Theory: An Introduction*. Oxford: Blackwell, 1997.

McRobbie, Angela. *Postmodernism and Popular Culture*. London: Routledge, 1994.

Wheale, Nigel. *The Postmodern Arts: An Introductory Reader*. London: Routledge, 1995.

Woods, Tim. *Beginning Postmodernism*. Manchester: Manchester University Press, 1999.

Chapter Nine

Lesbian and Gay Theories

Lesbian and gay theory and literary studies are closely linked to Black Aesthetics in terms of origins: both emerge primarily as political and social movements. Literary theories in the past have focused on issues of gender, race, class and nationality. However, in literary theory's emphasis on centring the marginalised (women, lower classes), there has been a curious silence on the matter of non-heterosexual relations, and those with sexual preference "outside" the heterosexual norm. Heterosexuality, as the above statement indicates, has been treated as the "norm" and homosexuality or same-sex bonds have been treated as deviant, perversion, and even criminal. The AIDs scare of the 1980s and 1990s has added a medico-legal angle to the issue, where the heterosexual norm is now able to see homosexuality as a threat and sickness-inducing "condition." The victimisation of the homosexual community over the centuries (a well documented fact, as the work of Michel Foucault, John D'Emilio, Lillian Faderman, Alan Bray, David Halperin and numerous others demonstrate) has meant that homosexual literature has never been part of the canon. Writers with homosexual tendencies could not express the same in their writings. And politically, the community of gays and lesbians was marginalised. Socially they were mocked, harassed and victimised. Gay and lesbian theory that emerges as a substantial body of work in the 1990s derived its sources in certain literary themes and ancient myths (such as Sappho's). Politically, the "coming out" of the gay/lesbian (a public acknowledgement of their sexual preferences, and the affiliation with the gay/lesbian community) has helped launch movements and organisations like the Gay Liberation Movement (GLF), Gay Activists Alliance (GAA), AIDS Coalition to Unleash Power (ACT UP) and the Mattachine Society. In terms of academics, there is now an M.A. programme in "Sexual Dissidence and Cultural Change" at the University of Sussex (run by Alan Sinfield), and centres like the Centre for Lesbian and Gay Studies at the CUNY. As in the case of Black aesthetics, gay and lesbian theories (like feminism before it) must be seen as the academic arm of the political gay liberation movement.

I Background and Origins

It is important to note that gay and lesbian theory begins in a social movement. The Stonewall Riots of 1969 may be described as the point of origin of the gay liberation movement. The riots broke out when police raided the Stonewall Tavern in New York City. Many gays, lesbians, transvestites fought back. The subsequent battles and riots received wide publicity. The first meeting of the British Gay Liberation Front took place at the London School of Economics on Nov 13, 1970, and the first Annual Gay Pride march on April 1, 1972. Since then, the gay liberation movement has sought to fight social, legal, medical and religious oppression and tried to locate a whole new cultural space for the thus far marginalised community. In the U.S., the lesbian and gay lobby was among the top fund raisers for President Bill Clinton's campaign in 1992. The founding of societies (listed above), furthered the cause of the gays and lesbians, and provided fora for political action. The history of male homosexuality is better documented than lesbianism.

The public antagonism to gays, the extraordinary life of Oscar Wilde (and his subsequent trial) in the nineteenth century, and the legal-religious rejection of the non-heterosexual norm meant that homosexuality was not something one admitted to in public life. It was literally a life in the closet (the closet becomes a crucial image in later gay writing and theory). The two wars of the twentieth century enabled numerous young men to discover their sexual preferences. A rereading of classic authors like Walt Whitman and nineteenth century ones like Edward Carpenter, the rise of overtly homosexual pop stars (Jasper Johns, Robert Rauschenberg, Andy Warhol), Hollywood stars (Rock Hudson), the poetry of W.H. Auden, the fiction of E.M. Forster, the plays of John Osborne (especially *A Patriot for Me*) in the 1950s and 60s suggested an alternate culture to the elitist, heterosexual one. Writers and critics began to detect homophobia (fear of homosexuality and homosexuals) in certain authors like Tennessee Williams. In the 1960s, pornography, including same-sex pornography, became more easily available. The journal *College English* brought out a special issue on gay writing and politics in 1974. The publication of Foucault's *The History of Sexuality* and the rise of feminist theory were also significant moments in the development of gay/lesbian theory. In the 1990s, the approaches included the racial aspect of homosexuality. Thus, homosexuality and the experience of immigrants, blacks, "border people" (such as those on the Mexican-U.S. border) began to be studied. The writing of Audre Lorde, Gloria Anzaldua, James Baldwin and Cherrie Moraga became significant texts. The plays of Tony Kushner, the fiction of Sarah Schulman and Edmund White, and the critical work of Steven Seidman and Lee Edelman sought to situate the AIDS crisis and its effects on homosexuals.

In feminism the radical feminists formed a new category, the *radicalesbians*. They argued that feminism was inherently heterosexual and never spoke of or even acknowledged the status of the lesbian woman. Thus (argue the radicalesbians) even feminist women suffer from homophobia. The radicalesbians collective suggested that lesbianism was the true reversal of patriarchy with its "woman identified woman" (also the title of their 1970 manifesto). The radicalesbians thus suggested a separatism. The work of Adrienne Rich, Judy Grahn, and theorists like Bonnie Zimmerman, Teresa de Lauretis, Judith Butler became important moments in the development of lesbian theory. A revaluation of earlier writers like Emily Dickinson, Gertrude Stein, Virginia Woolf, the explicitly lesbian work of Radclyffe Hall combined with the race-sexuality issue in lesbian theory. Lillian Faderman's classic *Surpassing the Love of Men* (1979) studies the development of a "*romantic friendship*" between women as seen in texts from the Renaissance to the present. In the 1990s "*Queer Theory*" combines a sociological, epistemological and historical mode of inquiry.

Since gay/lesbian theory is a relatively new area in critical theory, the "canon" of texts is still growing. Individual thinkers have produced single or maybe two influential works, but these are yet to coalesce into a whole "bibliography" by them. Thus the later discussion will necessarily be sketchy, outlining the central issues in gay/lesbian theory. Judith Butler, Jeffrey Weeks, Eve Sedgwick, Mary McIntosh, D.A. Miller, Ken Plummer, Diana Fuss, Adrienne Rich, and developments like Queer Theory, radicalesbianism, social constructionism will figure here.

II Assumptions and General Methods

Gay and lesbian theory assumes that sexuality plays a prominent role in the construction of social identity.

(1) The key assumption of gay/lesbian studies is best summed up thus in *The Lesbian and Gay Studies Reader* (1993): "lesbian/gay studies does for sex and sexuality what women's studies does for women." Here "[sexual orientation is] the fundamental category of analysis and understanding . . . informed by resistance to homophobia and heterosexism . . . and to the ideological and institutional practices of heterosexual privileges." Gay and lesbian studies suggests that the patriarchy which feminism contests is actually "*heteropatriarchy*" (Renee Hoogland's term). However, heteropatriarchy is not something feminism opposes because heterosexuality is taken as a given and natural. The gay finds some expression and acknowledgement in this discourse. But the lesbian is completely absent from the history (as noted in the introductory section). It is this invisibility that radicalesbians seek to understand and render visible.

(2) They argue, following Foucault, that the homosexual as a social category emerges essentially in the post-Renaissance. In the late nineteenth century several legal and medical texts speak of the homosexual as a deviant or a criminal, and homosexuality as a sickness and "condition." Homosexuality was seen merely as the dark Other of heterosexuality. The binary gender hierarchy of male/female is based upon the unquestioned assumption of a "natural" heterosexuality. Gender is always "*heterogender*" (Chris Ingraham), "the asymmetric stratification of the sexes in relation to the institution of patriarchal heterosexuality." Thus all sociological studies (even feminist ones) of gender relations in society rely upon what Chrys Ingraham famously termed "*the*

heterosexual imaginary." The heterosexual imaginary is "a way of thinking which conceals the operation of heterosexuality in structuring gender and closes off any critical analysis of heterosexuality as an organising institution." Heterosexuality is thus taken for granted. What is needed is an analysis of the material conditions (economic resources, cultural control) of *capitalist patriarchy that are linked to institutionalised heterosexuality*.

(3) Gay historians trace homosexuality back to the Greeks (especially well documented in K.J. Dover's 1978 work *Greek Homosexuality*). Thinkers and historians like Bernard Sergent read certain myths and rituals, especially those associated with Dionysus, as reflecting male-male desire. These historians are particularly careful to draw out evidence of "sexual dissidence" and social oppressive practices that kept homosexuality under wraps, or condemned it (and homosexuals) to fiendish tortures and execution. They try to trace the manner and context in which the homosexual retreats into the "closet." Like the feminist literary (and non-literary) historiographers, gay and lesbian historians seek to discover the gay tradition. Martin Duberman et al's *Hidden from History: Reclaiming the Gay and Lesbian Past* (1989) is an example of such a history.

(4) Social constructionist theorists like Jeffrey Weeks argue that homosexuality emerges as a discourse in the nineteenth century. Legal, medical and psychological studies and legislation were important instruments in their construction. Lesbian historiographers like Lillian Faderman likewise argue that the stigmatisation and victimisation of lesbianism begins primarily in the nineteenth century. Urbanisation, with its proliferation of clubhouses and meeting places, was an important factor in the formation of the "modern homosexual," according to the social constructivists.

(5) Lesbian theorists argue that even heterosexual women exhibit a certain fear (homophobia) of lesbianism. That is, even the feminist critiques of patriarchy are informed by an acceptance of heterosexuality as the standard, and homosexuality/lesbianism as a deviation (summed up in Adrienne Rich's 1979 essay "Compulsory Heterosexuality and Lesbian Existence"). Lesbi-

ans were seen as monsters or unnatural. They argue further that it is homophobia that remains at the root of all gender relations. The argument of the lesbian feminists is that the feminist movement so far has assumed heterosexuality to be the universal condition of *all* women. Moreover, the experience of the white, middle-class, urban woman was the "standard" subject of analysis. Lesbian feminists thus emphasise the need for accommodation of differences within a feminist practice: the difference of class, race, culture *and* sexual orientation.

(6) The real solution to the problem of patriarchy is lesbianism, for it rejects all forms of patriarchy. As Jill Johnston put it in *Lesbian Nation* (1973): "Feminism at heart is a massive complaint. Lesbianism is the solution." Radicalesbians suggest that lesbianism is as much a political identity as a sexual one. The rejection of heterosexuality is necessary to overturn patriarchy. The radicalesbian arguments may be summed up thus.

(i) They argue that the "malestream" conceptual framework, and even the *mainstream feminist* one, is built on the ideology of "sameness" (for an elaboration of the idea, see Luce Irigaray in the chapter on feminism). This is what Irigaray terms "*ho(m)mosexuality*"—a term that plays on the French *homme* (meaning man) and the Greek *homos* (meaning same). Ho(m)mosexuality thus suggests the economy of the same, where the female Other merely functions as the *object* of male exchange. Lesbianism represents a mode of psychosexual Otherness.

(ii) The radicalesbians argue that the gay males at least enjoy a certain cultural position as "prohibited objects" (Butler). Lesbian sexuality, on the other hand, is simply invisible, erased from the discussion and the social sphere. Lesbianism is not even a part of the discourse or the imagination. The lesbian is thus the "unthinkable." Malestream culture seeks to eradicate the threat of lesbianism by turning it into a titillating spectacle to be incorporated within the myth of masculinity.

(iii) Even mainstream feminism does not want to encourage or acknowledge the Otherness of lesbianism. Lesbianism is thus a spectre, a derivative figure, and a negative presence within the system of gendered heterosexuality. The Otherness of the lesbian is never admitted here. The lesbian is not recognised in either the dominant/masculinist discourse or the nondominant/feminist one. The "unthinkable" is outside the conceptual boundaries of the "straight mind" (Monique Wittig's term). The separatism of the radicalesbians has remained a controversial position within feminism. The lesbian epistemological subject thus seeks and threatens to undo the feminist theories based on a simple binary notion of sexual difference and the "heterosexual teleology" (the idea of means and ends, of purposes of being/existence and goals).

(7) Significantly, some lesbian studies have suggested that the woman-woman bond need not always be sexual. The concept of the "*lesbian continuum*" (Adrienne Rich) is a term that seeks to incorporate within itself the whole range of woman-woman relations: mutual help networks, camaraderie, woman's institutions, female friendships that are not necessarily sexual in nature. However, thinkers like Pauline Palmer oppose this "desexualising" of lesbianism, arguing that the *lesbian sexual experience* is and must remain the cornerstone of lesbianism.

(8) Increasingly, lesbian theory has found affinities with gay activists and thinkers rather than with other feminists. Here the debate is between the choice of *gender* (male/female) and *sexuality* (homosexuality/heterosexuality) as categories of political alliances and action.

   (i) If the emphasis is on *gender* as category then all women—homo- or heterosexual—are unified under one head, and opposed to patriarchy.

   (ii) If *sexuality* is the category, then the sexual preference unites both males and females, by their commonality of sexual preferences (homosexuality), against heterosexuality. Here gay and lesbian thinkers are aligned not on gender lines but along the axis of sexuality and sexual preferences.

   The affinity is the result of their identification of the other equally (sexually) marginalised from the emancipatory discourses. The result of this alliance is what is now termed Queer theory, or "*libertarian lesbianism*" (Pauline Palmer).

(9) Gays and lesbians locate an artistic and creative impulse in the particularity of their sexualities. Marginalisation, victimisation and the state of "hiding" are central themes in their work. Later theorists such as Diana Fuss and Judith Butler pay close attention to the state of "coming out" in gays and lesbians.

(10) The use of poststructuralism by queer theorists like Butler, Edelman and Fuss enables gay/lesbian theory to problematise issues of identity, marginality, authenticity and epistemology. There is an emphasis on the social context of identity. Queer theory rejects an "essentialism" of identity politics, and the binary opposition of heterosexual/homosexual in favour of a more fluid, and impermanent nature of the same (see section on Butler below).

(11) Queer theory is, as suggested above, an interdisciplinary approach to the issue of sexuality. Queer theory argues that gay/lesbian culture is a "*subculture*," which has the potential for effecting social changes. Queer theory also suggests the possibilities of political change, where gay/lesbian identities find a voice.

(12) The racial and class inflections to sexuality are also explored in the gay/lesbian theories of the 1990s. The crisis of immigrants, the Blacks and other marginalised groups are read against the experiences of the white homosexuals. The assumption here is that gay/lesbian individuals of, say, the economically disadvantaged working class Asian-immigrant population, are doubly marginalised: by the white race for being the racial Other, and within their own community for being not-heterosexual.

(13) Gay/lesbian theorists now seek to frame an alternative canon to the heterosexual one. Thus we have the retrieval of authors like Oscar Wilde, Walt Whitman, Virginia Woolf, Vita-Sackville West and Radclyffe Hall. There is also the attempt to incorporate into the gay/lesbian canon a multiplicity of racial and cultural variations—Jewish, Black, Mexican-American, Asian immigrants in the West—in the literary manifestation of homo-

sexuality. Thus non-white writers like Gloria Anzaldua, Audre Lorde, Firdous Kanga, Hanif Qureshi, find places beside Tony Kushner, Sarah Schulman, E.M. Forster and Randall Kenan. A similar work to anthologise gay/lesbian writing is taking place in other countries. The seminal volume, Hoshang Merchant's (ed.) *Yaraana: Gay Writing from India* (1999), is an important move in this direction.

(14) In addition to framing a homosexual canon, gay/lesbian theorists detect a veiled homosexual thematic in apparently heterosexual works. "Woman's friendship" (the title of Janet Todd's magnificent work on the area) and male bonding are located within classics such as *Jane Eyre*. As an extension, they also detect the homophobic tendencies in classic literary works.

(15) Gay/lesbian theory emphasises the liminal nature of identity. They stress the gay/lesbian identity as a "crossing-over" (with the evident parallel from transvestitism). Thus Robert McRuer analyses the borderfigure of the gay as one similar to the cultural "*mestiza*" (the term for "bordercrosser," in terms of the Mexican-American border) in the writings of Gloria Anzaldua. This hybrid and liminal nature of the gay/lesbian prevents an essentialist, unified or stable identity.

III Key Concepts and Thinkers

Gay/lesbian studies in the 1980s and 90s cover a range of areas: narrative theory, feminism, sociology, politics and activism, film studies and epistemology.

D.A. Miller: Miller's work on narrative and Western culture in *The Novel and the Police* (1988) and *Bringing Out Roland Barthes* (1992) is an important development in gay studies.

(i) Miller suggests that gays and lesbians have been excluded from the story of Western culture itself.

(ii) Western culture relies upon the myth of the Oedipal family and love leading to marriage.

(iii) Such a culture relies upon the "myth of life processes." By this Miller means the anchoring of cultural institutions of heterosexuality in a certain idea of the sexual. This idea suggests that the sexual is only biological reproduction. Naturally, with this overarching idea, non-reproductive sexuality—such as gay or lesbian—is rejected. Miller suggests that the "facts" of biology thus automatically valorise heterosexuality.

(iv) Further, the Western notion of the individual's progress through the cycle of love-marriage-family is the "*hetero-narrative*" which is based on the idea of the (biologically) reproductive nature of all sexuality and sexual relations. This results in the complete absence of the homosexual in the hetero-narrative of Western culture. Miller thus suggests a basic incompatibility between homosexuality and narrative itself.

(v) Miller suggests that the gay writing is fundamentally derivative for the above reasons. Stressing on narrative form rather than narrative content, Miler argues that what is needed is an "authentic" gay fabulation, "a series of experiments needing to tamper with the most deeply imprinted aspects of narrative form." Miller terms this *the novelesque*, a denaturalisation of the hetero-narrative. In the novelesque larger fictional structures like plot or character are abandoned in favour of small effects. The incident is privileged over plot, gesture is emphasised rather than character. The novelesque is the gay attempt to interrogate the so-called "naturalness" of narrative form.

Judith Butler: In *Gender Trouble* (1990) and *Bodies that Matter* (1993), Butler has consistently interrogated the notion of identity. Adapting Freud, feminism, Lacan and poststructuralism, Butler's work has focussed on the modes of representation of gay/lesbian identity and the idea of difference.

(i) Butler argues that "lesbian" becomes yet another sign that recolonises the (woman) subject. She states that she is "permanently troubled by identity categories" seeing them as "sites of necessary trouble." Butler argues that such identity categories tend to cohere into forms of control and regimentation. One needs therefore to use these identities/sites as rallying points for resistance (especially political) but remain vigilant that these same sites do become "regulatory imperatives."

(ii) Butler suggests that the issue is not of avowing or disavowing the category of gay or lesbian. Does avowing, asks Butler, imply a prior set of disavowals? Butler suggests that one needs to specify what "coming out" and such loose terms imply. If sexuality is to be disclosed, one may need to specify the true determinant of the meaning of sexuality itself: whether it means anatomy, the actual act, the phantasy structure, or the gender. Extending the argument, Butler asks: what exactly does lesbian theory seek to elucidate—the *specificity* of lesbian *experience*, lesbian *desire* or lesbian *sexuality*.

(iii) Butler argues that there is no causal or expressive connections between sex, gender, gender presentation, sexual practice, fantasy and sexuality. None of these terms "captures" the others.

(iv) Butler argues that lesbian sexuality is a process that reinscribes the power domain it resists. That is, lesbian sexuality is itself constituted partly from a heterosexual matrix. Therefore the specificity of lesbian sexuality has to be established not outside, but within the modalities of the discourse.

(v) Further, the so-called derivative nature of lesbian sexuality, where lesbianism is seen as bad copy of the original, can itself be reworked. One can demonstrate how heterosexuality that sees itself as the origin is itself composed of the Otherness of homosexuality. Thus the whole equation of original/ heterosexual and copy/homosexual can be displaced. This is the main argument in Butler, as we shall now see.

(vi) Identity is a switching of roles. Identity is not closed, stable or unitary thing which is separate from an Other. The Self and the Other are not mutually distinct species. Butler suggests that the Self emerges only with a separation. To deal with this loss, the Self retains the Other through a "melancholic incorporation." The Other is thus installed in the Self to attain a self-identity. The Self thus contains the Other within it. Without the disruption of the Other inside there would be no Self. This argument that suggests the insertion of the Other into the Self is extended to the gay/lesbian identity. The term "queer" which may be produced due to homophobia may itself be cited as the discursive basis of opposition. The citation/repetition of the queer identity may be used to destabilise the very discourse of heterosexuality. Identities thus escape the terms. The repetition of the terms "we" or "I" cannot be either summarily rejected nor can they be followed scrupulously. Butler is here suggesting an *aporetic* condition where one needs to both reaffirm and reject the identity "queer," as both acceptance of a certain subject-position and as the site of prospective resistance. A "citing" is also a "siting." One repeats (identities), but fails to repeat exactly (or "loyally," as Butler terms it).

(vii) Identity is constituted through a series of attempts to embody normative gender and sexual identities. The "injunction to be a given gender," the repetitions and parodies of the identity (male/female) in the form of drag thus reveal the "imitative structure of gender itself—as well as its contingency."

(viii) Butler argues for politics of "*dis*indentification." She describes this as "the uneasy sense of standing under a sign to which one does and does not belong." The failure of identification is itself the point of departure that respects internal difference. Thus to treat "'women' as a permanent site of contest . . . is to presume that there can be no closure on the category and that, for politically significant reasons there ought never to be."

(ix) There is no original or primary gender which is imitated (by, say, drag). Gender itself is a kind of imitation for which there is no original. Here *imitation creates the effect of the original.* What it imitates is the phantasy ideal of heterosexual identity. Heterosexuality is always the process of imitating its own idealisation, and *failing* in its imitation. Further, if homosexuality is not treated and constructed as the copy, there would be no way in which heterosexuality could see itself as original. Butler's argument thus comes to this: heterosexuality must *presuppose* homosexuality to construct itself. The inversion of the positions is very clear: for heterosexuality to state its original status, it needs to presuppose homosexuality. Thus, homosexuality is always present *within* the construction of heterosexuality itself, and unless the notion of the homosexual is spelt out there can be no "heterosexual" at all. Heterosexuality can no more see itself, or be seen, as cither pure or original, because the term/identity is constructed out of homosexuality. Butler's deconstructive argument thus reverses the hierarchy of priority and derivativeness.

(x) Heterosexuality is always the process of imitating its own idealisation, and *failing* in its imitation. Heterosexuality needs repetition, and repeated repetitions, to naturalise itself as original. Heterosexuality needs to elaborate itself because it fears being "undone." Heterosexuality is always afraid of its dependence upon homosexuality to construct itself.

(xi) Butler suggests that compulsory heterosexuality often presumes that there is first a sex, this sex is expressed through a gender, and then through a sexuality. But now we need to invert and displace this notion. Butler argues that the very categories of sex, sexual identity and gender are produced through the effects of the compulsory performance of sex.

(xii) Butler in *Bodies that Matter* recommends a *"critical queerness,"* a queerness that is both critically necessary and critical of itself. This queerness foregrounds and undermines identities. The term is necessarily overlapping: "the younger generation who want to resist the more institutionalised and reformist politics sometimes signifies by 'lesbian and gay'; . . . the predominantly white movement that has not fully addressed the way in which the 'queer' plays . . . within non-white communities; . . . a lesbian activism; . . . a false unity of women and men." Butler suggests that the use of the term must open up new possibilities for coalitional alliances that "do not presume that these constituencies are radically distinct form one another.

Eve Kosofsky Sedgwick: Sedgwick's *Epistemology of the Closet* (1991) was a pathbreaking work in the area of gay/lesbian studies. Sedgwick suggests that the relation between the known/unknown, explicit and implicit about homo/heterosexual definitions are revealing.

(1) Sedgwick argues that certain texts efface or render invisible their sexual charge in the form of gaps or silences. Silence here is as important as speech. The gaps in these texts are the points at which the discourse of the dichotomy of homo/ heterosexuality imposes a silence.

(2) Sedgwick argues that "coming out" is not a simple dichotomy. The term reflects the influence of the homosexual/heterosexual dichotomy on perceptions of public and private, secrecy and disclosure. Heterosexuality is the public face, homosexuality is restricted to the closet, a secretive and shameful act, forever threatened with disclosure. Degrees of hiding and openness co-exist in the same lives.

(3) Identity is necessarily a complex *mixture* of preferences, social and economic status and professional "roles" (on the "role" of homosexuals, see section on Mary McIntosh below). Sedgwick argues that forms of thought and knowledge in twentieth century Western culture are structured by "a chronic, now endemic crisis of homo/heterosexual definition . . . dating from the nineteenth century." Therefore any analysis of Western culture must incorporate an analysis of this definition.

(4) Sedgwick argues that homosexual practices come to mean differently in a society. Society insists that every individual, just as s/he occupies a particular gender, must also occupy one of the two categories of sexual orientation. This development around the late nineteenth century, meant that there was only the dichotomy of homo/heterosexual.

Sedgwick suggests the following axioms in the study of homosexuality. These axioms could become, suggests Sedgwick, the *informing principles* of the study.

(i) People are different from each other. Even identical (genital/sexual) acts mean different things for different people.

(ii) The study of sexuality is not coextensive with the study of gender. Anti-homophobic enquiry is not feminist enquiry.

(iii) There can't be an *a priori* decision about how far it will make sense to conceptualise lesbian/gay identities together or separately. This decision must necessarily be contingent.

(iv) The ritualised debates on nature versus nurture takes place against and within certain unstable assumptions and fantasies about both. There is no framework in which to ask about the origins and development of individual gay identity that is not already structured by an implicit Western project or fantasy of eradicating that identity.

(v) The historical search for a Great Paradigm Shift may obscure the present conditions of sexual identities.

(vi) The paths of *alloidentification* (Sedgwick's term for identification with/as the Other) is likely to be as "strange" as the one of *autoidentification*.

Mary McIntosh: McIntosh's classic essay "The Homosexual Role" (1968) suggested that the social labelling of persons as "deviant" operated a mechanism of social control.

(i) It helped to provide a "clear-cut, publicised, and recognisable threshold between permissible and impermissible behaviour." People were thus prevented from behaving in a "deviant" manner, for such an act would immediately elicit certain sanctions for being deviant.

(ii) It helped segregate deviants from others. The self-justifications for these deviant practices remained within the group. The bulk of the society was thus kept pure, because the "deviations" and "perverts" were segregated to be punished, despised. This meant that effectively, homosexuality and criminality attracted the same punishment form society.

McIntosh argues that the typology of people as homosexual (and as black, criminals, normal, white) helped polarise these groups. The homosexual must be seen as playing a social "*role*" rather than as having a condition. When a separate homosexual role is recognised, the society (and the homosexual) expect(s) the homosexual to be predominantly homosexual in his behaviour, attitudes and feelings. Expectations that he will be effeminate, that sexuality will play a part in his relations with other men, will also arise. Thus these *social* expectations will affect even the self-conception of the *homosexual individual* too. As McIntosh puts it, "the existence of a social expectation, of course, commonly helps to produce its own fulfilment."

Social Constructivism: The social constructivist reading of homosexuality is associated mainly with the work of those like Jonathan Katz, Jeffrey Weeks and Carroll Smith-Rosenberg.

(i) The social constructionist rejects the antithesis of sex and society. Sex is fundamentally social.

(ii) Heterosexuality and homosexuality are social and historical constructs. The idea that homosexual desire reveals a distinctive human type or identity or social .identity emerges in modern Western society (the influence of Foucault's work on sexuality is most visible here).

(iii) The social constructivists argue that homosexuals were made into some kind of ethnic minority. They seek, therefore, to analyse the social and material conditions that helped such an identity and status of the homosexual.

Jeffrey Weeks: Weeks' work, as noted above, is social constructionist. In works like *Coming Out* (1977) and *Sexualities and Its Discontents* (1985), Weeks suggested that it is no longer possible to talk of the universal history of homosexuality, for, as Weeks writes, the physical acts of homosexuality may be similar, but their social implications are different in different societies. The assumption is that "deviant" behaviour and sexual unorthodoxy is somehow inherent in the individual to which the social then *responds*. But the social actually *constructs* the deviance. The labelling of the homosexual as deviant is, in part, a construction of his/her homosexuality. Changing family norms, changing notions of childhood, of the role of parents have profound effects in the construction of the individual homosexual. Thus the emphasis on reproductive sex, the insistence on marriage, the laws against sodomy are factors that have to be seen as effecting changes in the social identity of the homosexual. That is, social categorisation may shape the experience of the homosexual in terms of the responses. What we need to do is to trace the various stages in the social stigmatisation of homosexuality and the individual and collective responses to this stigmatisation. Thus identities of the homosexual must be explored in terms of social specificities like class and gender. As Weeks sums it up, "the striking feature of the 'history of homosexuality' over the past hundred years or so is that the oppressive definition and the defensive identities and structures have marched together. Control of sexual variations has invariably reinforced and reshaped rather than repressed homosexual behaviour." Thus there has been individual anxiety and induced guilt, but there is also a social history of resistance and self-definition.

Diana Fuss: Fuss deconstructs the inside/outside opposition, where the inside stands for the heterosexual norm and the outsized is the realm of the homosexual (who is "outside the norm, is paradoxically closeted—inside—and needs to come out).

(i) Heterosexuality defines itself in opposition to what it is not—homosexuality.

(ii) Gay and lesbian theory interrogates the modes by which sexual boundaries of the inside and outside are constructed, sexual identities assigned and sexual politics formulated.

(iii) Language and law regulates the establishment of heterosexuality as both a practice and a system. It is the language of defence and protection: heterosexuality secures itself against the intrusion of the homosexual contaminant.

(iv) The homosexual is the excluded. However, the oppositional logic of the binary means that the Other/excluded is part of the inside. The exclusion can only be constructed in terms of the Other.

(v) The outside, suggests Fuss, is formulated as a consequence of the internal lack of the heterosexual. To protect against the recognition of the lack within itself, the self erects boundaries against an Other which is *made to represent this lack*. The homosexual is thus the ghost that haunts the heterosexual.

(vi) The paradox is that the first appearance of the homosexual as a "species" (in the nineteenth century) is also the moment when s/he disappears into the closet. The first coming out was also the first closeting.

Ken Plummer: Plummer's work adapts symbolic interactionism to analyse homosexuality. Plummer argues that homosexuality may be condition, but it cannot be considered in isolation from the reactions of society that stigmatises it. Hostile reactions that surround homosexuality and inhibit it may induce a homosexual "pathology." Homosexuality is thus a *process*, a role that something one adopts or drops depending upon the reactions of the society surrounding it. The issue one needs to address is: "under what conditions are homosexual roles adopted, sustained and stabilised?" Plummer identifies four "problem stages" in becoming a homosexual.

(i) Sensitisation: The child coming to perceive himself as "not like other men," the sense of "differentness" is the period of sensitisation. The reactions of peers, family and the social in general also sensitise the boy to his "condition." The *social* experiences create a potential base for a subsequent *sexual* interpretation. The boy incorporates the reactions into his own self-conceptions ("I am like this"), and translates it into sexual expression.

(ii) Signification and Disorientation: The process of coming out, the realisation of sexuality, the anxiety surrounding the realisation. It brings home the *significance* of the homosexual experience. Problems of reconciliation, access (to the gay community and other homosexuals), family acceptance will now trouble the young homosexual. Certain isolation takes place when the individual worries about the discovery.

(iii) Coming Out: The acknowledgement of his homosexuality and the exploration of the homosexual *community*.

Lesbian Feminism, the Lesbian Continuum and the Radicalesbians

(i) Lesbian feminism emerged with the recognition of the fact that classic feminism treated the sexual experience of all women as inevitably heterosexual. Thus there was no scope for female-female relations (sexual or otherwise) in this feminism. Also, there was no reference to the non-white woman's experiences. The stress on *difference* marks the rise of both black feminism (see chapter on Black Aesthetics) and lesbian theory. Lesbianism looks at the relations among/between women.

(ii) Adrienne Rich: Rich argues that "*compulsory heterosexuality*" is a "political institution" and a "lie" that ensures a woman's continued subordination because it privileges man's needs and issues. Rich wonders why the "mother-bond" of the daughter soon shifts to a man. Rich suggests that it is the ideology of the compulsory heterosexuality that forces the girl to turn to the man, forgetting her mother (and other women). The turning away of the girl from the mother/woman to the man is not natural or innate, rather her political environment forces it on her. The woman thus lives a "double life." This double life is characterised by "an apparent acquiescence to an institution founded on male interest and prerogative" and experiencing the strong pulls towards other women.

Rich then suggests the idea of the "*lesbian continuum.*" As Rich defines it, the lesbian continuum "include[s] a range . . . of woman identified experience; not simply that a woman has had or consciously desired genital experience with another woman." The lesbian continuum thus refers to a whole range of female relations—of mutual help groups, friendships and institutions and sexual relations. Rich also argues that the creative side of every woman is her lesbian self: "it is the lesbian in every woman who is compelled by female energy, who gravitates towards strong women. Who seeks a literature that will express that energy and strength . . . it is the lesbian in us who is creative, for the dutiful daughter of the fathers in us is only a hack."

(iii) The *radicalesbians* was a New York group which published a manifesto "The Woman Identified Woman" in 1971. They argued that the lesbian is really a natural "unconscious" feminist, a woman who devotes her energies to other women, who refuses to be identified in terms of a man. They thus refuse to accept identities that are conceived only in terms of a man's "power," "ego," or "status." Woman must forge identities with each other, that "only women can give to each other a new sense of self. That identity we have to develop with reference to ourselves, and not in relation to men." Such new women will therefore be "woman identified." The lesbian is the truly independent woman, and lesbianism is "a sign of mental health" (Martha Shelley).

Queer Theory: Queer theory, as already noted, emerges from the alliance between gay and lesbian theories, and sociology. The rise of queer theory in the 1990s has helped a broader analysis of the cultural practices of gender roles, the "construction" of gay/lesbian identities and the social-political implications of gay/lesbian activism. Queer theory suggests that twentieth century sociology has ignored the role of sexuality and sexual preferences. The sexual liberation of the 1950s and 60s was an indicator of social change. But conventional sociology looked only at the heterosexual sexualities, rarely at homosexuality in their analyses of social change. Queer theory seeks to reorient this approach. Steven Seidman's (ed.) *Queer Theory/Sociology* (1996) is the most important intervention and summary of the major debates in this new area in critical theory. It calls for a transformation of existing conceptual frameworks and the acceptance of these transformations in other areas. The essential features of queer theory may be summed up thus.

(i) A conceptualisation of sexuality which sees sexual power embodied in different levels of social life

(ii) The problematisation of gender and sexual categories, and identities. The destabilisation of identities is an important feature of queer theories (see section on Judith Butler above). In this queer theory id decidedly and consciously postmodern and influenced by poststructuralism.

(iii) A rejection of civil rights strategies in favour of the carnival, transgression and parody. The theorists favour decentring, deconstruction and revisionism. It is a politics of provocation where the limits of liberal tolerance may be tested.

(iv) A willingness to interrogate areas which are not generally seen as part of the discipline of sexuality. They also favour an approach where they practice queer readings of apparently non-sexualised or heterosexual texts.

(v) It is anti-assimilationist. It rejects the inclusion-project of lesbian and gay politics. It is oppositional, and resistant to the prevalent "normalising regime." Queer theory resists labelling for this reason, and for the identities a label imposes upon individuals.

(vi) It is co-sexual, meaning men and women are on equal footing. The term queer is now used to mean both gays and lesbians.

(vii) Arlene Stein and Ken Plummer in *Queer Theory/Sociology* offer three possible areas wherein queer theory may be assimilated into cultural and literary studies and sociology.

   (a) Reconsidering the Issues: To analyse the system of social stratification keeping in mind the issues and aspects neglected thus far. This includes: heterosexism, homophobia, and erotic hierarchies. As they put it, "lesbians and gay men are not simply persons with sexual identities; they also are raced, classed and situated in a wide array of different life contexts. Age, race, mobility, class, consumption studies, regional studies must include and be included in gay/lesbian studies.

(b) Rereading the Classics: Giddens, Habermas and Parsons need to be reread, keeping in mind the heterosexual assumptions that inform these works. What is needed is a revision of these texts to incorporate queer concerns. The heterosexual centre must be dismantled using these same theories about society and culture. As Michael Warner puts it, what is essential is "to make theory queer, and not just to have a theory about queers."

(c) Rethinking Pedagogy: Classrooms being heterosexualised, a queer pedagogy is necessary now. While refusing to organise classes around categories like gay/lesbian, the emphasis on the marginalised sexualities must inform teaching methods.

IV Relationship with Other Disciplines

As noted above gay/lesbian studies have influenced literary and cultural studies to a great extent. The retrieval of gay texts, anthologising and publication of gay texts, and tracing the history of gay themes has been an important development in the area. In New Historicism and Cultural Materialism, the work of Jonathan Goldberg, Alan Sinfield, among others, has focussed on homosexuality in Renaissance texts (as the title of Goldberg's book suggests: *Queering the Renaissance*, 1994), the repression of the theme and a gay resistance (especially in the life and work of Oscar Wilde and Andre Gide). Debates over the discipline of "Eng. Lit" itself as being heterosexual and homophobic have been common between scholars such as Eagleton and Sinfield-Goldberg (best known for Eagleton's savage response to Goldberg's controversial essay, "The Anus in Coriolanus," 1994). In sociology, Queer Theory as popularised by the work of Lee Edelman, Steven Seidman, Ken Plummer and Judith Butler has made important contribution to the socialisation of homosexuality. In film studies and popular culture, Teresa de Lauretis, Michele Aina Barale, Richard Meyer and others have made important contributions. Urban sociology, architecture and demographic studies have also been influenced by gay/lesbian theory, as seen in works like Daniel Bell and Gill Valentine's *Mapping Desire* (1995). Nationalism and sexuality has also been explored, notably in volumes like *Nationalisms and Sexualities* (1992). Edelman's work on AIDS and the effect on homosexual life, and the writings of Ellis Hanson, Thomas Yingling are explorations of the discourse of AIDS-health-homosexuality.

Further Reading

Abelove, Henry et al, ed. *Lesbian and Gay Studies Reader*. New York and London: Routledge, 1993.

Fuss, Diana, ed. *Inside/Out: Lesbian Theories, Gay Theories*. New York and London: Routledge, 1991.

McRuer, Robert. *The Queer Renaissance: Contemporary American Literature and the Reinvention of Lesbian and Gay Identities*. New York and London: New York University Press, 1997.

Munt, Sally, ed. *New Lesbian Criticism: Literary and Cultural Readings*. Harvester, 1992.

Chapter Ten

African-American Aesthetics and Literary Theory

The term African-American refers to the tradition of literary criticism in the geographical space of the U.S.A., but which finds its intellectual roots and myths in African traditions. "Black aesthetics," the other (earlier) term may also refer to the criticism that emerges from the African nations and the Caribbean's. Wole Soyinka, Ngugi wa Thiong'o, Kwame Anthony Appiah are prominent figures in the latter. The most important thinker in the area is Henry Louis Gates, Jr., who, while adapting traditional African tropes and myths to formulate his theories, prefers the term "African-American" as being less ethnocentric. African-American literary theory originates from the assumption that texts of Black writers cannot and must not be judged with criteria derived from the "white" tradition. Moreover, African-American literature has been inextricably linked to a political practice that has been in an oppositional relation with the established white Christian one.

I Background and Origins

To understand African-American literature and literary theory it is essential to chart the history of this "nation within a nation" position of the African in the U.S.A. The history of Black slavery in the New World begins in the 16th century. The first lot of slaves of African descent arrived at San Miguel de Gualdape, near Georgia, in 1526. They were actually Spaniards. The first permanent settlement at St. Augustine (1565) had slaves. From the 1760s, with plantations mushrooming all over the country, the slave trade also expanded. By 1860, the American South had the largest slave population in the New World. According to Seymour Drescher and Stanlcy Engerman (1998), there were nine systems of slavery in America. The Caribbean also saw its share of slave labour. The inhuman work conditions, the exploitative nature of relationships between the whites and the Blacks, the frequent tortures and legal penalties, the sexual exploitation of the Black women, the sale of children and the break up of Black families were the features of Black slave life.

By 1790s, organisations were formed to fight against the slave system. On March 2, 1807, a legislation banning African slave trade was passed. Some literature began to emerge from the Black population. Phyllis Wheatley (1753-1784) was one of the first known Black women poets. Conflicts arose between the American North and South on the issue of slavery. Numerous Black abolitionists took to extensive lecturing and pamphleteering to raise support (Frederick Douglas was the most significant of these). Numerous small "uprisings" took place, with John Brown's Harpers Ferry one becoming legendary (especially after Brown was hanged in 1859). With the civil war, the slave question became a major issue in American politics.

The twentieth century saw the rise of many thinkers and activists in the U.S.A. Extensive literature and polemical writing was also available. Racial segregation in social and cultural life began to be attacked. In certain parts of the American metropolis activists and artists came together to revive/launch a whole new cultural phenomenon. The Harlem Renaissance, as this early twentieth century movement came to be known, the Black Arts movements (the latter led by the poet Langston Hughes), the Black Arts Repertoire Theatre (which involved LeRoi Jones, Charles Patterson, William Patterson, Johnny Moore, Clarence Reed and others), helped the establishment of blues, rap, jazz as specifically African-American art forms. Talented writers and artists (Claude McKay, W.E.B. DuBois, Jean Toomer, James Weldon Johnson and several other writers grouped in New York, and were referred to as the "New York Wits"). J.E. Casely-Hayford's *Ethiopia Unbound*, believed to be the first African novel, was published around the same time (specifically in 1911). The debates over "assimilationist" views (that the Blacks were ultimately and indisputably a part of the white American nation, and they needed to adapt to this) and the "back to Africa" (negritude, Pan-Africanism and such, popularised by Marcus

Garvey) continued. In the 1970s, the Black Feminist movement began, rooting itself in the double oppression of the Black woman: of being Black *and* a woman.

Our survey of the critical stages in the development of Black thought will include: Black philosophy, Booker T. Washington, W.E.B. DuBois, Alain Locke, Hoyt Fuller, Larry Neal, Ron Karenga, Adam David Miller, Langston Hughes, Richard Wright, Ralph Ellison and Henry Louis Gates, Jr. A separate section on Black feminism will survey the central features and concerns of Black feminist thought. Addison Gayle's *The Black Aesthetic* (1971) brought together some of the most influential essays in the area.

II Assumptions and General Methods

The general assumptions that inspire a Black Aesthetics and literary theory are available in the Black philosophical tradition. Fred Lee Hord and Jonathan Scott Lee in *I Am Because We Are* (1995) provide a sketch of the basic assumptions in Black philosophy.

(1) They assume that there is a distinctive Black philosophical tradition.

(2) This assumption leads to two dangerous ideas, as Kwame Appiah sees them:
   - (a) It promotes false theories of race, especially in the development of a pan-Africanism
   - (b) It suggests a unity of tradition in Africa, and thereby underestimating the variety of African cultures and identities.

(3) Hord and Lee argue that the notion of race, itself a European one, is always linked to the notion of culture. There are three identifiable stages in the development of African and diaspora thought.
   - (a) The precolonial stage where the philosophical themes reflect the diversity of Africa's cultures. Here the ways of life are integrally linked to the geography and climate. The diversities are grounded in the "commonalties of civilisation." This is essentially lost today.

   (b) The imposition of the construct of race by Europeans and colonial intrusion. The population of Africa is homogenised as *one race* to facilitate slave trade and political policies.
   (c) The postcolonial stage where race is claimed at political and psychological levels in order to reconstruct the very notions of race. The concepts/movements of negritude and Black Aesthetics are the result of these new reconstructions.
(4) Certain "generative themes" may be located in Black philosophy.
   (a) The ideas that the individual is never separable from the socio-cultural environment. Identity is constructed not in self-obsessed consciousness but also partly in the set of shared beliefs, patterns of behaviour and expectations. The informing principle is not "I think therefore I am," but rather, "I am because we are." The community provides the basis for individual identity. This inspires most Black thinkers to speak of the collective identity and the duty of the artists to address the collective problems of Blacks as a whole.
   (b) A relational concept of reality. All dimensions of reality are interlinked. Physical objects, for example, cannot be separated from their uses, which are themselves human. Objects cannot be separated from the natural material that made them. The spiritual, the material, the spatial and the temporal are all linked together.
   (c) The central importance of religion and religion based ethics as dominant forms for social expression and philosophy Religious conceptions of human identity, portrayals of excellence in the community and expectations of the value of life are sources of philosophical reflections. The use of myths forms the African tradition (Ishmael Reed's voodoo, Gates' reliance upon traditional African gods and legends to develop an African-American literary theory are extensions of this idea).
(5) The emblem of the *sage* or the *griot* is crucial here. The Black philosopher assumes a visionary role, and offers a new redescription. The griot/sage is also the preserver of the cultural memory. He retells the tradition *and* critique of the same. Thus

it is balanced between past/tradition (memory, retelling) and future/destiny (fresh insights, revisioning). This dual role is very important in understanding Black philosophy (see section on Henry Louis Gates, Jr., for the use of the "revision motif" in Black theory).

(6) Leopold Senghor identifies three characteristics of African art. It is functional, *collective* and *committing* or *committed.* Ron Karenga, following Senghor, develops these ideas. All art must reflect the value system from which it emerges. Black art must carry the message of the revolution. It must give the everyday life of the Negro collective more colour and form.

(7) Black Aesthetics, then, may be summed up in Julian Mayfield's words, as "a search for a new program . . . because all the old programs spawned out of the Judaeo-Christian spirit have failed us. It is the search for anew spiritual quality, or the recapture of an old one, lost and buried in our African past."

(8) The development of a specifically African aesthetics, as in the case of Henry Louis Gates, Jr., therefore borrows from the African tradition and philosophy. While retrieving the cultural memory of the race, this aesthetic also tries to link art with the socio-political enslavement of the Blacks in America. Black aesthetics then tries to understand and reformulate the identities of Africans in the American context. The development of later strains of thought and theory such as multiculturalism and ethnocriticism (see appendix) owes much to the African-American aesthetics' negotiation between racial nationalism and integration with the American nation/way of life.

III Key Concepts and Thinkers

The tradition of Black Aesthetics or African-American criticism/theory has always been a socially relevant and politically charged one. "Pure" aesthetics and philosophy was never a part of the tradition. As such, a survey of the key positions in African-American thought must include non-literary figures/texts. Among the early writers Frederick Douglas, slave narratives such as those of Harriet Jacobs, the work of Sojourner Truth (see section on Black Feminism) are important documents. The first major academic critic in the African-American context was Benjamin Brawley, who became famous for his biography of the Black poet Paul Laurence Dunbar. However, to understand the evolution of African-American theory, one needs to backtrack a little. For our purposes the exploration of the African-American thought may begin with a general survey the work of Booker T. Washington and W.E.B. DuBois. Later thinkers and activists such as Martin Luther King, Jr. and Malcolm X were instrumental in raising a new Black consciousness. Authors like Alice Walker, Gwendolyn Brooks, Ida B. Wells (in the preceding era), Zora Neale Hurston, Richard Wright and numerous poets have played important roles in this field.

Booker T. Washington: Washington's autobiography, *Up from Slavery* (1900) provides the essential thought of Washington. The story of his "growth," the troubles he overcame and the success he achieved were documented to illustrate the opportunities that even the Blacks had in America.

Washington believed that for the Negro to achieve success, s/he must become socially useful. To this end he set up the Tuskegee institute where students learnt to be socially useful. Community service, self-reliance and the dignity of labour were Washington's main ideals. Students were to cook, help construct buildings and perform such socially necessary work.

(1) Washington wanted to assure the whites that the Negro could be a useful social human instrument. The aim was to reduce the white hostility towards the Blacks through the reiteration of their productivity and usefulness to the community. He supported industrial education for the Blacks, arguing that this would enable the Blacks to "enter the all-powerful business and commercial world." Washington deprecated institutions of higher learning, and emphasised the "little things of life."

(2) Washington criticised the movement of the Blacks from the country to the city. He also regarded the study of history and mathematics as impractical. The effort of the Black must be, said Washington, towards the study of proper cultivation.

(3) In his famous Atlanta Exposition address (1895), Washington claimed that education was "ruining . . . the Negroes." He urged the Blacks to "cultivate friendly relations with the Southern

white man." Washington was suggesting a liberal position for both the whites and the Blacks, where the Blacks seek to please the white with their selfless toil, and the whites exhibit greater understanding towards them as a result. Washington suggested to the whites that the Blacks could be of use to the nation, and that the white man should "cast down his bucket" (a favourite phrase of Washington) with the Blacks. Washington's argument may be summed up in his own words. "You [Washington is addressing the whites here] can be sure, in the future, as in the past, that you and your families will be surrounded by the most patient, law-abiding, and unresentful people that the world has seen. As we have proved our loyalty to you in the past . . . so in the future, in our humble way, we shall stand by you with a devotion that no foreigner can approach, ready to lay down our lives, if need be, in defence of yours, interlacing our industrial, commercial, civil and religious life with yours in a way that shall make the interests of both races one. This was a position that DuBois severely criticised.

(4) Washington accepted the dominant image/myth of America: that success is self-made and the result of individual effort. He urged the Blacks to compete and strive for success. To this end, he recommended industrial education for the Blacks. Washington however ignored the inequalities of opportunities that hindered the individual Black man's efforts. He refused to see that the labour of the Blacks in industries was slowly diminishing in importance with the advent of machinery. More importantly Washington did not acknowledge the problem of the labouring class in terms of the industrial revolution: where the capitalist economy simply reproduced the master-salve relationship of the past.

W.E.B. DuBois: DuBois led the Niagara Movement, was on the staff of the National Association for the Advancement of the Coloured People (NAACP) and an author. His *The Souls of Black Folk* (1903) is now a classic text in African-American literature.

(1) DuBois stated unequivocally that "the Negro people as a race have a contribution to make to civilisation and humanity which no other race can make." He argued that the African has a

deeper understanding of the human soul. He refers to the "intertwined community souls" of the Blacks (a concept that will figure in several later writers).

(2) He argued that the "imprisonment" within the racial identity meant that the racial group attained greater importance for the individual than the nation itself. Also, the segregation tends to inculcate a hatred of the other race. This prevents the mixing of the races.

(3) DuBois suggested that the Black in America lacks a true self-consciousness. He suffers from a "double consciousness," which DuBois defines as "the sense of always looking at one's self through the eyes of the others, of measuring one's soul by the tape of a world that looks on in amused contempt and pity. One ever feels his twoness—an American, a Negro, two souls, two thoughts, two unreconciled strivings."

(4) DuBois, writing in *Crisis*, the journal of NAACP (of which he was editor) insisted that for the Blacks, "art and propaganda be one." This call to make literature politically and socially relevant emphasises the *utilitarian* aspect of literature rather than the aesthetic one. Literature was to be a tool for political liberation. The conflict between the two functions of literature—of the presentation of beauty, and as propaganda—is very evident in DuBois.

(5) DuBois accepted a class-based interpretation of the artist's role. Thus the role of the intellectual acquires great prominence here (a trend that has persisted over the decades). DuBois therefore spoke of the "*talented tenth*," where the elite would represent the Black population. DuBois writes that America is unlikely to "yield" its racial prejudices, and the Negro must assert himself in collective action. This collective action is the domain of the intellectual. He says: "it involves the organisation of intelligent and earnest people of Negro descent for their preservation and advancement in America." He argues that the Negro race must discover a racial to prevent itself from being completely "beaten into submission and degradation."

(6) In his activist writings, DuBois also pleaded for the freedom of expression and adult suffrage. DuBois believed that it was not

possible for Negro businessmen and property owners to defend their rights and exist without suffrage, basic principles of human brotherhood and respect for the working man.

Alain Locke: Locke was the most important "historian" of the Harlem Renaissance. His *New Negro* anthology (1925), with his lead essay "The New Negro," is a manifesto for the movement.

(1) Locke seeks to explicate the rise of modern Black culture in America. The Old Negro was a caricature, a formula rather than a man. There was hardly any social or self-understanding.

(2) He outlines in this essay the transformation of a Black consciousness into a more heightened "progressive force."

(3) Unlike Booker T. Washington, Locke welcomes the movement of the Blacks from the South to the industrial towns. He treats it as the movement from "medieval America to modern," and as the move towards a greater "common consciousness." Harlem is the "race capital" for the Black masses, according to Locke. The earlier image of the Blacks as a "mass" could no longer be possible simply because like the rest of the nation, the Blacks were also in the process of class differentiation.

(4) Locke acknowledges that this common consciousness is at an early stage, but argues that it is bound to strengthen itself. However, he does not envisage a very great role for the Black intellectual (and here he differs from DuBois). Rather he suggests that "it is the rank and file who are leading, and the leaders who are following." Locke sees the "migrating peasant" as the symbol of the new leaders.

(5) Locke rejects the separatist ideas of Marcus Garvey. He sees the newly emergent African nationalism as very much a constructive part of modern American life. As Locke describes it, this new consciousness does not limit American life. In fact, the Negro's participation enables America to strengthen itself. He suggests that this new culture has a productive engagement with white culture. Locke is thus a believer in the democratic ideal of America. In fact, Locke describes it thus: "the New Negro is keenly responsive as an augury of a new democracy in American culture."

(6) The mixing of races in the progressive world of modernisation, has resulted in the fusing of "sentiment and experience." Previously, there was only the "common condition" of the Negro, now we have a "common consciousness."

(7) Locke recommends a new consciousness and self-awareness for the Negro. He should be more scientific in his attitudes, and not be a victim to "old sentimental interests." Locke also suggests a greater tolerance among and between races.

Langston Hughes: One of the best poets in the Afro-American tradition, Hughes' work has provided numerous images of race, inequality, consciousness in twentieth century America.

(1) Hughes suggested that the Negro artist's problem was to assert a Negro cultural integrity when faced with the "racial mountain." This mountain meant that a standardisation as "American" was sought rather than any African identity. As Hughes puts it, the "desire to pour racial individuality into the mould of American standardisation, and to be as little Negro and as much American as possible."

(2) This abandonment of race means that the Negro artists have no cultural material. He distances himself from the working class Negro life which is the very source of artistic creativity. Hughes therefore saw jazz as the true expression of Black aesthetics, since it originates in the Negro's working class life. Hughes was thus advocating a certain nationalistic doctrine of Black art, where racial art is not only the truly legitimate one, but also salsa (perhaps) inherently superior.

(3) Hughes blames the Black middle class for this move away from the actual working class roots in favour of a bourgeois work state. Even the artists, says Hughes, turn away from the race to white art and themes (which Hughes contemptuously describes as "run[ing] away from the painting of Negro faces to the painting of sunsets after the manner of academicians because he fears the strange un-whiteness of his own features."

Hoyt Fuller: In his famous essay "Towards a Black Aesthetic," Fuller suggested that revolutionary Black writers have turned their backs on old certainties and headed for a Black aesthetics.

(1) Fuller argues that racism, slavery and subjugation are old and established truths, the reactions to these are radically new.
(2) There may not be overt hostility, but there is the absence of clarity of vision. For, black life is viewed through a glass that is "befogged by the hot breath of history."
(3) Fuller argues that there can be no compatibility between the Black writer and the white critic (he is commenting upon Louis Simpson's review of Gwendolyn Brooks' poetry volume). This is so because the two occupy two "separate and naturally antagonistic worlds."
(4) The Black artists are aware of their "outsideness," of their political and economic powerlessness. They therefore find refuge in solidarity.
(5) The new consciousness of the Black suggests rebellion. They have now discovered that "Black is beautiful." They discover their heritage and history, and begin to pride themselves in their Blackness.
(6) The new consciousness of the artist also rejects the claims to universality of white literature, that Shakespeare is the appropriate frame of reference for even Black poetry. What is being formulated in this rejection of the white standards of judgements, forms and techniques, is a Black aesthetic.
(7) Black writers, writes Fuller, must accept immediately that white readers and critics cannot recognise or empathise with the subtleties of Black style. They need to therefore put things in proper perspective by developing new criteria for judging the work of the Black artist.

Larry Neal: Neal's "Some Reflections on the Black Aesthetic" is in the form of a table, which I shall summarise here. These constitute, for Neal, the elements of a Black aesthetic. The third column shows the development of the Black aesthetic from the early stages of African culture, displacement to America, through slavery, rebellion, rising consciousness and the present state.

Mythology	**Formal Manifestation**	
African voodoo, Spirit worship, Jesus Christ	Samba, Calypso, spirituals, Work songs, gospel songs	1. *Race Memory* Rhythm as expression of race, memory,

river spirits

As creative energy

2. *Middle Passage*
Diaspora, terror, landlessness

Neo-Mythology
Shamans, preachers, Blues singers, musicians

Black dance styles

3. *Transmutation and Synthesis*
Jigs, twist, Watusi, slow drag. Here dance as race memory.

Neo-Mythology
Legba, Oshun, woman as primarily Need/ man as doer, blues singer as Poet and moral judge, folk poet, priest, Priestess, hustler, soothsayer

4. *Blues God/Tone as Meaning & Memory*
Sound as racial memory, Blues as having same energy source as gospel, African voice transplanted

History as Unitary Myth
Shango, Nat Turner, Signifying Monkey, DuBois, Rap Brown, Bessie Smith, Ishmael Reed's hoodoo. Fanon's third world, expanded metaphors, revitalisation of the African styles in the West

5. *Black Arts and Aesthetics*
Energy intensifies, more concerned with the vibrations of the word, Black nation as poem, spiritual, rejects alienation, Black love conscious and affirmed. Change.

Neal writing on the Black Arts Movement suggests the following features.

(1) The Movement is radically opposed to any concept of the artist's work that alienates him from his community. This art must speak directly to the needs and aspirations of Black America. The Black artist's primary duty is to speak to the spiritual and cultural needs of his people.

(2) This requires a complete and radical overhauling of the western cultural aesthetic. It proposes a separate symbolism, mythology, critique and iconology.

(3) The Black Arts and Black Power concepts both relate to the Afro-American's desire for self-determination and nationhood. Both concepts are nationalistic, the former is concerned with the relationship between art and politics, and the latter with the art of politics.

(4) Certain assumptions inform the idea of a Black aesthetic.

(i) There is already in existence the basis for such an aesthetic. This is the African-American cultural tradition.

(ii) However, this is broader than tradition. It encompasses most of third world culture.

(iii) The motive behind the Black aesthetic is the destruction of the white thing, the white ideas and white ways of looking at the world.

(iv) The new aesthetic is predicated upon an ethics that asks: whose truth shall we express, ours or the white oppressors'?

(v) National and international affairs demand that we appraise the world in terms of our own interests. Thus the Black Arts movement is an *ethical* movement.

Richard Wright: Wright's fiction (especially the celebrated *Native Son*, 1940) and his prose have been very influential texts in their advocacy of a Marxist ideology for the Blacks in America. In his famous "Blueprint for Negro Writing" (in Gayle's *The Black Aesthetic*, 1971), Wright outlines the essential features that the genre should take.

(1) Wright suggests that the Negro writing thus far has demonstrated two characteristics:

(i) It became a conspicuous ornament, a hallmark of "achievement"

(ii) It became the voice of the educated Negro pleading with the whites for justice.

Thus the Negro himself was never addressed in this writing. The new writing must be directed towards the suffering and aspirations of the Negro.

(2) The Negro writers have rarely addressed the workers and the exploited. They have been distant from their people. Now they have to see society as becoming and not rely on a simple recounting of past achievements. They need to show solidarity with the Negro worker. Wright suggests that the distance between the artist and the worker should be reduced. The primary role of the artist was to reveal the economic oppression that haunts the Black worker's life. However, literature is not simply propaganda either. Thus Wright suggests that literature should not be simply an aesthetic achievement or polemical pamphlet,

but a mixture of the two. The Negro writer must turn to a Marxist conception of reality for this purpose.

(3) The vision of the Negro writer must be: that the writer must view the life of a Negro with the consciousness that one-sixth of the earth surface belongs to the working class. Their writing should be a "foreshortened picture" of the whole—their African roots, displacement, and their struggles. However, the writer should also try to retain some degree of professional autonomy.

(4) The Negro has a specific culture that has helped build his present consciousness: the Negro church and the folklore of the Negro people. The church was the mode of entry for the American Negro into western culture. They have since relied exclusively upon the Christian ideas of salvation. But complete expression has been achieved in his folklore, the vernacular wisdom and the human conditions of his own life. As Wright describes it, this folklore contains the "collective sense of Negro life in America." Negro writers have thus far ignored this folklore tradition which would have ensured a stronger relationship between them, and the Negro people. The two separate cultures that emerged—one for the Negro workers and one for the rising Negro bourgeoisie—is the result of this neglect of folk and native traditions.

(5) Wright supports the nationalist doctrine for Black art. This nationalism is visible, argues Wright, in the "whole of Negro culture and especially in folklore." Folklore embodies the "memories and hope of his struggle for freedom." Nationalism must rely on this fund of folklore wisdom. He rejects the work of Zora Neale Hurston because she accepts the roles thrust upon the Black since racism began. Wright disapproved of Black artists succumbing to the traditional models and redrawing the same stereotypes.

(6) Wright was also convinced of the integrity of African-American culture. While affirming the nationalist base of such a cultural integrity, Wright is also reluctant to accept a simplistic nationalism. Nationalism is not a final goal, but an intermediate one. As Wright describes it, the Negro writer will have a rather uneasy relationship with Negro nationalism. "they must accept the

concept of nationalism because, in order to transcend it, they must possess and understand it." They must be aware of the limitations of this nationalism. The Negro writer "must realise within the area of his own personal experience those impulses which . . . constitute the stuff of nationalism." The Negro writer must depict Negro life in all its complexity.

(7) Racism was a collective experience that helped the emergence of a nationalist perspective and culture. This culture was transmitted by numerous speech acts within the Black community and hence kept unified. Afro-American authors play an important role in this cultural transmission. They communicate the entire history and experience of the race.

(8) In conclusion Wright suggests that there is sense of isolation both among Negro writers as well as between Negro and white writers. The Negro writers must integrate themselves better with the "American scene" to prevent bitterness.

Ralph Ellison: Ellison is known more as a novelist than a critic-thinker. His *Invisible Man* (1953) is one of the most read (and celebrated) books of the twentieth century. In his essay collections, *Shadow and Act* (1966) and *Going to the Territory* (1986), Ellison develops his views on art, culture and politics.

(1) Ellison accepts the primacy of race in the artist's developments and creative activity. For Ellison, the work of art need not supply answers. It is merely the site for speculations and meditations on the conflicts.

(2) Ellison rejects naturalism as a suitable mode for the writer, preferring a magical narrative form.

(3) The work of art is important only so far as it engages with the central issues of the time.

(4) The Afro-American fictional character symbolises the essential dilemma of American life: the conflict between the professed *ideals* of democracy and equality and actual racist *practices*. This is the "irrepressible moral reality" of the Afro-American artist and her/his characters.

(5) Ellison supports liberalism because it suggests a degree of freedom.

Ron Karenga: Karenga's work on Black cultural nationalism, in close conjunction with that of LeRoi Jones, has been instrumental in the development of specific themes in African-American drama.

Karenga states that culture is the "basis of all ideas, images and actions." He adds, "without a culture Negroes are only a set of reactions to white people. Karenga identifies the following seven criteria for culture: Mythology, History, Social organisation, Political organisation, Economic organisation, Creative motif and Ethos.

(1) Black art must be part of the revolutionary machinery. It is a battle for the *minds* of Black people first.

(2) All art may be judged at two levels—the artistic and the social. It is the social that completes the picture. Any art that does not discuss and contribute to the revolution is therefore invalid. Art must be committed to revolution.

(3) The collectivity of art raises four questions, according to Karenga.

   (i) Popularisation: Art is of the people. One need not "lower" art to meet the people, contrary to common belief. Art and the people must develop at the same time.

   (ii) Individuality versus personality: Individualism of the artists is not something the Black Arts can now afford. The artist owes his existence to his context. He has no individuality, only personality. Individuality is useless isolation, and personality an important involvement.

   (iii) Diversity in unity: Unity does not mean that diversity is ignored. One does not seek standardisation of very creative act but a framework which one can create and avoid the European "gift of trial and error."

   (iv) Freedom *to* and Freedom *from*: When the artist demands freedom to do something or freedom from the restrictions that prevent him from doing something, he is essentially asking for a socio-political right. An artist may have the freedom to do what he wishes as long as it does not take the freedom from the people to refuse those arts that appear negative to them and their development.

Henry Louis Gates, Jr.: Gates' two important books on African-American literary theory, *Figures in Black* (1987) and *The Signify-*

ing Monkey (1988) have tried to formulate a specifically African-American theory using African myths and folklore. He is undoubtedly one of the most important theorist writing today and it is therefore imperative to discuss him in some detail.

(1) There are three significant motives in Gates' theory, as Theodore Mason points out:
   (i) The need to reform the study of African-American literature.
   (ii) The positioning of this reform as a revisioning of the dominant (that is, white Christian) critical theory. This is what Gates terms "Signifyin(g)."
   (iii) The development of a culturally specific theory of African-American literature.

(2) Gates' stated aim in *Figures in Black* is to "utilise contemporary theory to defamiliarise the texts of the black tradition, to create a distance between this black reader and our black texts." He argues that we need to translate contemporary theory, rename principles of criticism and name indigenous black principles of criticism to explicate Black texts.

(3) Gates discerns four "moments" in the development of Afro-American literary criticism.
   (i) *Repetition and Imitation*: The unimaginative borrowing of European theory to explicate black texts.
   (ii) *Black Aesthetics*: This rebelled against the above mode and concentrated on retrieving black texts, and the development of a genuine black aesthetic. This also explored the social and political implications relevance of Black literature. However, this emphasis on the status of a literary work as "a social document that bore witness to the political and emotional tendencies of the Negro victim of white racism" meant that literary theory itself became the "application of a social attitude." This emphasis became a "prescriptive canon": that all Black art must be social documents. As Gates wittily sums it up, this mode of criticism that emphasised on the link between the race and literature was borrowed from the Marxist idea of base and superstructure, and was made into a "race and superstructure" model!

(iii) *Repetition and Difference*: The use of contemporary theory to read black texts, but also, simultaneously critiquing this theory. Thus using poststructuralism to explicate a Black text would also suggest problems with poststructuralism. Houston Baker and Wole Soyinka are the best examples here, argues Gates.

(iv) *Synthesis*: The use of the Black vernacular tradition and African myths in tandem with contemporary theory to formulate a theory of African-American literature. Such a theory will address a "two-toned" audience: those who study black literature and those who study the institution of literature.

(4) Gates argues that the Western tradition has always linked rights with literacy and the ability to write. Emerson, William Lloyd Garrison, W.D. Howells and other intellectuals (both white and black) spoke of the need to develop the art of writing to enable emancipation (one recalls here Frederick Douglas' own triumphant acquisition of writing). The common belief was that Africans, and persons of African descent in America, did not create literature. Blackness and the absence of writing were thus synonyms. As Gates puts it, these were "readings of blackness as a trope of absence."

(5) Gates in *Figures in Black* and later in *The Signifying Monkey* develops two models for a black revision of literary history. This intensely intertextual, double-voiced tradition is what he terms "*critical signification*." The strategy outlined by Gates is termed *Signifyin(g)*. This derives from the tales of the Signifying Monkey. The signifying monkey is the counterpart of the Yoruba trickster figure, the Esu-Elegbara.

(6) *Esu-Elegbara*: This is a trickster figure who is supposedly the messenger of the gods figures in many Cuban, Haitian, Nigerian and Brazilian myths. Esu serves as the figure for interpretation and double-voicedness (for a discussion of double-voicedness as a critical concept, see section on Mikhail Bakhtin in chapter one). Esu interprets the messages of gods for man, carries the desires of man to the gods. He is the master of the stylus and the phallus (Esu is supposed to be an inveterate copulator), the guardian of the crossroads. The features of this figure are (ac-

cording to Gates): indeterminacy, open-endedness, parody, irony, magic, uncertainty, sexuality, chance, disruption and reconciliation, closure and disclosure. Esu is the indigenous black metaphor for the literary critic (*Esu-tufunaalo* is the methodological principles of the interpretation of black texts).

(7) The myths of instruction, of how writing was acquired by the white man, and how the greedy African chose gold, introduce the *Monkey*. The monkey is the figure who helped man acquire the sixteen palm nuts. These palm nuts represent the mode of interpretation in African myths, and is the *Ifa*. Esu and the Monkey are frequently interchanged in many myths. Gates suggests that Ifa is the metaphor for the *text*. Esu then stands for *interpretation*, which is open-ended and multiple.

(8) Gates summarises the uses of these myths for a theory. These myths and the characters therein (Esu, Ifa and the Monkey) function as focal points for black theories about formal language use.

   (i) The figure of *writing* is specifically to do with Esu. The figure of the Monkey is to do with *oral discourse* or speaking. The tension between the oral and the written modes of tradition is then represented as finding a *voice in writing*. This tension is the double-voicedness of all African texts.

   (ii) The role of the figurative is emphasised here. Esu and the Monkey symbolise the rhetorical nature of language. The tradition is itself made up of this rhetoric of undecidability and open-endedness. The literal, real, written and the figurative, mythic, spoken are always locked together in this tradition. All *writing*, in African theory, somehow signifies upon the *oral*. Even revision is always double-voiced.

   (iii) Esu and the Monkey stand for the indeterminacy of interpretation. Esu is the principle of language, of written discourse. Indeterminacy is the unavoidable feature of all interpretation.

(9) There are four types of double-voiced textual relations, according to Gates.

   (i) *Tropological Revision*: Where a specific trope is repeated with a difference in one or more texts. The trope of the "talking book," of the themes of ascent and descent (frequently seen as the movement between the American South and North) are some of them. Black texts of the nineteenth century exhibit this trope.

(ii) *The Speakerly Text*: The play of voices in a text, where "free indirect discourse" is used. The voice of the Black community, the standard ("received") English of the narrator combine to form a double-voiced narrative mode. Seen predominantly in Zora Neale Hurston's *Their Eyes were Watching God.*

(iii) *Talking Texts*: Black texts *talk to* other texts. Mimesis, revision and critique combine here. We have intertextuality between the texts of the same tradition. Ishmael Reed's *Mumbo Jumbo*, Ellison's *Invisible Man*, Wright's *Native Son* and Walker's *The Color Purple* are examples.

(iv) *Rewriting the Speakerly*: Direct and explicit revisions of earlier texts. Gates argues that Walker's *The Color Purple* explicitly revises Hurston's novel. Gates identifies two distinct modes here.

(a) *Parody*: seen mainly in the work of Reed. Gates terms this *motivated signifyin(g)*, where a *critique* is attempted of the predecessor text in order to clear a space for his own text.

(b) *Pastiche*: seen in the work of Walker. Gates terms this *unmotivated signifyin(g)*, where there is the *absence* of a negative critique. This is more in the nature of emphasising the relationship between the predecessor and the present text. This is frequently in the form of homage.

Black Feminism: The rise of Black feminism in the 1970s had two interlinked contexts. First, the feminist arguments and politics prevalent then focussed on the problems of women as a whole, assuming that the conditions of oppression were the same. This negated certain specific problems of the Black woman, whose experience of oppression was double of being woman and being black. Second, the Black aesthetic and Black power movement was inherently patriarchal, and left no space for the Black woman to voice her problems. Sexual oppression and exploitation of the Black woman remained unchanged even within the nationalist, "newly conscious" Black families and communities. Thus, Black feminist thought sought to interrogate the masculinist bias in Black thought and the racist bias in the feminist theory (as Patricia Hill Collins sums it).

(1) Reclaiming the tradition is a major point on the Black feminist agenda. This involves:
   (i) Discovering, reinterpreting and analysing the works of Black woman intellectuals for the first time. Alice Walker's retrieval of Zora Neale Hurston's work for the Black feminist movement is a good example for this activity.
   (ii) New interpretations of existing work through new theoretical frameworks. Hazel Carby's work on nineteenth century Black women novelists is an example.
   (iii) Redefining the role of the Black woman intellectual. Reconsidering and re-evaluating the work of early activists and thinkers like Sojourner Truth is an important aspect of this attempt to redefine the Black woman's intellectual tradition. This is based on certain criteria and assumptions.
      (a) The experiences of African-American women give them a unique standpoint inaccessible to other groups. They can thus provide insights into the conditions of their own oppression.
      (b) They provide a leadership for Black women's empowerment and resistance.
      (c) They can create group autonomy.

(2) Black feminist thought may then be defined as "specialised knowledge created by African-American women which clarifies a standpoint of and for Black women" (Collins). This standpoint includes the presence of certain core themes, the diversity of Black woman's experiences in encountering these core themes, the varied expressions of Black woman's Afrocentric feminist consciousness, the interdependence of Black women's experiences, consciousness and actions. It seeks to empower Black woman for political activism.

(3) There is a strong and recurring humanist vision that informs Black feminist thought. This solidarity with the human race as a whole is crucial to understanding Black feminism. Alice

Walker's term "*womanist*" (in *In Search of Our Mothers' Gardens*, 1984) indicates this. Womanist (derived from the Black vernacular "womanish"), for Walker, suggests a commitment "to the survival and wholeness of entire people, male and female." It suggests the qualities of independence, responsibility and toughness that have enabled Black women to resist racial and sexual oppression. A womanist is not, emphasises Walker, a "separatist, except periodically for health." The term thus universalises individual struggles when Walker redefines *all* people as "*people of colour*." Yet the scope for autonomous self-determination is also available here.

(4) The central themes addressed in Black feminist thought that derive from certain features of their existence may be summarised as:

   (i) The family, work and oppression: This involves the study of the interlocking nature of the Black woman's exploitation in the paid labour market and the unpaid family labour. This is thus an analysis that looks at the *class aspect* of the Black woman's life.

   (ii) The mammies, matriarchs and such stereotypes: Portraying Black women as stereotypical mammies, matriarchs, welfare recipients and "hot mommas" has helped oppress them. The Black woman is the Other. They are treated either as sexual objects or as children. The "mammy" is the faithful, obedient servant. She symbolises the dominant group's perceptions of the ideal Black female: even though she is well loved and may have considerable authority in the white man's family, but she remains a "faithful servant." The matriarch is the white culture's symbol of what is wrong with Black families. Aggressive, assertive and those who support their families economically are dismissed as matriarchs. This myth has been the subject of enormous intellectual debates, especially after the 1965 Daniel Moynihan report, which suggested that Black matriarchs prevented the development of white men. Finally, there is the stereotype of the whore. The image of the sexually aggressive Black woman helped justify the controls imposed upon the Black woman's sexuality by white males.

(iii) Self-definition: The need to find a voice, to attain visibility, and resisting objectification as the perpetual Other. This also suggests a culture of resistance. The community of Black women evolves as a close knit-groups at three "safe spaces" (Collins' term): informal friendships and family interactions; Black churches and Black women's organisations. The retrieval of the Black woman's tradition—Ma Rainey, Bessie Smith, Billie Holiday and Blues.

(iv) Motherhood: This is seen as a mode of self-expression and corrective to the stereotyping (see above). The woman-centred networks of *bloodmothers*, *othermothers* (women who assist bloodmothers by sharing mothering responsibilities) are important here. The emotional intensities involved here (especially between bloodmothers and daughters), the political activism and organisation of women's networks (especially groups of othermothers) play an important role in community rearing/caring of children. Thus individual separateness is rejected in favour of interconnectedness.

(v) Activism: This has two dimensions.

(a) The struggle for group survival which consists of actions taken to create Black female spheres of influence

(b) Struggle for institutional transformation.

(vi) Sexual Politics (Black lesbianism): Where heterosexuality is treated as the norm for all women, and Black lesbians are marginalised. This is so because, in the past, finding a man was perhaps the only "security" Black women had. Hence the unwritten acceptance of heterosexuality. Audre Lord and others have suggested that this "compulsory heterosexuality" (see Adrienne Rich under lesbian/gay theory)

(vii) Black Women's relationships: This focuses on the abuse of Black women by Black men. With their assimilation of Eurocentric ideologies of the gender differences and the stereotypes of the Black women, the Black men also objectify the Black women. The relationship between white and Black women is also caught up in a sexual politics, where the white woman does not see her own racism, or that of the white man's (because the white woman has herself benefited from racism).

IV Relationship with Other Disciplines

The work of bell hooks (Gloria Watkins) is located at the interface of cultural studies, civil rights and feminism. Hooks has written extensively on representation, postmodernism and race relations. Gloria Anzaldua, Cherrie Moraga and others analyse the issue of displacement, minority culture and "border cultures." The most important contribution of Black feminism is, of course, in activism.

Further Reading

Collins, Patricia Hill. *Black Feminist Thought: Knowledge, Consciousness and the Politics of Empowerment.* Cambridge, Massachusetts: Unwin Hyman, 1990.

Gates, Jr., Henry Louis. *The Signifying Monkey: A Theory of African-American Literary Criticism.* New York and Oxford: Oxford University Press, 1988.

Gayle, Addison, ed. *The Black Aesthetic.* New York: Doubleday, 1971.

hooks, bell. *Ain't I A Woman?: Black Woman and Feminism.* Boston: South End Press, 1981.

Hord, Fred Lee and Jonathan Scott Lee, ed. *I Am Because We Are: Readings in Black Philosophy.* Amherst: University of Massachusetts Press, 1995.

Appendix 1

Ecocriticism and Environmental Literary Studies

Earlier theories in literary and cultural studies focussed on issue of class, race, gender, region are criteria and "subjects" of critical analysis. The late twentieth century has woken up to a new threat: ecological disaster. The most important environmental problems that humankind faces *as a whole* are: nuclear war, depletion of valuable natural resources, population explosion, proliferation of exploitative technologies, conquest of space preliminary to using it as a garbage dump, pollution, extinction of species (though not a human problem) among others. In such a context, literary and cultural theory has begun to address the issue as a part of academic discourse. Numerous green movements have sprung up all over the world, and some have even gained representations in the governments. Large scale debates over "dumping," North versus South environmentalism (the necessary differences between the environmentalism of the developed and technologically advanced richer nations—the North, and the poorer, subsistence environmentalism of the developing or "Third World"—the South). Donald Worster's *Nature's Economy* (1977) became a textbook for the study of ecological thought down the ages. The historian Arnold Toynbee recorded the effect of human civilisation upon the land and nature in his monumental, *Mankind and Mother Earth* (1976). Environmental issues and landscape use were also the concern of the Annales School of historians, especially Braudel and Febvre. The work of environmental historians has been pathbreaking too. Richard Grove et al's massive *Nature and the Orient* (1998), David Arnold and Ramachandra Guha's *Nature, Culture, Imperialism* (1995) have been significant work in the environmental history of India and Southeast Asia. Ramachandra Guha is of course the most important environmental historian writing from India today. His

This Fissured Land (with Madhav Gadgil, 1992), *The Unquiet Woods* (1989) and *Environmentalism: A Global History* (2000) are seminal texts in the area. Third World concerns with development and environmental problems peculiar to their conditions were studied by Vandana Shiva (especially in *Staying Alive*, 1988) and Guha and Juan Martinez-Alier (*Varieties of Environmentalism*, 1998).

Various versions of environmentalism developed. Deep ecology and ecofeminism were two important developments. These new ideas questioned the notion of "development" and "modernity," and argued that all Western notions in science, philosophy, politics were "*anthropocentric*" (human-centred) and "*androcentric*" (Man/male-centred). Technology, medical science with its animal testing, the cosmetic and fashion industry all came in for scrutiny from environmentalists. Deep ecology, for instance, stressed on a "biocentric" view (as seen in the name of the environmentalist group, "Earth First!").

Ecocriticism is the result of this new consciousness: that very soon, there will be nothing beautiful (or safe) in nature to discourse about, unless we are very careful. In 1990, the University of Nevada, Reno (U.S.A.) created the first academic position in "Literature and the Environment," and soon a journal, *Interdisciplinary Studies in Literature and the Environment* (ISLE) was launched in 1993.

Ecocritics ask questions such as:

(1) How is nature represented in the novel/poem/play?

(2) What role does the physical-geographical setting play in the structure of the novel?

(3) How do our metaphors of the land influence the way we treat it? That is, what is the link between pedagogic or creative practice and actual political, sociocultural and ethical behaviour towards the land and other non-human life forms?

(4) How is science—in the form of genetic engineering, technologies of reproduction, sexualities—open to critical scrutiny in terms of the effects of science upon the land?

The essential assumptions, ideas and methods of ecocritics may be summed up as follows.

(1) Ecocritics believe that human culture is related to the physical world.

(2) Ecocriticism assumes that all life forms are interlinked. Ecocriticism expands the notion of "the world" to include the entire ecosphere.

(3) Moreover, there is a definite link between nature and culture, where the *literary* treatment, representation and "thematisation" *of* land and nature influence *actions on* the land. Literary studies with an environmental slant can help understand the modes through which culture has destroyed nature. Such an understanding may help reformulate policies and provide the basis for a sustained ecological "enterprise."

(4) Joseph Meeker in an early work, *The Comedy of Survival: Studies in Literary Ecology* (1972) used the term "literary ecology" to refer to "the study of biological themes and relationships which appear in literary works. It is simultaneously an attempt to discover what roles have been played by literature in the ecology of the human species."

(5) William Rueckert is believed to have coined the term "ecocriticism" in 1978, which he defines as "the application of ecology and ecological concepts to the study of literature."

(6) Cheryl Glotfelty adopts the Showalter model of three-stage feminism to chart the development of ecocriticism.

(i) The first stage is concerned with the representation of nature in literature. These include studies of nature as swamp, Eden, utopia, wasteland, hostile/paradise, alternative space for salvation, adventure site, tourist spot and so on. The representation of flora and fauna on the landscape is also analysed.

(ii) The second stage involves recovery of nature writing and ecologically minded texts. Thus the recovery of early texts like Gilbert White's *A Natural History of Selbourne* (1789) went along with the incorporation (where possible) of nature writing as part of the curriculum. This saw the inclusion not only of canonical "green writers" like Thoreau and Wordsworth, but also texts such as Aldo Leopold's *A Sand County Almanac* and Rachel Carson's *Silent Spring*. Environmental poets and novelists who either demonstrated an overt environmental concern, or whose works showed a remarkable understanding of the interconnectedness of all life, or whose focus on other life forms was important for ecological insight were re-read and canonised. Thus Richard Adams (*Shardik*), Gary Snyder (in all his poetry volumes) A.R. Ammons (known for his great poem, *Garbage*), W.S. Merwin (*Lice*), Don DeLillo (*White Noise*) and Graham Swift (*Waterland*) became part of the ecocritical canon. Several anthologies of nature writing were published: Jan Adkis' *Ragged Mountain Portable Wilderness Anthology* (1993), Karen Knowles' *Celebrating the Land: Women's Nature Writing, 1850-1991* (1992) and Peter Wild's *The Desert Reader* (1991), among others.

(iii) The third stage is the most theoretical stage. Poststructuralism (Sueellen Campbell), Foucauldian discourse analysis (Christopher Manes), Bakhtin (Michael McDowell) and other thinkers are employed here to question constructions of the "human" (defined, frequently, as *different* from an animal). Ecofeminism is the most important development in this area.

Ecofeminism: The work of Donna Harraway, Greta Gaard, Carolyn Mercahnt, Vandana Shiva, Maria Mies, Sandra Harding, Ariel Salleh, Ynestra King, Mary Mellor and several others can be grouped under this heading. Ecofeminism, like all other movements, has numerous strains: socialist ecofeminism, spiritual ecofeminism, radical ecofeminism and "Third World" ecofeminism (this last best exemplified by the brilliant work in India of Vandana Shiva) and others.

(1) Ecofeminism calls for an end to all oppression. They argue that no attempt to liberate women will be successful without an attempt to free nature. The nature/culture dualism is inherently patriarchal, for it links woman with nature. And nature, being projected as the all-giving *mother*, does not expect a return: it merely goes on giving. Thinkers like Linda Vance argue that ecofeminism must reconceptualise the relationship of woman

and nature as "sisters," based on the shared oppression of the woman and the non-human world.

(2) Ecofeminists divide the world into two groups—the privileged and the oppressed. The privileged group includes upper or middle class, human, technologically developed, male. The oppressed group includes poor, working class, non-human animal, "underdeveloped" nature and female. The ecofeminists link sexism, classism, speciesism (the stress on the human species) and naturism (the oppression of nature) as the main oppressors on earth

(3) They argue that men focus on rights, and women on responsibilities. This makes the women a more ecologically conscious human, for her attitude towards "utilisation" of nature is more responsible.

(4) They argue that technological and industrial disasters first affect women (especially their reproductive systems), children and nature.

(5) Ariel Salleh speaks of an identitarian politics where the equation reads: 1/0. Here 1= male and 0=female *and* nature. Thus all science, politics, ethics are anthropocentric, where women and nature are seen as objects for present for the use of man. Even liberal environmentalism, argues Salleh, recommends cautious utilisation of natural resources so that they may last longer for *man's use* (and not nature for the sake of nature).

(6) Sandra Harding, Donna Harraway and Vandana Shiva suggest that science is anti-nature and masculine. The woman's knowledge is rarely acknowledged. Vandana Shiva points out that in medieval times, one way of controlling woman's knowledge and the woman knower was to brand and burn her as a "witch."

Ecocriticism and ecofeminism promises to be one of the most radical and ethical of critical theories yet. Alongside Black Theory, feminism and multiculturalism, ecocriticism seeks to re-orient cultural and literary theory into addressing the most immediate concern of contemporary life.

Further Reading

Gaard, Greta, ed. *Ecofeminism: Woman, Animals, Nature*. Philadelphia: Tempe Press, 1993.

Glotfelty, Cheryl and Harold Fromm, ed. *The Ecocriticism Reader: Landmarks in Literary Ecology*. Athens and London: University of Georgia Press, 1996.

Guha, Ramachandra. *Environmentalism: A Global History*. Delhi: Oxford University Press, 2000.

Mellor, Mary. *Feminism and Ecology*. Cambridge: Polity, 1997.

Worster, Donald. *Nature's Economy: A History of Ecological Ideas*. Cambridge: Cambridge University Press, 1996.

Appendix 2

Technocriticism

The development of computer technology and the new versions of texts that are electronic texts to be read on screen rather than in the print form has had drastic impact in traditional literary studies. The influence of technology has always been visible in science fiction. The availability of WEB shopping, fiction (Judy Molloy's *Its Name Was Penelope*, to name one of them), chat shows, journals and essays on the web (example: MG Kirschenbaum's "The Cult of Print" in *Postmodern Culture* 6.1, 1995. Accessible at: http://128.220.50.88/journals/postmodern_culture/v006/6.1r_kirschenbaum.html) are electronic signs of the times. But the impact on the very nature and concept of textuality is a phenomenon associated with the 1980s and '90s. The age of the *hypertext*, simulation, computer aided designs and virtual reality requires a whole new theory of reading itself. Technocriticism is the result of these developments. In recognition of the "arrival" of a new age, *Modern Fiction Studies* brought out a special issue on the subject in 1997. The work of Katherine Hayles (especially in *Chaos Bound*) and Michael Joyce has been located at the interface of cyberstudies, cultural and literary studies. The study of narrative is undoubtedly the most fascinating area in technocriticism. The essential features and assumptions of "technocriticism" (in relation to narrative and reading) may be summarised as follows.

(1) Categories and notions like text, narrative, and linearity need to be rethought. The texts is no longer a linear narrative with a logical beginning, middle and end. Various parts of the text may be transferred, sequences rearranged, added to and subtracted from. Commentaries, other texts and notes may be displayed simultaneously, thus altering the way a text *looks* and is read (on screen). At the click of the mouse, the reader may switch

reading material, refer to an encyclopaedia, and compose/mark her/his comments.

(2) The text is now a *network*, or a "*city of texts*" (Michael Joyce). The reader is returned to the same "lexia" over and over again in the branching narrative. The reader "scans" a page, looking for a particular passage, word or image. Thus what the text should give you, or what the text means is already in the reader's mind when s/he clicks on the keyboard or mouse. Reading and re-reading a section of the text is thus a *reconfiguration* of the text itself. As a result, the "body" of the book is now a problematic concept. A hypertext, as defined by Jay Bolter in *Writing Space*, is "a network of texts which allows the reader to choose any path—all paths are equally valid."

(3) The change that occurs in narrative is that from a closed, linear, univocal authoritative aesthetic which renders the reader passive, to one which is multivocal, open, non-hierarchical, and non-linear and which is based on active "encounter" between reader and text. This new aesthetic is what Jaishree Odin terms "Net" or "hypertext" aesthetics.

(4) The reader can create her/his own narrative in the space of virtual reality. *Interactive* fiction and drama are examples of this. New pathways and solutions are offered by the reader/viewer, who is now a *player*. This is an intensely *visual* activity (so far!), where the writer organises a shape to the images, but which the reader reshapes on screen.

(5) Internet chatrooms and interactive dialogues suggest a whole new mode of reading. The solitary nature of reading and writing is no more available to us. Hence the definition of reading "space" requires redefinition.

(6) Simulation and virtual reality is not the obliteration of the object of representation. Rather, simulation brings the object into being, with the active participation of the reader. A new topology develops. This is full of gaps and "in-between spaces" which provide the potential for the reader's articulation and interruptions.

(7) The hypertext creates virtual spaces. Michael Joyce suggests two forms of these spaces:

(i) *Exploratory*: where readers create their own paths through a body of knowledge. On the Web, readers mark visited and unvisited sites by changing the highlighting colour of cue material. Destination codes for links are also displayed. Hints about where else to go are available. All this radically alters the way in which we read.

(ii) *Constructive hypertexts*: where writers collect, shape and act upon information and create visual maps of structures that anticipate what they are becoming. That is, they "write" a structure of something that does not yet exist.

(8) Hypertexts do not aim at reaching a destination. The art of "tracing" or "navigating" is itself the object. The lexias (units) are in random sequence, fragmented and discontinuous. The text and the reader therefore exist in the *in-between zone of transformation*, and navigation.

(9) The computer codes, programmed languages are involved in presenting certain "flickering signifiers" (Hayles) on the screen. A global command can rearrange the text in its entirety. Thus the relationship between the signifier and the signified is entirely arbitrary and temporary. One can retrace a link, "undo" a link or "recall" a lexia. The text can mutate itself instantly. This leads to a "reflexive body writing," where the path the reader traces is the materialisation of her/his subjectivity. The reader is thus an integral part of the topology. The gaps are the sites of potential where the reader may inscribe her/his body-subjectivity as s/he traverses along the paths.

More innovations in cyberculture will see corresponding developments in technocriticism. The relationship of the potential of cyberspace to subjectivity, postcolonialism, race and gender issues are now being tackled. Without a doubt, this is one of the most exciting areas of critical theory today.

Further Reading

Hayles, Katherine N. *Chaos Bound: Orderly Disorder in Literature and Science*. Ithaca: Cornell University Press, 1990.

Joyce, Michael. *Of Two Minds: Hypertext, Pedagogy and Poetics*. Ann Arbor: University of Michigan Press, 1994.

Landow, George P. *Hypertext: The Convergence of Contemporary Critical Theory and Technology*. Baltimore: Johns Hopkins University Press, 1992.

Landow, George P., ed. *Hyper/Text/Theory*. Baltimore: Johns Hopkins, 1994.

Modern Fiction Studies. Special Issue on "Technocriticism and Hypernarrative." Vol. 43, No. 3, Fall 1997.

Select Bibliography

Adas, Michael. *Machines as the Measure of Man: Science, Technology and the Ideologies of Western Dominance*. Ithaca: Cornell, University Press, 1989.

Adkins, Jan, ed. *Ragged Mountain Portable Wilderness Anthology*. Maine: International Marine Press, 1993.

Adorno, Theodore. *Negative Dialectics*. Trans. E.B. Ashton. London: Routledge, 1990.

—. *Prisms*. London: Neville Spearman, 1967.

Adorno, Theodore and Max Horkheimer. *The Dialectic of Enlightenment*. Trans. John Cumming. New York: Herder and Herder, 1972.

Ahmad, Aijaz. *In Theory: Nations, Classes, Literatures*. Delhi: Oxford University Press, 1994.

Althusser, Louis. *For Marx*. Trans. Ben Brewster. New York: Pantheon, 1969.

———. *Lenin and Philosophy and Other Essays*. Trans. Ben Brewster. New York: Monthly Review Press, 1971.

Anderson, Benedict. *Imagined Communities: Reflections on the Origin and Spread of Nationalism*. London and New York: Verso, 1991.

Appiah, Kwame Anthony. *In My Father's House: Africa in the Philosophy of Culture*. New York: Oxford University Press, 1992.

Arac, Jonathan. *Postmodernism and Politics*. Minnesota: University of Minnesota Press, 1986.

Arnold, David. *Colonising the Body: State Medicine and Epidemic Disease in Nineteenth Century India*. Berkley: University of California Press, 1993.

Arnold, David and Ramachandra Guha, ed. *Nature, Culture, Imperialism: Essays in the Environmental History* of South Asia. Delhi: Oxford University Press, 1998.

Ashcroft, Bill et al. *The Empire Writes Back: Theory and Practice in Post-colonial Literatures*. London: Routledge, 1989.

Baber, Zaheer. *The Science of Empire: Scientific Knowledge, Civilisation and Colonial Rule in India*. New York: State of New York Press, 1996.

Baker, Houston. *Afro-American Poetics: Revisions of the Harlem and the Black Aesthetic*. Madison: University of Wisconsin Press, 1988.

Bakhtin, Mikhail. *The Dialogic Imagination: Four Essays*. Trans. Caryl Emerson and Michael Holquist. Austin: University of Texas Press, 1981.

———. *Problems of Dostoevsky's Poetics*, ed. and trans. Caryl Emerson. Minneapolis: University of Minnesota Press, 1984.

———. *Rabelais and His World*. Trans. Helene Iswolsky. Bloomington: Indiana University Press, 1984.

Ballhatchet, Kenneth. *Race, Sex and Class Under the Raj: Imperial Attitudes and Policies and Their Critics, 1793-1905*. London: Weidenfeld and Nicolson, 1980.

Barrett, Michele. *Women's Oppression Today: Problems in Marxist Feminist Analysis*. London: Verso, 1988.

Bart, Moore-Gilbert. *Postcolonial Theory: Contexts, Practices, Politics*. London: Verso, 1997.

Barthes, Roland. *Writing Degree Zero*. Trans. Annette Lavers and Colin Smith. London: Cape, 1967.

———. *S/Z*. Trans. Richard Miller. New York: Hill and Wang, 1974.

———. *Image, Music, Text*. Trans. Stephen Heath. Glasgow: Fontana, 1977.

———. *Mythologies*. Trans. Annette Lavers. New York: Hill and Wang, 1994.

Barry, Peter. *Beginning Theory: An Introduction to Literary and Cultural Theory*. Manchester: Manchester University Press, 1999.

Baudrillard, Jean. *The Illusion of the End*. Cambridge: Polity, 1994.

———. *America*. Trans. Chris Turner. London: Verso, 1988.

———. Simulations. Trans. Paul Foss et al. New York: Semiotext(e), 1983.

———. *Seduction*. Trans. Brian Singer. London: Macmillan, 1990.

Bauman, Zygmunt. *Intimations of Postmodernity*. London: Routledge, 1991.

Baym, Nina. *Women's Fiction: A Guide to Writing by and about Women in America, 1820-1870*. Ithaca: Cornell, 1978.

Beauvoir, Simone de. *The Second Sex*. Trans. H.M. Parshley. Harmondsworth: Penguin, 1984.

Beck, Ulrich. *The Reinvention of Politics: Rethinking Modernity in the Global Order*. Trans. Mark Ritter. Cambridge: Polity, 1997.

Bell, David and Gill Valentine, ed. *Mapping Desire: Geographies of Sexualities*. London and New York: Routledge, 1995.

Belsey, Catherine. *Critical Practice*. London: Methuen, 1980.

Benjamin, Walter. *Illuminations*, ed. Hannah Arendt. Trans. Harry Zohn. London: Jonathan Cape, 1970.

Bennett, Tony. *Formalism and Marxism*. London: Methuen, 1979.

Benveniste, Emile. *Problems of General Linguistics*. Trans. Mary E. Meek. Miami: Miami University Press, 1971.

Bhabha, Homi K, ed. *Nation and Narration*. London and New York: Routledge, 1990.

———. *The Location of Culture*. London and New York: Routledge, 1995.

Bijker, Wiebe et al, ed. *The Social Construction of Technological Systems: New Directions in the Sociology of Technology*. Cambridge, Massachusetts: MIT Press, 1989.

Bloom, Harold. *A Map of Misreading*. New York: Oxford University Press, 1975.

———. *Agon: Towards a Theory of Revisionism*. Oxford: Oxford University Press, 1983.

———. *The Anxiety of Influence: A Theory of Poetry*. New York and Oxford: Oxford University Press, 1984.

Boehmer, Elleke. *Colonial and Postcolonial Literature*. Oxford and New York: Oxford University Press, 1995.

Bonaparte, Marie. *The Life and Works of Edgar Allan Poe: A Psychoanalytic Interpretation*. Trans. John Rodker. London: Imago, 1949.

Bourdieu, Pierre. *The Field of Cultural Production: Essays on Art and Literature*, ed. Randall Johnson. Cambridge: Polity, 1993.

Bray, Alan. *Homosexuality in Renaissance English*. Boston: Gay Mens' Press, 1988.

Britt, David, ed. *Modern Art: Impressionism to Post-Modernism*. London: Thames and Hudson, 1989.

Brown, Norman. *Love's Body*. New York: Vintage, 1966.

Brunette, Peter and David Wills, ed. *Deconstruction and the Visual Arts*. Cambridge: Cambridge University Press, 1994.

Bruster, Douglas. *Drama and the Market in the Age of Shakespeare*. Cambridge: Cambridge University Press, 1992.

Bulbeck, Chilla. *Re-Orienting Western Feminisms: Women's Diversity in a Postcolonial World*. Cambridge: Cambridge University Press, 1998.

Butler, Judith. *Gender Trouble: Feminism and the Subversion of Identity*. New York and London: Routledge, 1990.

———. *Bodies that Matter: On the Discursive Limits of "Sex*." New York: Routledge, 1993.

Carby, Hazel. *Reconstructing Womanhood: The Emergence of the Afro-American Woman Novelists.* New York: Oxford University Press, 1987.

Caudwell, Christopher. *Studies and Further Studies in a Dying Culture.* New York: Monthly Review Press, 1972.

Cesaire, Aime. *Discourse on Colonialism.* Trans. Joan Pinkham. New York: Monthly Review Press, 1972.

Chatterjee, Partha. *Nationalist Thought and the Colonial World: A Derivative Discourse.* London: Zed, 1986.

———. *The Nation and Its Fragments: Colonial and Postcolonial Histories.* New Jersey: Princeton University Press, 1993.

Chodorow, Nancy. *The Reproduction of Mothering: Psychoanalysis and the Sociology of Gender.* Berkley: University of California Press, 1978.

Chow, Rey. *Writing Diaspora: Tactics of Intervention in Contemporary Cultural Studies.* Bloomington: Indiana University Press, 1993.

Cixous, Helene. *The Newly Born Woman.* Trans. Betsy Wing. Manchester: Manchester University Press, 1987.

———. *"Coming to Writing" and Other Essays*, ed. Deborah Jenson. Cambridge, Massachusetts, 1991.

Clifford, James and George E. Marcus, ed. *Writing Culture: The Poetics and Politics of Ethnography.* Delhi: Oxford University Press, 1990.

Collins, Patricia Hill. *Black Feminist Thought: Knowledge, Consciousness and the Politics of Empowerment.* Cambridge, Massachusetts: Unwin Hyman, 1990.

Cooke, Miriam and Angela Woolacott, ed. *Gendering War Talk.* New Jersey: Princeton, 1993.

Crosby, Alfred. *Ecological Imperialism: The Biological Expansion of Europe.* Cambridge: Cambridge University Press, 1986.

Culler, Jonathan. *Barthes.* London: Fontana, 1983.

Danto, Arthur. *After the End of Art.* Princeton: Princeton University Press, 1997.

Dasgupta, Probal. *The Otherness of English: India's Auntie Tongue Syndrome.* New Delhi: Sage, 1993.

D'Emilio, John. *Making Troubles: Essays on Gay History, Politics and the University.* New York: Routledge, 1992

De Lauretis, Teresa. *Alice Doesn't: Feminism, Semiotics, Cinema.* Bloomington: Indian University Press, 1984.

———. *Technologies of Gender: Essays on Theory, Film and Fiction.* Bloomington: Indiana University Press, 1987.

Deleuze, Gilles and Felix Guattari. *Anti-Oedipus: Capitalism and Schizophrenia.* Trans. Robert Hurley et al. Minneapolis: University of Minnesota Press, 1983.

———. *A Thousand Plateaus: Capitalism and Schizophrenia.* Trans. Brian Massumi. Minneapolis: University of Minnesota Press, 1988.

De Man, Paul. *Allegories of Reading: Figural Language in Rousseau, Nietzsche, Rilke, Proust.* New Haven and London: Yale University Press, 1979.

———. *The Rhetoric of Romanticism.* New York: Columbia University Press, 1984.

———. *The Resistance to Theory.* Minneapolis: University of Minnesota Press, 1986.

———. *Blindness and Insight: Essays in the Rhetoric of Contemporary Criticism.* London: Routledge, 1989.

Der Derian, James and Michael J Shapiro, ed. *International/Intertextual Relations: Postmodern Readings of World Politics.* New York: Lexington, 1989.

Derrida, Jacques. *Of Grammatology.* Trans. Gayatri Chakravorty Spivak. Baltimore and London: The John Hokpins University Press, 1976.

———. *Writing and Difference.* Trans. Alan Bass. Chicago: University of Chicago Press, 1978.

———. *Speech and Phenomena and Other Essays on Husserl's Theory of Signs.* Trans. David Allinson. Evanston: Northwestern University Press, 1973.

———. *The Other Heading: Reflections on Today's Europe.* Trans. Pascale-Anne Brault and Michael B. Naas. Bloomington: Indiana University Press, 1992.

———. *Specters of Marx: The State of the Debt, the Work of Mourning and the New International.* Trans. Peggy Kamuf. New York and London: Routledge, 1994.

———. *Margins of Philosophy.* Trans. Alan Bass. Brighton: Harvester, 1982.

Dollimore, Jonathan. *Radical Tragedy: Religion, Ideology and Power in the Drama of Shakespeare and His Contemporaries.* Hemel Hempstead: Harvester, 1986.

Donaldson, Laura. *Decolonising Feminism: Race, Gender and Empire-building.* London: Routledge, 1993.

Drakakis, John, ed. *Alternative Shakespeares.* London and New York: Methuen, 1985.

Drescher, Seymour and Stanley Engerman, ed. *A Historical Guide to World Slavery*. New York: Oxford University Press, 1998.

Duberman, Martin, et al, ed. *Hidden from History: Reclaiming the Gay and Lesbian Past*. New York: New American Library, 1989.

During, Simon. *Foucault and Literature: Towards a Genealogy of Writing*. London and New York: Routledge, 1992.

———, ed. *The Cultural Studies Reader*. London and New York: Routledge, 1993.

Eagleton, Terry. *Literary Theory: An Introduction*. Oxford: Blackwell, 1983.

Eco, Umberto. *A Theory of Semiotics*. Bloomington: Indiana University Press, 1976.

———. *The Role of the Reader: Explorations in the Semiotics of Texts*. London: Hutchinson, 1979.

Edney, Mathew. *Mapping an Empire: The Geographical Construction of British India, 1765-1843*. Chicago: University of Chicago Press, 1997.

Eisenstein, Zillah. *The Radical Future of Liberal Humanism*. New York: Longman, 1981.

Engels, Friedrich. *The Origin of the Family, Private Property and the State*. Harmondsworth: Penguin, 1985.

Faderman, Lillian. *Surpassing the Love of Men: Romantic Friendship and Love Between Women from the Renaissance to the Present*. New York: Morrow, 1981.

Fanon, Frantz. *Black Skins, White Masks*. Trans. C.L. Markmann. New York: Grove Press, 1967.

———. *A Dying Colonialism*. Trans. Haakon Chevalier. Harmondsworth: Penguin, 1970.

———. *The Wretched of the Earth*. Trans. Constance Parrington. Harmondsworth: Penguin, 1977.

Felman, Shoshana. *Jacques Lacan and the Adventure of Insight: Psychoanalysis in Contemporary Culture*. London: Harvard University Press, 1987.

Felperin, Howard. *Beyond Deconstruction: The Uses and Abuses of Literary Theory*. Oxford: Clarendon, 1990.

Fiske, John. *Television Culture*. London: Methuen, 1987.

———. *Understanding Popular Culture*. Boston: Unwin Hyman, 1989.

Foster, Hal, ed. *Postmodern Culture*. Massachusetts: Pluto, 1985.

Foucault, Michel. *Discipline and Punish: The Birth of the Prison*. Trans. Alan Sheridan. London: Allen Lane, 1977.

———. *Power/Knowledge: Selected Interviews and Other Writings*, ed. Colin Gordon. Trans. Colin Gordon et al. New York: Pantheon, 1980.

———. *The History of Sexuality: An Introduction*. Vol. I . Trans. Robert Hurley. New York: Vintage, 1990.

Freud, Sigmund. *The Standard Edition of the Complete Psychological Works of Sigmund Freud*. Trans. James Strachey. London: Hogarth, 1974.

Friedberg, Anne. *Window Shopping: Cinema and the Postmodern*. Berkley: University of California Press, 1993.

Frug, Mary Joe. *Postmodern Legal Feminism*. New York: Routledge, 1992.

Gadgil, Madhav and Ramachandra Guha. *This Fissured Land: An Ecological History of India*. Delhi: Oxford University Press, 1999.

Gates, Jr., Henry Louis. *The Signifying Monkey: A Theory of African-American Literary Criticism*. New York and Oxford: Oxford University Press, 1988.

Geertz, Clifford. *The Interpretation of Culture*. London: Fontana, 1993.

Genette, Gerard. *Narrative Discourse: An Essay on Method*. Trans. Jane E. Lewin. London: Basil Blackwell, 1980.

Geuss, Raymond. *The Idea of a Critical Theory: Habermas and the Frankfurt School*. Cambridge: Cambridge University Press, 1981.

Gibson, Andrew. *Towards a Postmodern Theory of Narrative*. Edinburgh: Edinburgh University Press, 1996.

Giddens, Anthony. *Beyond Left and Right: The Future of Radical Politics*. Cambridge: Polity, 1994.

Gilbert, Sandra and Susan Gubar. *The Madwoman in the Attic: The Woman Writer and the Nineteenth-Century Literary Imagination*. New Haven: Yale University Press, 1979.

———. *No Man's Land: The Place of the Woman Writer in the Twentieth Century*. 2 vols. New Haven: Yale University Press, 1988.

———, ed. *The Norton Anthology of Literature by Women: The Tradition in English*. New York: Norton, 1985. .

Girard, Rene. *Deceit, Desire and the Novel: Self and Other in Literary Structure*. Trans. Yvonne Freccero. Baltimore: Johns Hopkins, 1984.

Gleick, James. *Chaos: Making a New Science*. London: Sphere, 1988.

Goldberg, Jonathan. *James I and the Politics of Literature: Jonson, Shakespeare, Donne and their Contemporaries*. Baltimore: Johns Hopkins, 1983.

———. *Queering the Renaissance*. Durham: Duke University Press, 1994.

Goldman, Lucien. *The Hidden God*. Trans. Philip Thody. London: Routledge and Kegan Paul. 1964.

Gramsci, Antonio. *Selections from the Prison Notebooks*, ed. and Trans. Quintin Hoare and Geoffrey Nowell-Smith. London: Lawrence and Wishart, 1971.

Green, Martin. *Dreams of Adventure, Deeds of Empire*. London: Routledge, 1980.

Greenblatt, Stephen. *Marvelous Possessions: The Wonder of the New World*. Chicago: University of Chicago Press, 1991.

Greimas, A.J. *On Meaning: Selected Writings in Semiotic Theory*. Trans, Paul Perron and Frank Collins. London: Pinter, 1987.

Groden, Micahel and Martin Kreiswirth, ed. *The Johns Hopkins Guide to Literary Theory and Criticism*. Baltimore and London: Johns Hopkins University Press, 1994.

Grossberg, Lawrence et al, ed. *Cultural Studies*. London: Routledge, 1992.

Grosz, Elizabeth. *Volatile Bodies: Towards a Corporeal Feminism*. Bloomington: Indiana University Press, 1994.

Grove, Richard et al, ed. *Nature and the Orient: The Environmental History of South and Southeast Asia*. Delhi: Oxford, 1998.

Guha, Ranajit et al, ed. *Subaltern Studies*. Vols. 1-9. Oxford: Oxford University Press, 1982.

Habermas, Jurgen. *Communication and the Evolution of Society*. Trans. Thomas McCarthy. London: Heinemann, 1979.

———. *The Philosophical Discourse of Modernity*. Trans. Frederick Lawrence. Cambridge: Polity, 1987.

Hall, Stuart. *Critical Dialogues in Cultural Studies*, ed. David Morley and K.H. Chen. London and New York: Routledge, 1996.

Harding, Sandra. *Whose Knowledge? Whose Science? Thinking from Women's Lives*. Milton Keynes: Open University Press, 1991.

Harari, J.V. *Textual Strategies: Perspectives in Poststructuralist Criticism*. London: Methuen, 1980.

Haraway, Donna. *Primate Visions: Gender, Race and Nature in the World of Modern Science*. London: Routledge, 1989.

———. *Simians, Cyborgs and Women: The Reinvention of Nature*. London: Free Association, 1991.

Hartman, Geoffrey, ed. *Deconstruction and Criticism*. New York: Seabury, 1979.

———. *Saving the Text: Literature/Derrida/Philosophy*. Baltimore: Johns Hopkins, 1981.

Hassan, Ihab. *Paracriticisms: Seven Speculations for The Times.* Urbana: University of Illinois Press, 1975.

———. *The Postmodern Turn: Essays in Postmodern Theory and Culture.* Ohio: Ohio State University Press, 1987.

Hawkes, Terence. *That Shakespeherian Rag: Essays on a Critical Process.* London: Methuen, 1986.

Hebdige, Dick. *Subculture: The Meaning of Style.* London: Routledge, 1979.

Heelas, Paul et al, ed. *Detraditionalisation: Critical Reflections on Authority and Identity.* Oxford: Blackwell, 1996.

Heller, Agnes and Ferenc Feher. *The Postmodern Political Condition.* Cambridge: Polity, 1991.

Hirschkop, Ken and David Shepherd, ed. *Bakhtin and Cultural Theory.* Manchester: Manchester University Press, 1989.

Hoffman, Frederick J. *Freudianism and the Literary Mind.* New York: Grove, 1959.

Hoggart, Richard. *The Uses of Literacy.* Harmondsworth: Penguin, 1958.

Holderness, Graham. *The Shakespeare Myth.* Manchester: Manchester University Press, 1988.

Holland, Norman N. *The Dynamics of Literary Response.* New York: Norton, 1975.

———. *The I.* New Haven: Yale University Press, 1985.

hooks, bell. *Ain't I A Woman?: Black Woman and Feminism.* Boston: South End Press, 1981.

———. *Feminist Theory: From Margin to Centre.* Boston: South End Press,1984.

———. *Talking Back: Thinking Feminist/Thinking Black.* Boston: South End Press,1989.

———. *Yearning: Race, Gender and Cultural Politics.* Boston: South End Press,1990.

Hord, Fred Lee and Jonathan Scott Lee, ed. *I Am Because We Are: Readings in Black Philosophy.* Amherst: University of Massachusetts Press, 1995.

Hutcheon, Linda. *A Poetics of Postmodernism: History, Theory, Fiction.* London: Routledge, 1995.

Irigaray, Luce. *Speculum of the Other Woman.* Trans. Gillian C. Gill. Ithaca: Cornell University Press, 1985.

———. *This Sex which is Not One.* Trans. Catherine Porter. Ithaca: Cornell University Press, 1985.

———. *An Ethics of Sexual Difference*. Trans. Carolyn Burke and Gillian C. Gill. Ithaca: Cornell University Press, 1993.

Jakobson, Roman. *On Language*. London: Harvard University Press, 1990.

Jameson, Fredric. *Marxism and Form*. New Jersey: Princeton University Press, 1971.

———. *The Political Unconscious: Narrative as a Socially Symbolic Act*. London: Methuen, 1981.

———. *Postmodernism, Or the Cultural Logic of Late Capitalsim*. London: Verso, 1991.

Jencks, Charles. *Post-Modernism: The New Classicism in Art and Architecture*. London: Academy, 1987

Jenkins, Keith. *On 'What is History'? From Carr to Elton, Rorty to White*. London: Routledge, 1995.

———. *Why History?: Ethics and Postmodernity*. London: Routledge, 1999.

Johnston, Jill. *Lesbian Nation*. New York: Simon and Schuster, 1973.

Jones, Ernest. *Hamlet and Oedipus*.

———. *Psycho-Myth, Psycho-History*.

Johnson, Pauline. *Feminism as Radical Humanism*. Boulder: Westview, 1994.

Joshi, Svati, ed. *Rethinking English: Essays in Literature, Language, History*. New Delhi: Trianka, 1991.

Kamps, Ivo. *Shakespeare Left and Right*. London: Routledge, 1991.

———. *Materialist Shakespeare: A History*. London and New York: Verso, 1995.

Katz, Jonathan. *The Invention of Heterosexuality*. New York: Dutton, 1995.

Kellner, Douglas. *Jean Baudrillard: From Marxism to Postmodernism and Beyond*. Cambridge: Polity, 1989.

King, Anthony D. *Colonial Urban Development: Culture, Social Power and Environment*. London: Routledge and Kegan Paul, 1976.

———. *Urbanism, Colonialism, and the World-Economy: Cultural and Spatial Foundations of the World Urban System*. London and New York: Routledge, 1990.

Knowles, Karen, ed. *Celebrating the Land: Women's Nature Writings, 1850-1991*. Flagstaff, Arizona: Northland, 1992.

Klein, Melanie. *Guilt and Reparation and Other Works, 1921-1945*. London: Hogarth and Institute of Psychoanalysis, 1975.

———. *Envy and Gratitude and Other Works, 1946-1963*. London: Hogarth and Institute of Psychoanalysis, 1975

Kristeva, Julia. *Desire in Language: A Semiotic Approach to Literature and Art*. Trans. Thomas Gora et al. New York: Columbia University Press, 1984.

———. *Revolution in Poetic Language*. Trans. Leon S. Roudiez. New York: Columbia University Press, 1984.

———. *The Kristeva Reader*, ed. Toril Moi. Oxford: Basil Blackwell, 1986.

Krupat, Arnold. *Ethnocriticism: Ethnography, History, Literature*. Berkeley: University of California Press, 1992.

Kuhn, Annette and Ann Marie Wolpe, ed. *Feminism and Materialism*. London: Routledge and Kegan Paul, 1978.

Kumar, Deepak. *Science and the Raj, 1857-1905*. Delhi: Oxford University Press, 1997.

Lacan, Jacques. *Ecrits: A Selection*. Trans. Alan Sheridan. London: Tavistock, 1977.

———. *The Four Fundamental Concepts of Psychoanalysis*. Ed. Jacques-Alain Miller. Trans. Alan Sheridan. New York and London: W.W. Norton, 1981.

Laclau, Ernesto and Chantal Mouffe. *Hegemony and Socialist Strategy: Towards a Radical Democratic Politics*. London: Verso, 1987.

Leask, Nigel. *British Romantic Writers and the East: Anxieties of Empire*. Cambridge: Cambridge University Press, 1993.

Le Doeuff, Michele. *Hipparchia's Choice: An Essay Concerning Women, Philosophy, etc*. Trans. Trista Selous. Oxford: Blackwell, 1991.

Leitch, Vincent B. *Deconstructive Criticism: An Advanced Introduction*. London: Hutchinson, 1983.

Lenin, V.I. *Imperialism: The Highest Stage of Capitalism*. New York: International, 1939.

Levi-Strauss, Claude. *Structural Anthropology*. London: Penguin, 1977.

Lodge, David, ed. *Twentieth Century Literary Criticism: A Reader*. London: Longman, 1972.

———. *After Bakhtin: Essays in Contemporary Criticism*. London: Routledge, 1990.

Lotman, Yuri. *Analysis of the Poetic Text*. Ann Arbor: University of Michigan Press, 1977.

Lukacs, Georges. *History and Class Consciousness: Studies in Marxist Dialectics*. London: Merlin, 1971.

———. *The Theory of the Novel*. Trans. Anna Bostock. London: Merlin, 1971.

———. *The Historical Novel.* Trans. Hannah Mitchell and Stanley Mitchell. Lincoln and London: University of Nebraska Press, 1983.

Lyon, David. *Postmodernity.* Buckingham: Open University Press, 1994.

Lyotard, Jean-Francois. *The Postmodern Condition: A Report on Knowledge.* Trans. Geoff Bennington and Brian Massumi. Minneapolis: University of Minnesota Press, 1984.

———. *Just Gaming.* Trans. Wlad Godzich. Minneapolis: University of Minnesota Press, 1985.

———. *The Differend: Phrases in Dispute.* Trans. George Van Den Abeele. Minneapolis: University of Minnesota Press, 1988.

Macherey, Pierre. *A Theory of Literary Production.* Trans. Geoffrey Wall. London and Boston: Routledge and Kegan Paul, 1978.

Machin, Richard and Christopher Norris (ed). *Post-Structuralist Readings of English Poetry.* Cambridge: Cambridge, 1987.

Mannoni, O. *Prospero and Caliban: The Psychology of Colonisation.* Trans. Pamela Powesland. London: Methuen, 1956.

Marcuse, Herbert. *One-Dimensional Man: Studies in the Ideology of Advanced Industrial Society.* Boston: Beacon, 1964.

Marks, Elaine and Isabelle de Courtivron, ed. *New French Feminisms.* Brighton: Harvester, 1981.

Marshall, Barbara L. *Engendering Modernity: Feminism, Social Theory and Social Change.* Cambridge: Polity, 1994.

Martinez-Alier, Juan and Ramachandra Guha. *Varieties of Environmentalism: Essays North and South.* Delhi: Oxford, 1998.

Massey, Doreen. *Space, Place, Gender.* Cambridge: Polity, 1994.

Marx, Karl and Friedrich Engels. *Selected Works.* London: Lawrence and Wishart, 1968.

McClintock, Anne. *Imperial Leather: Race, Gender and Sexuality in the Colonial Contest.* New York and London, 1995.

Meeker, Joseph. *The Comedy of Survival: Studies in Literary Ecology.* New York: Charles Scribner's Sons, 1972.

Mellor, Mary. *Feminism and Ecology.* Cambridge: Polity, 1997.

Memmi, Albert. *The Coloniser and the Colonised.* Boston: Beacon, 1963.

Merchant, Carolyn. *The Death of Nature.* New York: Harper and Row, 1983.

Merchant, Hoshang, ed. *Yaraana: Gay Writing from India.* New Delhi: Penguin, 1999.

Metcalfe, Thomas. *An Imperial Vision: Indian Architecture and Britain's Raj.* Cambridge: Cambridge University Press, 1989.

Mies, Maria and Vandana Shiva. *Ecofeminism.* London: Zed, 1993.

Mill, John Stuart and Harriet Taylor Mill. *Essays on Sex Equality*. Ed. Alice S. Rossi. Chicago: University of Chicago Press, 1970.

Miller, J. Hillis. *Fiction and Repetition: Seven English Novels*. Oxford: Basil Blackwell, 1982.

———. *Ariadne's Thread: Story Lines*. New Haven: Yale University Press, 1992.

Millett, Kate. *Sexual Politics*. New York: Avon, 1971.

Mitchell, Ju!iet. *Psychoanalysis and Feminism*. New York: Random House, 1974.

———. *Woman's Estate*. Baltimore: Penguin, 1974.

Mitchell, Juliet and Jacqueline Rose. *Feminine Sexuality: Jacques Lacan and the Ecole Freudienne*. London: Macmillan, 1985.

Mitter, Partha. *Much Maligned Monsters: History of European Reactions to Indian Art*. Oxford: Oxford University Press, 1977.

———. *Art and Nationalism in Colonial India, 1850-1922: Occidental Orientations*. Cambridge: Cambridge University Press, 1994

Moers, Ellen. *Literary Women: The Great Writers*. New York: Doubleday, 1976.

Moi, Toril. *Sexual/Textual Politics: Feminist Literary Theory*. London and New York: Methuen, 1985.

Mongia, Padmini, ed. *Contemporary Postcolonial Theory: A Reader*. Delhi: Oxford University Press, 1997.

Moraga, Cherrie and Gloria Anzaldua, ed. *This Bridge Called My Back: Writings by Radical Women of Colour*. Watertown, Massachusetts: Persephone, 1981.

Nandy, Ashis. *The Intimate Enemy: Loss and Recovery of Self Under Colonisation*. New Delhi: Oxford University Press, 1989.

Nehring, Neil. *Popular Music, Gender, and Postmodernism*. London: Sage, 1997.

Nelson, Cary and Lawrence Grosberg, ed. *Marxism and the Interpretation of Culture*. Urbana: University of Illinois Press, 1985.

Niranjana, Tejaswini. *Siting Translation: History, Post-Structuralism and the Colonial Context*. Berkley: University of California Press, 1992.

Norris, Christopher. *The Deconstructive Turn: Essays in the Rhetoric of Philosophy*. London and New York: Methuen, 1983.

Ohmann, Richard. *English in America: A Radical View of the Profession*. New York: Oxford University Press, 1976.

Pandey, Gyanendra. *The Construction of Communalism in Colonial North India*. Delhi: Oxford University Press, 1996.

Papadakis, Andreas, ed. *Deconstruction in Architecture*. London: Academy, 1988.

Paranjape, Makarand, ed. *Nativism: Essays in Criticism*. New Delhi: Sahitya Akademi, 1997.

Parker, Andrew et al, ed. *Nationalisms and Sexualities*. London and New York: Routledge, 1992.

Patterson, Dennis, ed. *Postmodernism and Law*. Aldershot: Dartmouth Publishing, 1994.

Peirce, C.S. *Selected Writings*. Ed. Philip P. Wiener. New York: Dover, 1958.

Peterfreund, Stuart, ed. *Literature and Science: Theory and Practice*. Boston: Northeastern University Press, 1990.

Prakash, Gyan, ed. *After Colonialism: Imperial Histories and Postcolonial Displacements*. New Jersey: Princeton University Press, 1995.

Pratt, Mary Louis. *Imperial Eyes: Travel Writing and Transculturation*. New York: Routledge, 1992.

Propp, Vladimir. *Morphology of the Folktale*. Ed. Louis Wagner. Trans. Laurence Scott. Austin: Texas University Press, 1968.

Rengger, N.J. *Political Theory, Modernity and Postmodernity*. Oxford: Blackwell, 1995.

Rich, Adrienne. *Blood, Bread and Poetry: Selected Prose, 1979-1985*. New York and London: W.W. Norton,1986.

———. *Of Woman Born: Motherhood as Experience and Institution*. New York: Norton, 1976.

Ridley, Hugh. *Images of Imperial Rule*. London: Croom Helm, 1983.

Rimmon-Kennan, Shlomith. *Narrative Fiction: Contemporary Poetics*. London: Methuen, 1983.

Rorty, Richard. *Contingency, Irony and Solidarity*. Cambridge: Cambridge University Press, 1989.

———. *Consequences of Pragmatism*. Minneapolis: University of Minnesota, 1982.

Rose, Jacqueline. *Sexuality in the Field of Vision*. New York: Verso, 1986.

Ryan, Michael. *Marxism and Deconstruction: A Critical Articulation*. Baltimore: Johns Hopkins, 1982.

Said, Edward. *Orientalism*. London: Penguin, 1985.

———. *Culture and Imperialism*. London: Vintage, 1994.

Salleh, Ariel. *Ecofeminism as Politics: Nature, Marx and the Postmodern*. London: Zed, 1997.

Sandler, Irving. *Art of the Postmodern Era: From the Late 1960s to the Early 1990s*. New York: Harper Collins, 1996.

Sangari, Kumkum and Sudesh Vaid, ed. *Recasting Women: Essays in Colonial History*. New Delhi: Kali for Women, 1989.

Saussure, Ferdinand de. *A Course in General Linguistics*. Trans. Wade Buskin. New York: McGraw, 1966.

Schreiner, Olive. *Women and Labour*. New York: Johnson, 1972 (Reprint).

Seidman, Steven. *The Postmodern Turn: New Perspectives on Social Theory*. Cambridge: Cambridge University Press, 1994.

———, ed. *Queer Theory/Sociology*. Cambridge: Blackwell, 1996.

Sedgwick, Eve Kosofsky. *Epistemology of the Closet*. Berkley: University of California Press, 1990.

Seldon, Raman. *A Reader's Guide to Contemporary Literary Theory*. Brighton: Harvester, 1985.

Shapiro, Michael J. *Reading the Postmodern Polity: Political Theory as Textual Practice*. Minneapolis: University of Minnesota Press, 1992.

Sharpe, Jenny. *Allegories of Empire: The Figure of Woman in the Colonial Text.* Minneapolis; University of Minnesota Press, 1993.

Shiva, Vandana. *Staying Alive: Women, Ecology and Development in India*. New Delhi: Kali for Women, 1995.

Shklovsky, Viktor. *Theory of Prose*. Trans. Benjamin Sher. Illinois: Dalkey Archive Press, 1991.

Showalter, Elaine. *A Literature of their Own: British Women Novelists from Bronte to Lessing*. Princeton: Princeton University Press, 1977.

———, ed. *The New Feminist Criticism: Essays on Women, Literature and Theory*. London: Virago, 1986.

———, ed. *Speaking of Gender*. London: Routledge, 1989.

Sim, Stuart. *Beyond Aesthetics: Confrontations with Poststructuralism and Postmodernism*. New York: Harvester Wheatsheaf, 1992.

Soja, Edward. *Postmodern Geographies: The Reassertion of Space in Contemporary Critical Social Theory*. London: Verso, 1989.

Spivak, Gayatri Chakravorty. *In Other Worlds: Essays in Cultural Politics*. London: Methuen, 1987.

———. *The Post-Colonial Critic: Interviews, Strategies, Dialogues*. Ed. Sarah Harasym. New York: Routledge, 1990.

———. *A Critique of Postcolonial Reason: Towards a History of the Vanishing Present*. Calcutta: Seagull, 1999.

Sprinker, Michael, ed. *Ghostly Demarcations: A Symposium on Jacques Derrida's "Specters of Marx."* London: Verso, 1999.

Steiner, Peter. *Russian Formalism: A Metapoetics*. Ithaca: Cornell University Press, 1984

Sunder Rajan, Rajeshwari. *Real and Imagined Women: Gender, Culture, Postcolonialism*. London: Routledge, 1993.

———, ed. *The Lie of the Land: English Literary Studies in India*. Delhi: Oxford University Press, 1992.

Tabbi, Joseph. *Postmodern Sublime: Technology and American Writing from Mailer to Cyberpunk*. Ithaca and London: Cornell, 1995.

Taylor, Brandon. *Modernism, Post-modernism, Realism: A Critical Perspective for Art*. Winchester: Winchester School of Art Press, 1987.

Teltscher, Kate. *India Inscribed: European and British Writing on India, 1600-1800*. Delhi: Oxford, 1997.

Tharu, Susie, ed. *Subject to Change: Teaching Literature in the Nineties*. Hyderabad: Orient Longman, 1998.

Tharu, Susie and K. Lalitha, ed. *Women Writing in India. 2 vols*. Delhi: Oxford University Press, 1999.

Thompson, E.P. *The Making of the English Working Class*. Harmondsworth: Penguin, 1977.

Tillotson, G.H.R., ed. *Paradigms of Indian Architecture: Space and Time in Representation and Design*. Surrey: Curzon, 1998.

Thiong'o, Ngugi wa. *Decolonising the Mind: The Politics of Language in African Literature*. Nairobi: Heinemann, 1986.

Tiffin, Chris and Alan Lawson, ed. *De-Scribing Empire: Post-colonialism and Textuality*. London and New York, 1994.

Todd, Janet. *Feminist Literary Historiography: A Defence*. Cambridge: Polity, 1988.

Todorov, Tzvetan. *Introduction to Poetics*. Trans. Richard Howard. Brighton: Harvester, 1981.

———. *The Fantastic: A Structural Approach to a Literary Genre*. Trans. Richard Howard. Ohio: Case Western Reserve University Press, 1982.

Toynbee, Arnold. *Mankind and Mother Earth: A Narrative History of the World*. New York and London: Oxford University Press, 1976.

Traub, Valerie. *Desire and Anxiety: Circulation of Sexual Energy in Shakespearean Drama*. London: Routledge, 1992.

Trilling, Lionel. *The Liberal Imagination*. New York: Harcourt, Brace, Jovanovich, 1979.

Trinh T Minh ha. *Woman, Native, Other: Writing Postcoloniality and Feminism*. Bloomington: Indiana University Press, 1989.

Trivedi, Harish and Meenakshi Mukherjee, ed. *Interrogating Post-Colonialism: Theory, Text and Context*. Shimla: Indian Institute of Advanced Study, 1996.

Ulmer, Gregory. *Teletheory: Grammatology in the Age of Video*. Illinois: Northwestern University Press, 1989.

Vachek, Josef V. *The Linguistics School of Prague: An Introduction to Its Theory and Practice*. Bloomington, 1966.

Viswanathan, Gauri. *Masks of Conquest: Literary Studies and British Rule in India*. London: Faber and Faber, 1990

Walker, Alice. *In Search of our Mothers' Gardens: Womanist Prose*. New York: Harcourt, Brace Jovanovich, 1983.

Weeks, Jeffrey. *Coming Out: Homosexual Politics in Britain from the Nineteenth Century to the Present*. London: Quartet, 1990.

Wellek, Rene. *Discriminations: Further Concepts in Criticism*. New Haven: Yale University Press, 1970.

West, Cornel. *Race Matters*. Boston: Beacon, 1993.

White, Hayden. *Metahistory: The Historical Imagination in Nineteenth-Century Europe*. Baltimore: Johns Hopkins, 1973.

———. *Tropics of Discourse: Essays in Cultural Criticism*. Baltimore: Johns Hopkins, 1987.

Whitford, Margaret. *Luce Irigaray: Philosophy in the Feminine*. London: Routledge, 1991.

Wild, Peter, ed. *The Desert Reader*. Salt Lake City: University of Utah Press, 1991.

Williams, Raymond. *Culture and Society, 1780-1950*. London: Penguin, 1958.

———. *Marxism and Literature*. Oxford: Oxford University Press, 1977.

———. *Keywords: A Vocabulary of Culture and Society*. London: Fontana, 1989.

Wiitig, Monique. *The Lesbian Body*. Trans. David Le Vay. London: Peter Owen, 1975.

Wolfe, Susan J. and Julia Penelope, ed. *Sexual Practice/Textual Practice: Lesbian Cultural Criticism*. Cambridge: Blackwell, 1993.

Wolstonecraft, Mary. *A Vindication of the Rights of Woman*. Baltimore: Penguin, 1975.

Woolf, Virginia. *A Room of One's Own*. New York: Harcourt, Brace, Jovanovich, 1957.

———. *Three Guineas*. New York: Harcourt, Brace, Jovanovich, 1938.

Worton, Michael and Judith Still, ed. *Intertextuality: Theories and Practices*. Manchester: Manchester University Press, 1991.

Yegenoglu, Meyda. *Colonial Fantasies: Towards a Feminist Reading of Orientalism*. Cambridge: Cambridge University Press, 1998.

Young, Robert. *Colonial Desire: Hybridity in Theory, Culture and Race*. London: Routledge, 1995.

Zaretsky, Eli. *Capitalism, the Family and Personal Life*. New York: Harper, 1976.

INDEX